John Frederick Adolphus McNair

Perak and the Malays

John Frederick Adolphus McNair

Perak and the Malays

ISBN/EAN: 9783337310486

Printed in Europe, USA, Canada, Australia, Japan

Cover: Foto ©Suzi / pixelio.de

More available books at **www.hansebooks.com**

PERAK AND THE MALAYS:

"SĀRONG" AND "KRĪS."

BY

MAJOR FRED. McNAIR

(Late Royal Artillery)

COLONIAL ENGINEER AND SURVEYOR-GENERAL, STRAITS SETTLEMENTS ;
LATE OFFICIATING H.M. CHIEF-COMMISSIONER, PERAK ;
FELLOW OF THE LINNÆAN SOCIETY, ETC. ETC.
ASSOCIATE INSTITUTE CIVIL ENGINEERS.

Illustrated with Thirteen Engravings by R. Knight, from Photographs taken by the Author.

LONDON:
TINSLEY BROTHERS, 8, CATHERINE STREET, STRAND.
1878.

PREFACE.

BEING in England on a few months' leave of absence, for the purpose of recruiting my health, after a severe attack of jungle fever, contracted in Perak, it occurred to me that a brief account of that comparatively unknown country and its people might not be altogether unacceptable to the English reader.

This Malayan State, it will be remembered, came into public notice in 1875–76, through the murder there of the British Resident, and the despatch by our Government of a combined naval and military force to exact satisfaction for the outrage.

As I accompanied the Governor of the Straits Settlements on his progress through the country just prior to the disturbances, and was also with the force subsequently sent there, I enjoyed exceptional opportunities for observation, of which I availed myself, in making the notes which have since been embodied in this work.

A*

I may say in addition, that my general knowledge of the manners and customs of the Malays has been acquired during a residence of over twenty years in the Straits Settlements.

I am indebted to the Reports which have been made from time to time by the various officers of the Government for the confirmation of my own opinions, and also for much valuable information gleaned by them in portions of the country which it was not my good fortune to visit.

For much of the past history of the Malays I have consulted the works of Crawfurd, Newbold, Loubere, Pritchard, Pickering, Marsden, and Dr. Vincent; Moor's "Notes on the Archipelago," and the Colonial State Papers—these being among the principal authorities that have treated of the origin and progress of this peculiar and wide-spread race; while, as the work is intended for general reading, I have thought it better to omit all scientific terms.

CONTENTS.

CHAPTER XXXII.

CHAPTER XXXIII.

CHAPTER XXXIV.

CHAPTER XXXV.

CHAPTER XXXVI.

CHAPTER XXXVII.

LIST OF ILLUSTRATIONS.

"SĀRONG" AND "KRĪS."

CHAPTER I.

IT is hardly too much to assume that, prior to 1875,
when the sad news reached England of the rising of a
people under British protection, and the murder
of Mr. Birch, the state of Perak was, to the majority of people, a *terra incognita.* They knew, of
course, that the Malay peninsula was a long tongue
of land stretching nearly to the equator, and that it
was in close proximity to Sumatra and Java, with
innumerable islands generally known as the Malay
archipelago ; but saving those interested in the British
Straits Settlements—Singapore, Malacca, and Penang
—it may be taken for granted that few people were
aware that a large and rich territory, ruled over by a
sultan and his petty chiefs, had been, so to speak,

B

placed under the wing of the British Government, whose representatives, under the name of residents and assistant-residents, were at the court of the ruler, to counsel and advise for the better management of a country whose people were suffering from anarchy and misrule.

Picture this tropical land : Not a sun-baked region of parched desert and insufferable drought ; but a rich moist country, almost touching the equator, but rarely suffering from excessive heat ; a land of eternal summer, where refreshing rains fall ; where the monsoons blow regularly ; where the frightful tempests of the east are unknown ; and which is, for the most part, covered with a luxuriant vegetation, the produce of a fertile soil.

This Perak—pronounced as though spelt Payrah—is one of the largest of the native states into which the Malay peninsula is divided, and lies upon the western coast, having there, for its ninety miles' boundary-line, the bright prau-traversed waters of the Straits of Malacca. To be geographically accurate, its boundaries—north, south, and east—may be named as the states of Quedah or Keddah, which in the native language signifies an elephant-trap ; Salangore ; Pahang, and Tringanu. These are all native states, whose rule and people are very similar to those of the land in question.

Perak signifies silver—a name given to it not from the abundance of that metal, for its existence has been little traced, but probably from the vast amount of silvery-looking tin which has been, and promises still to be, one of its principal productions. Taken roughly—for we are yet dependent upon native sources for our knowledge of its unsurveyed boundaries —the depth inland of the state is about forty-five miles, thus giving an area of somewhere about 4000 square miles, of a land metaphorically flowing with milk and honey; but badly ruled, thinly inhabited, poorly cultivated, and asking the direction of Western capitalists, and the busy hands of the Chinese people to make it one of the most productive under the sun.

The nature of the country may be seen if we take a rapid glance through it by means of its great waterway, the Perak river, which intersects the wide central plain from north to south, and fairly divides the state, having west the fertile lands reaching to the sea, and on the east the gradually-rising country to the central ridge of mountains—the backbone, or watershed, of the whole peninsula—whose mineral resources are only known from the rich treasures in gold and tin that have been, in the course of ages, washed down into the alluvial lands.

Sailing, steaming, or even paddling up one of these Perak rivers, we have on either hand, if the tide be down, the regular mud-banks of a tropical shore, with the dense mangrove forest standing up in its labyrinth of water-washed roots, as if nature had set the example, followed by the dwellers in the land, of building a rough scaffold, on which to support the tree-trunks, high and dry above the flood. If, on the contrary, the tide be up, right and left the mangrove forest seems to be growing directly out of the river, the stream passing unhindered among the roots. The silence is solemn in its intensity; for, save the plashing of the water to paddle or screw, not a sound is to be heard, and the traveller seems to be penetrating into one of nature's unexplored retreats, as he looks in vain for some trace of life beside that of the dense vegetation on either bank.

At last he sees it in the shape of a white eagle, gliding with silent wing athwart the stream; and farther on, suddenly, from some exposed mangrove root, there is a flash of blue, and, like a vivid azure streak, away darts a kingfisher, one of the brilliantly-feathered birds of the country, disturbed while waiting for its gorgeously-scaled prey. As the light-winged bird disappears, and the eye is still filled with its beauty, the ear is at last saluted with a sound to break the utter stillness of the river, for there is a dull heavy splash, an eddying in the water, as, from amidst the mud or mangrove roots, a huge alligator rushes into the stream, the traveller being, perhaps, in time to see a portion of its rugged, muddy-hued, loathsome body; and he may be fortunate enough to see, just upon the surface, the two hill-crowned eyes and long snout of some other reptile, the head turning slightly from side to side, as its owner sends a shudder through the spectator, who knows that the monster is on the watch for prey.

As the boat glides on and on, beyond the tidal influence, the character of the forest changes : the mangroves give place to jungle growth, and on either side, columnar and beautiful, rise the stately growths of palm, with their wondrously-straight trunks and tufted heads.

Suddenly the first trace of human habitation appears, in the shape of a Malay campong or village —a cluster of houses of bamboo and other wood, in a grove of cocoa-nut palms and other fruit-trees. The huts are raised on posts, so as to be beyond the reach of flood and noxious beast, and look neat with their woven sides of split bamboo or reed, while their roofs are thatched with attap, an arrangement of the palm-leaves, that grow close at hand.

If the campong be of any extent, there is probably a mosque ; while, secured to bamboo posts, or run up safely on the mud, are the boats of the people. These boats play a prominent part in the daily life of the Malay ; for, roughly speaking, Perak is now a land of jungle, and its rivers are the highways, upon which its villages are built ; while its roads are only a few elephant-tracks but little used, and pathways through the jungle known to the country people alone.

Continuing our course either up the main stream

or one of its tributaries, the jungle disappears here
and there, to give place to traces of cultivation,
where padi or rice is grown in the low, moist, alluvial
soil. As we still ascend, the native boats, or sampans,
may be met coming down with the stream, laden
with produce, or containing some fisherman, equipped
for his pursuit.

As we ascend higher, it is to find that the stream
grows more rapid, and if in a small boat, poling, or
as we should call it punting, our skiff against the
stream, is the custom adopted. And now, from time
to time, fresh traces of the sparse population of the
country appear, battling with the ever-encroaching
primeval forest. Buffaloes are seen, standing knee-
deep in the river-edge; children approach the river-
bank to stare at our boat; and then there is the
forest once more, the gliding river with increasing
shallows, and higher still the rapids.

The coast-line is broken with endless numbers of
mangrove-fringed creeks, and small tidal estuaries,
and these have ever been the hiding-places of the
much-dreaded praus, those famous piratical craft
with which the name of the Malay has so long been
associated. The principal rivers that here form
estuaries are the Perak; the Krean and Bernam,
which form the northern and southern boundaries of
the state; the Laroot river, which drains the principal
tin-land; and the Dinding, off which lie the islands of
the same name.

These islands, like Penang to the northward, have now become British territory, and afford capital anchorage between them and the shore, with an ample supply of fresh water to be obtained on the principal island, Pulo Pangkore. This is the largest of the group, and, unlike the greater proportion of the mainland, is now becoming rapidly peopled by the Malays and Chinese; these latter making a busy home wherever there is gold or tin to be mined, or money to be earned by straightforward industry. Here at Pulo Pangkore they are mostly employed as woodcutters, and in making lime, for which abundant material is found all round the island, in the shape of the limestone coral and madrepores.

This zoophyte-produced limestone, as seen from a boat, when peering down through the limpid water, presents a scene of wondrous beauty, with its many tints and shades of colour, forming a perfect submarine garden of endless loveliness, through whose flowers and shrubs glide the brilliant fish of the tropic region, clad in armour whose hues are at times dazzling, and far outrival the corals amongst which they rove. The dry coral is easily burned by the Chinese into lime, and procures a high price for building purposes at Penang. The Malays, on the contrary, occupy small tracts of land, which they plant with fruit-trees, principally the plantain or banana, and the chumpada or small jack-fruit, a variety of the bread-fruit of Polynesia.

The Dutch were the former occupants of this island at the time that they held Malacca, and the remains of their fort and factory are still to be seen close to the shore, and within reach of Anson Bay.

The Perak river is a fine broad stream, averaging for the first fifty miles about one-fourth of a mile in width, navigable for about one hundred and eighty miles from its mouth—an assertion that sounds somewhat paradoxical, when the limits of the country are given as only ninety miles from north to south. Its serpentine wanderings, however, fully account for this. Although navigable to so great a distance, this is only for boats : still goodly vessels may make their way up for forty miles to Durian Sabatang, after which the draught of boats must become smaller and smaller, while in Ooloo, or Upper Perak, rapids are encountered in several places, long before the sources are reached, at a range of hills, called Titti-Wangsa, in the adjacent state of Quedah.

These rapids in the ascent of the river are generally passed on rafts, which are very skilfully constructed by the Malays, out of the large hollow bamboos of the country, lashed securely together with rattans. They will readily make a raft of this kind fifty feet long and six feet wide, containing upon it a palm-thatched house. Two men paddle, while two more stand fore and aft with long poles, by means of which they keep the raft clear of boulders, as on entering the rapids it glides frequently between rocks only eight or ten feet apart, contact with which would mean an utter collapse of the light raft, and too probably a fatal accident.

The most dangerous of these rapids is one known by the Malays as Jeram Panjang, at the present known boundary of Perak, towards the state of Patani. Here there is a huge boulder, and before attempting to pass it the boatmen make certain propitiatory offerings, in the shape of bananas and betel-nuts, accompanied by a speech, in which leave is asked to go down the rapid. It is no light task this rapid, for the fall amounts to a dozen feet in the space of forty yards, through a passage only from ten to fourteen feet wide. To prevent accidents rattans are secured to the raft to hold it back; but in spite of this many accidents occur amid the rush and turmoil of the hurrying waters, which eddy and form dangerous whirlpools, and lives have occasionally been lost. Some idea of the difficulties of the navigation in these higher parts of the river may be formed, when it is announced that according to a late voyager—Mr. Daly—down the stream, there were over fifty rapids —the most dangerous being the above-named, and one known as Jeram Kling.

These rapids are not the only obstacles to the navigation, for after the freshets the trunks of large trees are frequently brought down, many of which strand in the shallows, and form those dangerous impediments which the Americans call " snags," and

" sawyers," and which are fatal to the unfortunate boat
that encounters them in its way.   Like most rivers of
its kind, the Perak has a large bar at its mouth, of
sufficient importance to necessitate careful pilotage
through the channel, for large vessels inward or
outward bound.

Of its tributaries the principal are the Plus,
Kungsa, Kinta, and Batang Padang rivers, all rising
in the east and north-east, amongst the heights of the
central range; while numerous streams of minor growth
tend to make the state an admirably-watered country,
and, as already intimated, form the highways for the
limited commerce that is carried on.

This is no land of huge volcanic peaks, for the
mountains only attain to an average altitude of 5000
or 6000 feet; 7000, as far as present surveys
go, probably being the extreme.   Here the ancient
forest reigns supreme in all its grandeur ; in fact,
with few exceptions, as soon as the river-banks,
with their sparse villages, are left behind, the
traveller plunges into the jungle, and then finds the
land almost wholly uninhabited, save by a few wild
tribes, who migrate from spot to spot, as they are
moved by their superstitious reverence for good or
evil omens.

The general knowledge of the eastern portion of
Perak is at present very imperfect ; and though the
Malay peninsula has been crossed to the north and
south, so far it is probable that no European has

made his way through Perak to the opposite coast, thus leaving open a goodly exploration for anyone of adventurous mind. The indefatigable Russian traveller, Baron Maclay, has traversed a considerable portion of the interior; but the information he obtained from native sources was, on the whole, so contradictory and untrustworthy as to be but of little value.

There are two minor ranges between the higher mountains and the seaboard, and, running almost parallel with the backbone of the peninsula, they form the valleys of the Perak and Kinta rivers. The range nearest the sea contains several tolerably high mountains, the principal of which are Gounong Booboo and Gounong Hijau—"gounong" being the Malay term for a mountain, as "bukit" is for a hill. The ascertained height of Gounong Booboo is 6100 feet, the latter being only a little lower. Other eminences are known, as the North and South Mounds, and Bukit Sigari, or the False Dinding. The most peculiar mountain of the country, however, is one known as Gounong Pondoh, lying a little north of the direct route between the mouth of the Laroot river and Qualla Kungsa, one of the principal stations of the upper Perak river.

Gounong Pondoh is a singular eminence, standing alone, and rising out of the plain like a huge beehive; for it is one mass of red and white limestone, about 1000 feet high, bare and time-worn in places,

and perforated with the caves peculiar to this formation. This eminence is distinctly seen on entering
the mouth of the Laroot river, and also forms a
very prominent object from Qualla Kungsa on the
Perak river. A similar hill is found in the neighbouring state of Quedah, and is there known as the
Elephant Rock. It is likewise of limestone, and its
peculiar formation must be a problem for geologists.

The caverns of these limestone hills are well
worthy of a visit, and make no great demand on the
explorer. In the case of the Elephant Rock there is
first a stiff climb over the rocks to reach the arched
entrance, which is richly fringed with the stalactites
common to limestone caves. One of these stalactites
has been broken, and on being struck by the club of
the Malay guide, the peculiar sonorous tone emitted
reverberates through the cavern with a hollow roar.
During a visit in 1872, torches were lit which displayed
on all sides the peculiar shapes taken by the congela-
tions of lime-charged water, these shapes being
grotesque in the extreme, some even assuming a
strong resemblance to the human profile, with flowing
beard and locks, carved in white marble by some
clever sculptor's hand. Some idea of the extent
may be gained when it is mentioned that the roof is
some seventy feet above the floor, while large unexplored passages extend in different directions.
Prevalent as are the stalactites, their corresponding
stalagmites are comparatively few. Many, however,

are doubtless buried beneath the excreta of bats,
which covers the floor to a great depth ; and doubtless
below this the geologist will find many relics of the
older fauna of the peninsula when the time for excavation comes.

On the occasion of this visit the party had a
narrow escape, for one member was moved with a
strong desire to let off a rocket in the interior of the
cave; a proceeding which would probably have resulted in bringing down tons of stalactites on his companions' heads. He was however stopped in time.

The cavern is entered from the land side, and the
mountain is completely pierced, so that the explorer
comes at length upon an opening of some fifty feet by
thirty, looking straight out to sea through a glorious
fringe of stalactites and ferns, giving the opening, with
its ferny and mossy terraces, the aspect of a beautiful
proscenium, from which the eye is taken with regret.

The road mentioned as extending from the mouth
of the Laroot river to Qualla Kungsa is notable as
being one of the principal in the state, and has been
developed, under the management of the British Resident, from a mere elephant-track into one suitable for
the transport of produce. The mention of a road
some twenty-seven miles in extent may sound a trifle,
but in a land where the rivers form almost the sole
means of intercommunication, the existence of one
good road, setting aside the military advantages,
means the opening out of the country to a new form

of traffic. This road leads through the pass of Bukit
Berapit, a ravine of great beauty though of no
vast extent. The granite crops out here of a fine
gray variety, similar to our Aberdeen ; tall forest trees
tower up, rich in their gorgeous greens, whilst at their
feet cluster ground-orchids quaint and curious in form,
and far more beautiful than the stunted kinds seen
in our hothouses at home. In clearings where the
forest gives place to the traces of former cultivation,
fruit-trees are found in abundance, the Malays
planting extensively wherever they settle. Clump
after clump of fruit-bearing trees is passed, lending the beauty of their foliage and burdens to the
scene, already brightened here and there by bubbling
streams of delicious water, rushing over the rocks of
the narrow gorges on their way to swell the Laroot
river below the pass.

The trees here are frequently grand in their growth,
rising up without a branch a hundred feet before inter-
weaving with their fellows to form a shade so dense,
that farther in the forest a dim twilight reigns even at
noonday.

This road passing through Bukit Berapit divides
the district of Laroot·from Perak proper. It was
commenced by Captain Speedy, Her Majesty's Assistant-resident at Laroot, with the aid of the Muntri
of Perak, one of the principal officers of the Sultan's
little court, and one who has for many years claimed
to be the governor of the above district. It was

pushed on with vigour by the civil and military authorities during the disturbances of 1875–76, and a line of telegraph was laid along it to connect the military post of Qualla Kungsa with the anchorage in the Laroot river at Teluk Kartang, the nearest point to our old settlement at Penang.

A good idea may be formed of the primitive nature of the country, when it is considered that this is the only road worthy of the name. There are, however, certain tracks important from their communications, not from their condition. One of these leads from a place called Boyah, north of Sengang, on the Perak, to Kinta, a place of importance from its having been the old seat of the Government of Perak. This track passes through several villages during its course of about forty miles ; while a back pathway of about twenty miles in length will take the traveller again to the river at a village called Blanja, where, if the Perak be crossed, a couple of fresh tracks diverge, each of which leads to the sea by communication with the rivers Trong and Dinding, whose mouths are about twenty-five miles apart.

A road to connect the mouth of the Perak river with Banda Baru, the Residency, is in course of construction, and this will do away with the necessity for a long and tedious journey along the serpentine windings of the lower reaches of the river. Besides this there are a few jungle pathways, as intimated, only known to the natives, and but little used.

CHAPTER II.

LIBERALLY supplied as they have been, then, by nature
with water-ways, in the shape of rivers, the necessity
for roads does not seem to have occurred to the
Malays, especially as they are by nature essentially a
sea-going and boating people ; and consequently they
for the most part build their campongs or villages on
the river-banks ; and where elephant-tracks do exist
they are mostly in places where it has been found
convenient to carry tin to the nearest market, obtaining in return rice, salt, and salt-fish, which form
the staple food of the Malays.

During the petty war which followed the murder
of Mr. Birch, one of these elephant-tracks was
traversed by General, now Sir Francis, Colborne,
K.C.B., with his little force, which marched through
the jungle from Blanja to Kinta ; but it was only
with great difficulty—a difficulty which will be
understood when it is stated that the elephant, from
notions of safety, always plants his feet in the

tracks of his fellows who have gone before, from time immemorial, with the natural result that the track becomes a series of pit-holes, almost impassable for travellers on foot.

Before quitting the subject of the rivers, a few words must be said respecting the more important tributaries of the Perak—namely, the Kungsa, at whose confluence the important station of Qualla Kungsa, or mouth of the Kungsa, is situated—the Bidor and Batang Padang, which unite and enter the Perak about fifty miles from its mouth. Up to this point ships drawing not more than thirteen feet of water may be navigated. It was here that Her Majesty's war vessels lay at anchor during the disturbances. This place—Durian Sabatang as it is named—has been chosen from its natural advantages as a most desirable place for a permanent station, and it is believed that the authorities have definitely decided upon erecting one here.

The river Kinta, perhaps after the Perak the most important of those in the state, rises in the main range, and after running in a southerly direction, enters the Perak at Qualla Trus; but it bifurcates about six miles before joining the main stream, and forms a delta, upon which is situated the village of Banda Baru, the seat of the Residency. This is no very cheerful spot, lying low, and being uncomfortably swampy, and it is probable that on the erection of a station at Durian Sabatang, the Residency will be

removed to what will probably become the principal
port of the south. This is the more probable that
at this point an alteration becomes necessary in the
navigation, vessels of lighter draught being required,
and from the swift nature of the stream the process of
poling being adopted ; though after what has been
done in the way of constructing large steamers
drawing only a foot or two of water, and with stern-
paddles, for the shallow American rivers, the want of
depth in the Perak will not stand in the way of its
becoming the great water-way of a large commerce,
running as it does north and south through the whole
state, and even at Qualla Kungsa, one hundred and
fifty miles from its mouth, being over two hundred
yards wide.

The Bernam and Krean have already been mentioned, not as tributaries of the Perak, but as running
direct into the Straits, and important, the former as
forming the southern boundary between Perak state
and Salangore—the latter as dividing the state from
Province Wellesley, our British possession, and the
state of Quedah on the north.

The soil on the banks of these rivers is generally
a light sandy loam, which easily washes in during the
annual freshets, with the natural consequence that
sandbanks frequently obstruct the navigation. These,
and the many other hindrances in the shape of tree-
trunks, will doubtless be cleared as the country becomes more opened up ; but, in spite of the admirable

supply of water-ways, and the convenience of the streams for bringing down the mineral produce of the central ridge of mountains in which they rise, the necessity becomes every day more apparent for the construction of large trunk-roads, with cross-roads communicating with the river.

Abundance of material exists for this purpose, except on the actual banks of the rivers near the sea, where the constant recurrence of mangrove swamps necessitates the formation of the well-known road composed of trunks of trees laid side by side, and called " corduroy," or else the excavation of deep trenches, to obtain sufficient soil to raise the surface of the road above the reach of the water in the tidal swamps ; for unless this is done to the extent of at least two-and-a-half feet above high-water mark, the road is soon perforated by land-crabs, and becomes useless.

The rivers become swollen with mountain torrents during the rains, rising several feet, for the average rainfall in Perak is from sixty to ninety inches ; and at such times navigation becomes difficult or impossible. There is no distinction of spring, summer, autumn, and winter here ; for the year is divided into two seasons, ruled by the prevalence of the monsoons, that from the north-east beginning about the middle of October and lasting to the middle of April, while that from the south-west prevails during the rest of the year. The word " monsoon " is too often associated in people's minds with a time of storms, but in these regions it

c 2

applies only to the direction of the winds, which blow steadily from these quarters for six months alternately. For Perak is no land of typhoons and hurricanes, but is an equable region, a land, as has been intimated, of eternal summer to the European, which, by the way, is looked upon by him as no advantage ; for the monotony of such an unchanging season becomes wearisome in the extreme.

The north-east monsoon is, so to speak, the dry season, though a dry season proper does not exist ; for there are constant showers which lighten the air and make the climate pleasant and easy to bear. The day perhaps has been hot, steamy, and oppressive, when towards evening the clouds are seen to gather blackly over the mountains, and a steady downpour sets in, accompanied by thunder and lightning, the latter mostly of the kind known as "sheet." As the rain ceases there is a delicious freshness in the atmosphere, the oppression passes away, and the air is for the time being redolent of the sweet after-shower scent ; though it must be said that the flowers of this region are greatly wanting in the delicious odours of those of temperate climates—a fact probably to be attributed to their rapid growth and development from a well-watered soil, and from an atmosphere laden with moisture to the greatest degree.

During the prevalence of the south-west monsoon the heavy rainfalls occur, with storms and electrical discharges, which last for many hours.

The heat is never great, and bears no comparison with that of India, a singular fact when it is considered how near Perak lies to the equator. On the plains the mean annual temperature is about 79 degrees, but in the morning the thermometer frequently falls as low as 74 degrees; while in the ascents of the mountains that have been scaled the Malays have been known to complain bitterly of the cold. There is this peculiarity in the climate, that before rain the air becomes very oppressive, from the amount of moisture with which the atmosphere is saturated; and this, with the sudden nightly falls of the mercury, is the principal cause of disorders amongst the Europeans.

These diseases take the form of fever and rheumatism. On the whole, however, the climate is decidedly healthy; though, as in almost any part of the world, a night's rest at the foot of hills, or any low-lying swampy ground, may result in an attack of fever. These are facts apparently known to the natives, as shown by the construction of their huts upon piles of bamboo; though the seeking of protection from wild beasts and from floods doubtless has had its influence.

Lakes seem to have, so far as is at present known, little to do with the physical features of Perak. Here and there the rivers widen into lagoons, and a lake of some extent has been seen, but not surveyed, in the central part of the country; but probably such lakes as exist are dependent upon the freshets of the rainy season.

Very little has been ascertained as yet as to the geological features of the country ; but one of nature's singular changes of surface is very plain here in the way in which she is constantly denuding the higher grounds, and carrying down, by means of the rivers, the superabundant soil which constantly adds to the coast-line. This is especially marked in the Laroot district, where small tracts of new land have been brought under cultivation, so that where at no very distant period the tide ran, padi, or rice, is now showing its luxuriant growth.

The primitive rock—that which forms the main range of the country—seems to be that hard stone so familiar to us in the sculptures of the Egyptians, and known as syenite, while here and there, as in the pass at Bukit Berapit, a fine-grained granite crops out, equal to our own Aberdeen. In this pass there is also quartz rock, and it is possible that here the granite passes into syenite. The most important rock, however, is an argillaceous talcose schist, for in this is to be found the principal mineral deposits of the country.

For some distance from the coast the land is low and swampy, but, gradually rising, a better class of country is reached, where the soil has been washed from the hills, and this is as fertile as that towards the sea is sterile and unproductive. There are, how-

ever, plains near the coast of higher elevation than
the ordinary tracts, and these are cultivated by the
natives, who plant maize and fruit-trees, and, where
irrigation is available, they grow their staple food—
rice.

Farther inland, the plains, which are to be found
of greater extent in the Perak than in the Kinta
valley, are broken up with natural sand-ridges, which
lighten the soil, and make it very well suited for the
cultivation of rice ; and, from their appearance of
having been more under the plough than at the
present time, give evidence of the existence of a far
larger population than now exists in the country.
Undoubtedly the richest soil in the valleys is that composed of the *débris* of the mountains proceeding from
the decomposition of the felspar in the granite. This
débris, mixed with the decayed vegetable matter, has
gradually subsided into the low lands, and now offers
itself for cultivation. There is no trace of volcanic
action in the peninsula, saving a few hot springs existing at Malacca ; and, near as Perak lies to the great
volcanic band which contains the craters of Java and
Sumbawa, earthquakes are unknown, though slight
shocks have been felt at Singapore. The country is,
however, peculiarly rich in minerals, and these will
undoubtedly lay the foundation of its future prosperity.

Fossils are rarely found ; but at the mouth of one
of the rivers there are very curious deposits of the
ordinary cockle-shell, raised up into heaps many feet

high, and looking as if they had been left there by
the action of some eddy ; though when and how, it is
impossible to say, for they lie high and dry upon the
shore.

In northern Perak a limestone formation is pretty
prevalent, as opposed to the ferruginous sandstones
and shales of the south. Large slabs of slate are to
be found in certain of the rivers :· it is tolerably soft,
but not bituminous. From indications, there seems
to be a rich deposit.

Hard sandstone and ironstone rocks are to be
found jutting out from the banks of the upper reaches
of the Perak river, but the ironstone is not affected by
the magnet. Here again, too, quite inland, traces of
shells are found in positions eight or ten feet above
the level, as if left by the receding sea. This is
especially noticeable at the base of Gounong Wang, a
huge limestone hill.

On the whole, so far as the country has been
explored, the palæontologist does not find rich and
curious stores awaiting him, and has to be content with
examining boulders of granite, veined with quartz,
sprinkled with large grains of felspar, and showing
their character plainly in the smooth-washed sides in
the rapids above Qualla Kungsa. Now and then,
though, he may be rewarded with a fossil, traces being
seen of what is evidently petrified wood; but until
the country is more opened out, organic remains are
not likely to reward his search.

CHAPTER III.

IF the visitor to Perak turns his attention to mineralogy, rich stores doubtless await him, especially as a scientific search, although proposed, has not yet been undertaken by the Government. In 1854, the writer discovered graphite or plumbago, in one of the states south of Perak; and though brought into notice at the time it has since passed out of mind, but there is every reason to believe that deposits exist. The same may be said of galena, which has been found in the Dindings, and of which there are valuable mines in Patani, just to the north. This ore of lead was known to be a mineral of the peninsula as far back as 1616, but its actual site and locality never appear to have been traced until very recently by Mr. Fisher.

This may seem a poor argument as regards Perak, till it is understood that the states north and south are really only portions of the same country, pierced by the same range of mountains, and separated only by a comparatively few miles.

What is wanted is for exploring-parties to trace eastward and examine the mountain-ranges with their ravines, so as to reach the matrices of the metallic stores that are tolerably-plentifully obtained even now in the lower lands. Traces of hidden wealth have frequently been found. Of gems, there are diamonds and garnets, in what number it is impossible to say, and amethystine quartz exists in great beauty.

A curious discovery of silver antimony was made not far south of Perak. On one occasion when a quantity of stones were taken into Singapore jail for the convicts to break, one was found to be a mass of antimony. The explanation given was that the lump was one of the stones that had been used by the Malays for attaching to the anchors of their boats; and in this way it had probably been brought over from Borneo, where the ore is known to exist. Search near the spot where the stone was picked up proved fruitless; but it is a far more reasonable surmise that silver antimony exists in the Malay peninsula if not in Perak, and that it will some day reward the explorer's zeal. This is, of course, surmise, but to it may be added the reports that in the mountain-ranges of the Laroot district copper with bromide and sulphide of silver have been found. There is no reason why they should not exist, though in a land of gold and tin.

On the whole, iron is abundant in Perak, and exists in the form of the peroxide, and as a cellular clay ironstone known as laterite; but so far no attempt has been made to reduce these to the metallic form. The late Mr. Westerhout stated that he had had specimens of copper brought to him from the interior of the country; but he died before it was possible to take advantage of the discovery, and the rich metal therefore lies waiting for the explorer's hand.

Coal has been found, though as yet small in quantity, and of no great commercial value. Investigation, however, would probably result in the discovery of any or all of the above minerals in abundance; and even if it were barren of result, the prospecting-parties would be amply rewarded by the opening out of new lodes of tin and gold, which not only exist, but have been mined here from time immemorial.

The bright silvery metal tin is worked in Perak to a great extent, and though obtained in a clumsy primitive way, the yield is very abundant, and would be far greater but for the evident depopulation of the country. The metal has been attractive enough to bring the busy Chinaman by the thousand, and go where you will through Perak, he is to be encountered, patient and busy, digging, washing, and melting the ore.

It seems odd in a land where gold is found in tolerable quantities, that tin should be looked upon as the principal metal. This however is easily explain-

able from the greater ease with which it is obtained.
A chief here reckons his wealth in his bhars or slabs
of tin; and when, as in a late act of piracy, a rajah
was brought to book by one of Her Majesty's cruisers,
the offender was mulcted, not in so many hogsheads
of palm-oil as on the west coast of Africa, nor in so
many peculiarly-shaped dollars as in China, but in a
certain number of slabs of tin.

All over the country deserted tin mines are to be
found. In the south, in the neighbourhood of the
Batang Padang, and Bidor rivers, they are frequent,
but at the same time there are many mines being
worked. In each case examination shows that the tin
gravel has been brought down by floods from the
mountains some miles to the east and north; but the
idea of going to the mineral fountain-heads never
seems to have occurred to the Chinese, though sometimes, like the Malays, they object to any such
proceeding on account of the mountain jungle being
infested with evil spirits, to whom they might give
offence. Yet at the same time it is found that the
nearer the mountain, the better is the yield of the
ore, which is found in small black granules, similar to
those seen in a quartz specimen of tin ore from
Cornwall.

In these southern parts, want of capital and the
difficulties of carriage seem to prove great drawbacks
to the successful carrying out of the work; and the
consequence is that Laroot, in the extreme north of

the state, where the deposits are rich, and carriage comparatively easy—which last has its due effect on the food supply—draws to itself the principal portion of the tin-mining energy.

The principal mining stations of Laroot are Thaipeng and Kamunting. This portion of the state is well deserving of a visit, from its being the busiest and most thriving; standing out, as it does, in strong contrast to the sleepy agricultural portions, where the ubiquitous Chinaman is not at work. At Thai-peng is the dwelling of the Assistant-resident, Captain Speedy, a gentleman who, by his energy, has produced peace amongst the rival factions of the Chinese, given protection and safety, and fostered the mining energy to such an extent that the mining towns are thronged, there are Chinese shops, and the general air of the place betokens prosperity.

The Resident's house here is a large native structure upon an eminence. It looks, with its wooden supports, palm-thatch, and extensive verandahs, precisely adapted to the climate; and here the eastern element shows out strongly, in the Chinese going and coming in their peculiar costume and parasol-shaped hats, while the Resident's police—swarthy Sikhs, in white puggarees—stand about awaiting orders, or on duty.

Thai-peng village, or town, as seen from the Assistant-resident's house, is a busy place, with long thatched buildings by the hundred. Fences and

watercourses intersect the land, and here and there
supplies of water are dammed up for the purpose of
washing the tin.

Much will have to be done to improve the process
of obtaining and smelting the tin, as the natives are
wasteful and extravagant, with the consequence that
high prices result. · Unfortunately the trade has of
late been bad, the duty high, and Australian tin
has begun to compete favourably with that of the
Straits; but as the latter is stream tin, and in abundance in Laroot, without seeking in the matrix, it is
probable that it may soon recover its old position in
the market, though perhaps not at the earlier prices.

What is really wanted to make the tin deposits of
Laroot highly profitable is the introduction of British
capital and machinery, with British enterprise. Then
the ore would be obtained, washed, and smelted with
the smallest loss; and here, in a land where shafts
that take years to dig, and require fortunes to be
sunk, are not needed, but where the ore is reached
after removing a few feet of superficial soil, there must
be temptations enough for the Cornish miner, whenever a settled rule has made the country safe—and
this must ultimately come.

The method of procuring the ore or "biji timah"—
tin seeds—is very simple. The Malays dig a few feet
down in ·a favourable spot at the base of the hills,
take up the clay, which contains the tin in small
nodules, and carefully wash it in running water, made

to flow over it by means of artificial channels. The ore is then, when dry, ready for smelting, which is also performed in a very primitive manner. A furnace is built up of clay, with a hole beneath; the ore is placed in the furnace between layers of charcoal; fire is applied, and forced into a powerful glow by means of very homely bamboo bellows, which keeps up sufficient blast to cause the golden-orange molten metal to trickle into the receptacle below, from which it is ladled into moulds, to form slabs or ingots, weighing two catties (equal to 2¾ lb.). Sometimes, however, the Chinese mould is adopted, in which a slab weighing fifty catties is cast.

The Chinese are wasteful enough in their way of obtaining the tin, but they are far in advance of their unprogressive neighbours, bringing simple machinery to bear where necessary; and their process is admirably described by Captain Speedy, the Assistant-resident at Laroot.

According to his report, the tin lies at a distance of from twenty to fifty feet from the surface, gradually diminishing towards the hill-sides, where it is not more than six feet down; and as it lies horizontally, the following arrangements are made : The jungle is cleared and the mine marked, water is brought by a ditch from the nearest stream, and then the excavating commences.

At about six feet down water begins to rise from the soil; and to get rid of this, and also to utilise the water from the stream as a motive power, an ingenious chain-pump is made, by constructing a long wooden trough of three planks, each one hundred feet in length ; and this is placed with one end resting on the bank, the other sloping to the water in the lowest part of the mine.

"A wooden chain with small oblong pieces of wood placed at right angles to the line is fitted accurately into the above-named trough. The wooden chain is endless, and is passed round two wheels, a small one at the lower end of the trough and a larger one at the upper end. This latter is a water-wheel, and is turned by a constant stream flowing over it. Round the axle of this wheel are cogs, each of which in turn, as the wheel revolves, draws up a joint of the endless chain through the trough, and as each joint fits accurately into the trough, they bring up in succession a quantity of water, which, on reaching the mouth of the trough, falls into the channel by which the water which turns the wheel is carried off, and is thus also taken away out of the mine and conducted to the next, where the process is repeated. The small wheel at the lower end of the trough regulates the chain, and guides the wooden joints into the trough, causing each to take up in succession its quantum of water, and by this means the mine is emptied."

Their tools are very poor, consisting of only a common hoe and a small flat cane basket. With these the whole of the work is done, the baskets when full holding about four pounds of earth. One of these baskets is placed at either end of a stout bamboo, balanced over a labourer's shoulders, carried off and emptied, while the men with the hoe scrape together more soil and fill other baskets.

What an English navvy, armed with spade, barrow, and pick would think of the oblique-eyed, childish-faced Chinaman and the amount of work he does may easily be imagined. Still the slow tortoise won the race; and whereas our navvy demands so many pounds of meat and so many pots of beer per diem, Ah Sin is content with a little rice, some fresh water, and, for his grand relaxation, a tiny pipe of opium.

The washing, as performed by the Chinese, is very simple. The ore is found at Laroot in a stratum of whitish clay, which is washed in long open troughs, water passing freely through, carrying off the soil, and leaving the ore at the bottom, for it is prevented from running down the inclined trough by means of bars of wood nailed across the bottom, and against which the heavy grains rest. On this plan the Chinese seem in advance of the washing on inclined planes at the Cornish tin mines, the crossbars being a very efficient way of arresting the ore.

The melting process is very similar to that of the Malays, but more elaborated, and is carried out on rather a larger scale, and in place of the bamboo bellows a very ingenious plan is adopted. The trunk

of a tree about eighteen inches in diameter, and ten
feet long, is carefully hollowed out, and closed at either
end. "A long pole with a circular piece of wood at one
end, fitting exactly into the bore of the tube, acts as a
piston. In order to secure the tube being perfectly
air-tight, the end of the piston is well padded with
feathers. Valves are placed at each end to allow the
air to enter, and in the centre the nozzle of the bellows
communicates with the furnace by means of a small
air-passage. On the piston being drawn out, the air
in the higher portion of the tube is forced down the
nozzle, and on being drawn back the air in the further
part of the tube is similarly drawn into the furnace."
The charcoal is soon brought to a white heat, and as
the molten tin drips through, fresh layers of ore and
charcoal are added, the fluid tin being ladled out into
the moulds already mentioned as being sometimes
adopted by the Malays.

The value of the tin exported in the seven years
prior to 1874 was upwards of a million and a quarter
sterling, this being the produce of thirty mines. It
must however be added that these figures were
derived from native sources, and may have been
exaggerated; for Captain Speedy's estimate of the
produce for 1875 was in money value a million and a
half of dollars. Since then, however, the number of
Chinese miners has largely fallen off, probably in
consequence of the disturbances. Under a more
favourable system there is every probability of their

being re-collected, and the works attaining to great prosperity.

Anyone who has had experience of the lamentably-slow process of obtaining Cornish tin, and the vast sums of money adventured without result in that granitic peninsula, will see what an opening is here in Perak for British capital, especially as the climate is healthy and Coolie labour comparatively cheap.

Much store as the Malays of Perak lay by tin, they are not blind to the charms of gold, and, to their taste, it is best of a dark-red colour. It is no un-common thing, when journeying through the interior, to come upon a Malay, or even a boy, washing the soil left by some ancient flood. The quantity obtained in this way is necessarily very small; but still it is to be procured, and the nearer the mountains are approached the richer is the find; of course pointing to the fact that there lies the matrix from which, by the decomposition of the quartz, the gold has been washed down.

In some of the tin mines worked by the Chinese, especially in the south, in the neighbourhood of the Batang Padang river, the soil is first washed for the tin ore, and afterwards undergoes a second washing for gold, which is found in small quantities, but still sufficient to repay the labour. One peculiarity in con-nection herewith is that the gold is found at depths of thirty to forty feet below the surface, and invariably in connection with the trunks of large trees, in every

stage of decay—a fact pointing to the tremendous
floods that must have taken place at the time of the
deposition of the metal.

In the north, one of our Government officials
describes the neighbourhood of the Krean river as
showing a formation having much the appearance of a
gold-bearing country, such as he had seen in Australia,
and offering tempting places for a prospecting-party to
examine the junction of the granite and slate ; adding
that, if gold were not found, the search would probably result in the discovery of tin or some other
metal.   That gold has been found in large quantities
in the Malay peninsula, is proved by the vast number
of old workings surrounding the base of Mount Ophir,
to the north-east of Malacca ; and if with their primitive ways of working, sufficient could be found by
the people of bygone ages, modern appliances should
result in securing a rich return.

On the eastern side of the Perak river itself, at
a place called Kleian Bronsong, there is an alluvial
deposit which yields gold, and it is washed out of the
creek, during the rainy season, by the Chinese and
Malays, who however are idle during the dry times,
for want of water.   Among other places on the Perak
river where gold is found, washing of the deposit is
carried on by Chinese at Campong Cherako, and there
are several abandoned gold mines at a place called
Chigar Gala, one of the largest villages on the river,
and lying above the station at Qualla Kungsa. In fact,

so abundant is gold, that before now the writer, when wandering about, has with very little difficulty washed specimens of the precious metal from the river beds, where it mostly occurs in little globular forms, like small or dust shot. Mr. Daly, the Government surveyor, who observed this during a journey taken to determine the northern boundaries of Perak, remarks that it would be interesting to thoroughly investigate these gold deposits, and describes the metal he has seen as being "rough and shotty," and having the appearance of not having travelled far; while, judging from the quartz, slate, and other pebbles found in the river, he believes that the matrix will be found in the quartz reefs lying embedded between the granite and slate.

Enough has been said to show that plenty of traces of gold are to be found, little as the country has been explored. What stores the jungle-hidden streams, running up to the mountains, conceal in olden mines or untouched virgin pockets, time and the ceaseless energy of the Anglo-Saxon alone will show. As to the Malays, they are too accustomed to a *laissez-aller* style of life to make any energetic attempts to discover and work the metallic treasures, while the efforts of the Chinese, with their primitive tools, are not likely to greatly influence the yield of the precious metals.

Recompense of some description is almost certain to reward the explorer, for, as has been before remarked,

the finding of a rich lode of metal of any kind is a
reward not to be despised; and it is questionable
whether the discovery of the Burra Burra copper
mines in Australia was not a more worthy one than
that of the gold; while as to Perak, if instead of
metal a good vein of coal could be found, the finder
would be a benefactor to the state.

CHAPTER IV.

BRITISH tin was an article of export to the islands of
the Eastern Archipelago up to the year 1618, and it
is difficult to trace the time when it was first discovered in Perak and the other portions of the Malay
peninsula. De la Loubere, the French envoy to the
King of Siam, in the years 1687–88, wrote an account
of that people, and he states that all the calin or tin
in Siam—which country then embraced a considerable
portion of the Malay peninsula—was sold by the king
to strangers as well as to his own subjects, except that
which was dug out of the mines of Jon Salam or
Junk Ceylon, in the gulf of Bengal, "not above the
distance of a man's voice from the coast of Siam," and
where there is loadstone; for this being a remote
frontier, he leaves the inhabitants in their ancient
rights, so that they enjoy the mines which they dig,
paying a small profit to the prince.

Mr. Walckenaer, the German traveller, thinks that

the word *kalah—calin—*tin, was derived from the
modern Quedah, the Portuguese corruption of Keddah.
Masudi speaks of the fourth sea of India—that of
Kalah Bao or the sea of Selahat, which had shallow
waters, and was full of small islands containing tin
mines, where the natives used poisoned arrows; an
exact description of the straits of Malacca—and selahat
is certainly the Malay for a strait.

The Arabian term *cassider*, derived from the
Sanscrit *kastina*, applied by the Phœnicians to tin,
as in our own Cassiterides, or tin islands, off Cornwall,
seems to imply that they derived their knowledge of
metal in the first place from the East, or through the
Arabians; and tin is not found anywhere nearer to
them than in the Indian Archipelago. These latter,
in the Middle Ages, seem to have adopted the Hindoo
term *kala* or *quala* for tin, although *kasdin* is the true
Arabic. Our name *tin* is traced to the Malay word
timah, but how this came to pass is not very clear.

The Sanscrit *kala* literally means *black*, so that
it does not seem necessary to go far to trace the
application of the word by the natives immigrant
from India, to the black mineral grains found as
stream tin; and its adoption by the Siamese and
Arabians at a later day, to distinguish the tin of the
Indian Archipelago from that of Great Britain.

Among other writers, Dr. Vincent, in his "Periplus,"
published in the year 1800, speaks of tin as being an
import into Africa, Arabia, Scindi, and the coast of

Malabar ; and as an article of commerce brought
from Britain in all ages, and conveyed through the
Mediterranean by Phœnicians, Greeks, and Romans, to
the Eastern seas ; but says it was only during the past
few years that it had reached China in British vessels.

Of the ancient history of the gold of the Malay
peninsula much may be said, for it has been famed
for its production from all ages. This peninsula was
the Aurea Chersonesus of the ancients, and although
the evidence is not conclusive that Josephus is right
when he says that the Mount Ophir of Malacca, some
hundred and fifty miles south of Perak, and called by
the modern Malays Gunong Ledang, is the Ophir of
Solomon, there is much that is in favour of this supposition ; and being a subject of such great interest,
it may be worth while to investigate the question,
even at the risk of being somewhat tedious.

It may be taken as a matter of fact, that from the
very earliest ages there was intercourse between the
Arabians and Malays ; and hence it is reasonable to
suppose that the precious metal gold, would, with
spices, be amongst the articles of trade. From the
earliest times we know that the Arabians sent into
Sabea both spices (frankincense) and gold, but whether
the latter came from Sofala, on the east coast of Africa
—the sea-port of the Mount Ophir of Bruce and Le
Grande—or from the Mount Ophir of Malacca, is an
open question. There is also, it should be added, a
Mount Ophir, or the Golden Mountain, in Sumatra ;

but this may be left out of the argument, as the name was conferred upon it by Europeans at a comparatively recent date.

Lassen, the orientalist, has placed Ophir, the origin of Solomon's gold, somewhere about the mouth of the Indus; and his hypothesis, says Mr. Crawfurd, is founded on some resemblance between the Hebrew and Sanscrit names of the commodities brought from this ancient spot. The nearest resemblance is in the words for an ape, that in the Hebrew being *koph* or *kof*, and in Sanscrit, *kâpi* or *kopi*. Mr. Crawfurd, however, in view of all the difficulties connected with its geographical position, comes to the conclusion that the Ophir of Scripture is simply an emporium where Solomon's fleet obtained "gold, silver, ivory, apes, and peacocks;" and he fixes this emporium somewhere in Arabia, either at Sabea, or at a spot on the southern coast. But as we read that the ships of Solomon "came to Ophir," it is more natural to conclude that they went to a place bearing that name, and not to a convenient emporium, where the gold of Ophir and the other commodities were exposed for sale. The question then seems to lie between the Ophir of the eastern coast of Africa and that of Malacca.

There are many things in favour of the mount in the Malay peninsula being that of Scripture, and the idea is supported by many writers. For instance, Dr. Kitto, in his Encyclopædia, states that the natives of Malacca call their gold mines "Ophirs;" to which may be added, that the Malays being a decidedly non-progressive people, their term probably comes from time immemorial. De P. Poivre, a French author, writing in 1797, gives the same statement, adding of the natives of Sumatra—*on y trouve plusieurs mines d'or, que les habitants de Malacca et de Sumatra nomment "Ophirs."* He, too, adds that the mines of the adjacent places are richer than all those of Brazil and Peru.

When we consider the objects sought, we find that they were apes, peacocks, ivory, and gold. Now, though the ape proper is not indigenous to the Malay peninsula, monkeys of large size abound; it is the home of one of the most beautiful of the peacocks; ivory, if not abundant, is procurable, for elephants are plentiful; spices follow as a matter of course, for this is the very centre of the production; and gold is worked to the present day. Gold, apes, and ivory are certainly found in Africa, but the other articles would have to be brought from the Eastern seas.

To go back to the ancients for support of the theories that Solomon's vessels may have traded with the Malays: Pliny tells us that Eratosthenes speaks of Meroe, India, and the Thinoe; and Agatharcides, a contemporary of the latter, about 104 B.C., says of Sabea, now Yemen, or "the blest": "The people are robust, warlike, and able mariners. They sail in very large vessels to the country where the odoriferous commodities are produced; they plant colonies there,

and import from thence the 'larimma,' an odour
nowhere else to be found ; in fact, there is no nation
upon earth so wealthy as the Gerrhei and Sabeî, as being
the centre of all the commerce which passes between
Asia and Europe." The same writer also refers to the
Maldive and Laccadive islands, and coupled with these
is a reference to Malacca or the Golden Chersonese.

According to Dr. Vincent, the Chinese had not
then passed the straits of Malacca ; but the Malays
seem in all ages to have traded with India, and
probably with the coast of Africa, and he ends by
saying :

" All this induces a belief that in the very earliest
ages, even prior to Moses, the communication with
India was open, that the intercourse with that continent was in the hands of the Arabians, that Thebes
had owed its splendour to that commerce, and that
Memphis from the same cause came to the same pre-
eminence, and Cairo succeeded to both in wealth,
grandeur, and magnificence."

If then, as this evidence would show, the communication with India and its isles was open before
the time of Moses, and in the hands of the Arabians,
who from the earliest ages had an intercourse with the
Malays, the inference that can be drawn from this
may be left to everyone to judge of as he pleases.

There is, however, another significant point which
favours the belief that the gold of Ophir was obtained
from Malacca, for amongst the articles of export to the

Red Sea in the time of the "Periplus," which gives
an account of the navigation of the ancients, from the
east coast of Africa down to Sofala, gold is not
mentioned, but only "ivory, rhinoceros-horn, and
tortoise-shell of a good sort, but inferior to that of
India." Dr. Vincent, the last editor and exponent of
the work, is so struck with this fact, that he confesses
to feeling "some degree of disappointment in not
finding gold, as the fleets of Solomon are said to have
obtained gold from this coast." He however gets over
the difficulty by saying : "Our present object is not
the trade but the geography."

In later days—namely, in the fourteenth century
—Barbosa says that gold was so abundant in Malacca
that it was reckoned by the bhar of four hundred
weight. In 1615, also, we read in the State Papers
that at Acheen, in Sumatra, the admiral's galley had
a turret built in the stern, covered with plates of gold
—a sure sign of the plentiful supply of the metal.
Later still, in "Herbert's Travels," printed in 1677,
he says that Malacca had the name Aurea given to
it, on account of the abundance of gold carried thither
from Menang Kabau, in the neighbouring isle, Sumatra;
and again, Valentyn says, in 1737, Acheen exported
gold by the thousand ounces at a time.

To come down to our own days : Mr. Logan estimated the total produce of gold in the Malay peninsula
as twenty thousand ounces per annum only. This
does not arise from the mines being worked out, but

from the gradual depopulation of the country, and the facile way in which tin is obtained and sold by the Chinese, leading to the temporary abandonment of the search for the more precious ore.

In addition to this, the discoveries of gold in other parts of the world have taken off the attention of European capitalists from the mines of Malaya; and though an attempt was made recently to work the gold mines of Chindrass, near Malacca, the adventure failed from the want of mining skill and proper appliances. What is required for the proper development of the acknowledged valuable mineral resources of the peninsula is—as was some time since suggested —that a practical mineralogist and geologist should be sent out from England, to examine and give copious reports of the capabilities of the country, so as to draw public attention to it at home. This step has not yet been taken, but it is not too late to adopt the suggestion; and the outlay on such a survey, if judiciously carried out, would be amply returned to the Government and to the colony.

CHAPTER V.

In few parts of the world are the wonders of the
vegetable kingdom to be seen in greater perfection
than in the Malay archipelago; and Perak possesses
its full share of these glorious productions, for the
moist hot climate favours rapid growth, to an extreme
degree.

On quitting the river-ways, and plunging into the
jungle, the traveller is at once in a world of wonders.
In almost every instance he is confined to the forest
track, for the jungle is literally impenetrable. Huge
trees tower up a hundred and a hundred and fifty feet
without a branch, and then weave and interweave in
the most extraordinary manner. These are the pillars
and supports of creepers and parasites innumerable,
among which the most prominent are the various
varieties of the rattan cane—the common cane of the
shops, but which here winds and runs to the length
of two and even three hundred feet. A soft greenish
twilight generally prevails in these dense parts of the

forest; but where there are openings that admit of
the sun, flowers—principally orchids—add their beauty
to the scene.

Wherever a watercourse is found, there, with their
lace-like fronds, tree ferns spring up to fifteen and
twenty feet in height, drooping gracefully over the
mossy rocks, and beneath them may be seen an
abundance of the lesser variety of ferns, chiefly of
the Pteris family.   Soon, again, appear the beautiful
quaint-blossomed orchids, principally the Dendrobium
and Vanda varieties, hanging in rich clusters from the
trunks and branches of the forest trees.   The elk-horn
hangs pendent in masses of many feet in length,
and, deeper in the jungle, lycopodiums, and the many
varieties of moss which flourish in moist situations,
carpet the earth.

It is a carpet, however, that is untrodden; for
unless a way be cut by means of the heavy knife or
parang of the Malay, progress even of the slowest
nature is impossible, and the beauties of the ground
orchids which spring up in the clearer spots are
doomed to flourish and fade unseen.   In these dense
woods ebony is sometimes found, though not in any
great profusion, and it is not used by the Malays.
There is an abundance, though, of excellent timber
for building purposes, which to a great extent is
felled and squared by the Chinese.   The chief of these
woods—some of which are hard and very durable—
are the marbow, and the damar laut, the maranti, and

the serayah. There are many others of admirable quality which it is needless to name.

One timber tree promises well. It is known by the Malays as the *seum*. They say that if placed over piles used for jetties it will resist the action of the teredo, or boring-worm; for the worm, after devouring the wood attacks that of the ordinary piles, and is killed from the action of the acids of the two, and if this be the case it will be a valuable timber to possess. Further proof however is needed of its qualities.

Teak, though found at Penang and Singapore, and abounding in the jungles of Siam, oddly enough does not grow in Perak. There are plenty of fine durable woods, though, to make up for the deficiency. Neither has the camphor tree been found, though believed to exist at Salangore, but the gutta tree is tolerably plentiful, and its curious gum is extracted by cutting down the whole tree, tapping it on the under side, and allowing the gutta to exude into vessels placed for its reception. This gum is frequently used by the young Malays to catch birds, forming a most glutinous bird-lime. The name by which it is known in England—gutta-percha—many people may not be aware, is rather a redundant one, percha being only the native name for Sumatra, whence the gutta was perhaps originally brought. The indiarubber tree, with its glossy green leaves, is one of the many trees of the wood; but its juices are not com-

monly extracted, though used also occasionally as
bird-lime.

One very hard wood, called by the Malays
kamooning, is obtained from a slow-growing flower-
bearing tree. It is of fine grain, takes an admirable
polish, and is used to ornament the hilts of krises,
and to make into fancy or useful articles, such as
boxes, cigar-holders, and watch-cases : the late rajah of
a neighbouring state was a great adept at turning
this wood in his lathe.

It is no uncommon thing in the depths of these
jungles, as night sets in, to see glades lit up with what
seem in the distance to be so many pale lamps burning
with a mild radiance, but which prove on closer
inspection to be a very curious kind of phosphorescent
fungi, of considerable size, the light being probably
produced by their decomposition. At times too,
during a journey, the native guide points out the ipoh,
or upas tree, and announces that it is poisonous; but
the stories of its deadly nature are apocryphal; and
though the tree may possess poisonous qualities,
beyond tradition the Malays seem to know very little
about it.

Another famous tree flourishes here, namely, the
banian; but, growing as it does in the dense jungle,
where it has to struggle for its existence in a very
small space, there are none of the wonderful wide-
spreading specimens such as are said to shelter a
regiment on an Indian plain. To revert however for

a moment to the upas: it is perhaps too much to say
that an approximation to its branches, or sleeping
beneath its shade, may not be highly injurious,
especially when it is an established fact that the
poison alder of Virginia acts upon the skin, if ever so
lightly touched, with the greatest virulence, producing
all the symptoms of poisoning to a marked degree.
The upas, however, does not seem to have been
tested, and possesses perhaps a far worse name than it
deserves.

The bombax, or cotton tree, is here in two varieties,
but probably imported. The kayoo puteh, literally
wood white, is a tree whose name has been corrupted
into the cajeput of the Pharmacopœia. It yields a
very valuable green oil, which is used for medicinal
purposes. Large quantities of wood oil, or kayoo
minyati, are also obtained by the Malays, by cutting
a triangular hole right into the trunk of a forest tree,
and placing therein a cup or half a cocoa-nut shell.
Fire is then applied, and the oil is melted and drips
into the cup. This oil forms a kind of varnish, and
is used for the interior woodwork of their houses,
and sometimes as a medicine.

One of the prettiest trees is the waringhan, with its
birch-like growth ; it is a species of ficus, and deserves
to be called the most ornamental in the peninsula,
though the beautiful growths are endless, even as they
are peculiar. Amongst the ornamental trees, though,
must be classified those which blossom. One of the

finest of these is called by the Malays *dadap*. It
bears a beautiful flower of a brilliant scarlet, and is
utilised largely in the coffee plantations of Java as a
protection to the young trees from the ardent sun.
Another blossoming tree is the chumpaka, of which
there are two varieties, the one bearing a yellow, the
other a pure white flower, and both diffusing—what
is comparatively rare—a delicious scent. These are
favourite flowers, and are often used—like the white
blossoms of the jasmine and the sweet-scented star-
shaped bunga tanjong—by the women to ornament
their hair, while the natives of India in the peninsula
offer them at the shrines of their god.

One of the especial features of the jungle is the
beauty of tint and mottling of the foliage, and this
relieves greatly what would otherwise seem sombre
and monotonous. Almost side by side may be seen
growing leaves of a bright yellow and others of richly-
tinted reds, while close by are displayed infinite
variegations, in different shades, of purple mixed with
splashes of white, as if all colour had been withdrawn
from the leaves. Undoubtedly the beauty of nature's
gardening in these eastern forests has had something
to do with the taste that has of late set in for foliaceous
plants. The foliage, too, of the hill-sides in Perak is
wondrously beautiful, displaying every tint of leafage,
from pale yellow, through infinite shades, to the
darkest green, with here and there clusters of bright
blossoms peering out, amongst which may frequently

be seen what is known as the Pride of the Forest, a blossom of a deep red and yellow. There is also the blossom of the kamooning tree, which strongly resembles that of the orange, and emits as sweet a scent. Though no scented flower, there is a modest plant found occasionally that is a pretty and familiar object to every European, and takes attention when its tree-like relatives weary the eye. This is our adiantum, the pretty little maiden-hair fern, and it is principally found growing in the laterite clay iron-stone soil. The first discoverer of this little favourite is said to have been Archdeacon Hose, and the habitat was Malacca.

Though Perak can hardly be called a land of flowers, still there are many of very great beauty, and this want of gorgeous petals is made up for by the colours of the leaves. The orchids however are very beautiful, both the large parasitical and the ground varieties. The scorpion orchid—a wonderfully-accurate copy of the poisonous creature from which it takes its name— abounds, as does a magnificent creeper which would be a great acquisition to a European garden, from its rich maroon blossoms. Climbing plants are very common in the jungle, running up the trees in a straight line similar to the strands of our close small-leaved ivy, and often to a height of thirty or forty feet. But perhaps of all the climbers the most striking are the nepenthes, or monkey-cups, which are seen in every opening. Those grown in our hothouses

poorly set forth the beauty of the varieties of this
singular plant. Here they may be seen growing in
clusters of fifty or sixty together, close to the ground,
and with pitchers of ten or twelve inches in length.
Others, again, are seen ascending the forest trees,
sun-seeking from a shady spot. They are generally
green, but variegated with purple and red, speckled,
splashed, and striped, and many of them fringed in a
most beautiful manner. They all contain water, many
over half a pint in quantity; but it generally seems
to be of a viscid nature, and not tempting as a
beverage.

Water-lilies abound wherever they find a suitable
habitat in the lagoons formed by the many streams;
while the lotus is found in great perfection, sending
up from its floating leaves its bright blossom-cups of
red, blue, and silvery-white. There is a fine display
of this plant in a small lake fronting the house of one
of the native chiefs, at Bukit Gantang, while these
and the water-lilies lend great beauty to some of the
smooth open reaches in the wilder portions of the
country.

Arums, and that beautiful plant the calladium,
with its arrow-shaped variegated leaves, also play their
part in diversifying the jungle. The sensitive-plant
grows largely too on the peninsula; and it has this
peculiarity, that wherever it abounds it destroys the
lallang grass—a knowledge of which fact may be of great
service where the land is infested with this growth, for

good grass can readily be grown around the sensitive-plant, after the lallang is destroyed. The hibiscus grows to the size of a tree, and the gardinia flourishes well, its large white flowers being great favourites with the Malays.

A flower-bearing tree, known as the *Poinsiana regia*, flourishes well here; it is small in leaf, but bears a magnificent bloom, which grows in clusters on every bough; in fact, like the azaleas of our green-houses, there are often more flowers than leaves. Mr. Dunman, a former inspector-general of police at Singapore, introduced this largely into the town, where it now grows to great perfection.

The nipah-palm grows in company with the mangrove in brackish water, by the muddy shores, and is often washed off to go floating about the straits, looking in the distance like a boat under sail. These mangroves, whose singular roots have already been mentioned, have a peculiarity in their seed-pods, which deserves mention. There are apparently two varieties, the one having a seed something like a cocoa-nut, the other, pods of a large size, rather in the shape of a boy's skittle, but pointed at the bottom; and so wonderfully are these balanced, that as they drop from the mangrove branch they fall upright in the mud, literally planting themselves, and rapidly taking root.

Another very beautiful shore-loving tree is the casuarina, which flourishes amid the sand, being a kind of fir. It is peculiar for the way in which the wind

sighs through it, reminding the settler of the old
Scottish fir of far away, with its roar as of surges in
its dark green crown.

Perak may be looked upon as a paradise of palms,
of which there are many varieties. The nipah, which
has just been mentioned, fringes the rivers up to tidal-
mark, and forms the chief thatching material of the
Malays, while its fruit makes a preserve. Then there
are the sago, which is allowed to grow for about
fifteen years, and then cut down to obtain the farina
from the pith in its trunk; the jaggary, from which
coarse sugar is made; and the areca, a slender, very
graceful tree, yielding the betel-nut, which the Malays
chew for its stimulating qualities. The blossom of
one of the wild arecas has a most delicious odour, and
there are several varieties. The penang, or areca, is
the palm which is utilised in a variety of ways by
the Malays, its leaf-sheath affording them a horny
material, which they use for water-buckets and baskets.
The cocoa-palm grows luxuriantly, and fruits well at
long distances from the sea. In addition, there is a
rare variety which bears a cocoa-nut, whose fruit is
pink instead of white. The gamooty-palm is also very
common, and the black fibres of this tree are of
endless use to the Malays, for making cordage, ropes,
and the open strands with which they take their
enemy the alligator. The most graceful of the family,
however, is the nibong, which in beautiful clusters
shades the jungle dwellings of the Malays, supplies

56

CAMPONG ON PERAK RIVER.

the posts for their houses, and is cut into strips to make their floors.

The various palms are the most striking features of the river-banks, and wherever they are clustered in any number there are sure to peep out the pointed roofs of the attap-thatched houses. The wonder is that the large cocoa-nuts, in their great fibrous coating, and heavy falling leaves, are not frequently the cause of accidents to the children playing beneath them in the villages; but somehow they seem to escape, for injuries are rarely known to the writer as having occurred.

Next to the palms in value to the Malays come the bamboos, which graceful ornaments to the jungle, towering up like Brobdingnagian grass, are utilised in a variety of ways : building, boat-making, raft-constructing, and also for cutting up into various domestic implements. It is also of great service to the natives for their fences and stockades, and if used as a hedge it acts admirably, those that have been made about the settlements adding greatly to the attractions of the lanes and country roads. Fine clumps of bamboo add to the beauty of the river Perak, seen as they are, feathering against the pure sky. But great as is the beauty of this cane it has its bad qualities. The Malays use the large hollow joints to hold water; but in its wild-growing state it is frequently the cause of fire; for where pieces of large growth, or even plants of similar silicious nature, are in a position to be fretted and rubbed together by the wind, a serious jungle fire will often result. This no doubt taught the aborigines how to obtain fire by rubbing a couple of pieces together. The rotans, or rattans, have already been mentioned as among the great obstacles to progression through the jungle; but to the Malays they are of infinite value, supplying them, when twisted by means of a lever, and then dried, with their strongest ropes.

CHAPTER VI.

THE fruits of Perak are almost endless, and embrace
some of the most delicious under the sun; but many
of them bear names that would be little better than
puzzles to the reader. Some of the principal must
however be given by their native titles.

Mr. Wallace, in his "Malay Archipelago," says
that the durian, which he seems to have found in a
great many of the islands, is the king of fruits, and
the orange the queen. To give *place aux dames*, the
queen of fruits does not exist in Perak at present;
but the country is eminently suitable for its growth,
and those specimens which are brought in from
Tringanu, on the east coast, are little inferior in flavour
to those of St. Michael.

The king of fruits, however, flourishes largely, and
is peculiar to the archipelago. It grows upon a large
tree something similar to a walnut, ripe fruit and flowers
being seen upon the tree at the same time; and, as if

to startle the learned gentleman who is said to have
refuted. the atheist about the acorn, the durian will
grow as large as a man's head, is covered closely with
terribly sharp spines, set hexagonally upon its hard
skin, and when ripe and it falls, if it should strike
anyone under the tree, severe injury or death may be
the result. So fully awake are the natives, to the
danger of a blow from a falling durian, that in populous
places they take the trouble to stretch nets at some
distance from the ground, where a road or pathway
leads beneath a durian grove, so as to catch the ripe
fruit as it falls. Five faint marks exist on the shell,
which show the line of the carpels, like those of an
orange, and following these the fruit can be opened with
a heavy knife. Inside there are, to each carpel or
division, two or three seeds as big as chestnuts, and
these are surrounded by a rich thick cream, upon
the flavour of which opinions are wonderfully divided.
The natives are excessively devoted to it, and some
Europeans declare it to be like a rich buttery custard
flavoured with almonds ; while Mr. Wallace says,
"with it come wafts of flavour that call to mind
cream-cheese, onion sauce, brown sherry, and other
incongruities."

The writer's testimony is that it is, no doubt, to
some palates a very delicious fruit or food, as it
may be termed, but when over ripe, its odour is
fœtid to a degree. The disagreeable odour of this
fruit has formed the basis of many an anecdote, and if

one or two are given in passing, it is only what would be expected when the durian is mentioned.

A high official, on his way from England to China, was sumptuously entertained by the then resident councillor at Penang. This gentleman was a great admirer of the fruit, and had one of the very best his garden could produce placed upon the table. On his lordship being asked his opinion of it, he replied sharply to his host: "It may have been very good last season, Mr. L., but, if you will excuse me, I would rather not venture on it now."

Ladies are supposed to look upon this production with extreme disgust, but get the credit of being very partial to it nevertheless. The story goes that a lady, the descendant of one of the old settlers of the peninsula, made a confession in an unguarded moment, when, being condoled with upon the question of having to go and live in a very out-of-the-way bungaloh, she declared she should not feel dull, for there would be plenty of durians there.

So strange and unwholesome is the odour of this fruit, that it is possible it may possess the quality of temporarily destroying the sense of smell in those who partake of it; otherwise this intense fondness for the fruit seems almost a mystery. It may be detected at a considerable distance, and about the nearest approximation to its peculiar smell is that of a brick-kiln when in full burning. The natives cultivate it largely, and esteem it above all others. An old writer says that the Siamese would barter their liberty to obtain it; certain it is that a Malay would give a considerable portion of his day's pay to obtain one.

The mangosteen too deserves special notice, for its inviting appearance and delicious flavour. It is a fruit that would be highly esteemed in England; and the writer is glad to announce that plants of this fruit-tree which have been sent to British Guiana are now growing, favoured by the latitude; and probably by the time these pages appear will be in full fruit at Trinidad, whither they were sent. The distance from Demerara or Trinidad is comparatively so short that there is the possibility of the mangosteen at length finding its way to an English table. This it is hoped may prove to be the case, as all efforts made by the writer, who tried various methods, failed to get the fruit home from Singapore in decent condition.

The pine-apple flourishes well wherever planted, but grapes are only produced with great difficulty. The varieties of the custard-apple, guava, pome-granate, alligator-pear, mango, and a number of native fruits, grow abundantly at the Settlements, and fruit-trees of many kinds are carefully planted round their homes by the Malays. The pommeloe, or shaddock, flourishes well, but is an importation from the East and West Indies; there are several kinds too of citrons and limes, while the plantain, banana, or pisang, as the Malays call it, exists in a great many varieties, the best known being those bearing the names of the stone, gold, sweet, egg, king, sultan, monkey, and finger plantain.

The bread-fruit is of two kinds, only one of which is edible, but it is not held in the same esteem as in the South Sea Islands. There is a pandanus too, which bears a fruit as large as a durian. It is a fine object in the marsh lagoons of Perak. The fruit is, however, smooth, and not in favour with the Malays, though much sought after by the monkeys. Perhaps one of the most singular of the fruits of the peninsula is the cashew-apple, which abounds, and is remarkable for being like two fruits in one ; an apple above, with the familiar kidney-shaped nut below. The dookoo is a large round fruit, and grows on a comparatively small tree. The nam-nam, an acid apple-like fruit, has the peculiarity of growing on the stem of the parent-tree ; while, for some unknown reason, the papaya is said to possess the quality of giving tenderness to meat placed beneath its boughs.

A curious seed-pod growing commonly in Perak deserves mention. It is only a little over an inch from tip to tip ; but it is peculiar from its taking the exact shape of a buffalo's horns and frontal. It is one of those freaks of nature that are so hard to explain, for in this case no possible reason can be assigned for its eccentric shape.

Very few cases of injurious symptoms seem to arise from partaking of fruit. There is one kind however, the rokam, which is very unwholesome if taken in an unripe state, and cases of death from its effects are not unknown amongst children. When ripe however it resembles a gooseberry in flavour, and though hard, becomes very pulpy on pressure, and is eaten in this state by the Malays and some Europeans.

The indigenous fruits of the peninsula are however almost endless, and a full description of all would be far beyond the limits of this work.

CHAPTER VII.

ONE of the first things a settler thinks of in a new
country is the supply of food to which he has been
accustomed. When, however, the resident in Perak
looks for the homely old vegetables of his native land,
he is doomed to be disappointed. Still, if he be not
too strictly wedded to conventionality, he will find
that nature has, in withholding the produce of a
temperate region, been prodigal in her supplies of
that belonging to the tropics. A stranger will look
in vain for the simple potato, even though it was
originally the growth of a foreign shore, for all
attempts to cultivate it here result in the production
of wretched little tubers not much larger than peas. In
its place, however, there is the dry-eating, farinaceous
yam, which flourishes abundantly.

The great dish of the east is curry; but let not
the reader imagine that it is composed with a dry

F

yellowish powder, for nothing is farther from the
truth.   The fact is, that the native curry more
resembles the preparation for a salad, inasmuch as it
is composed of vegetables in their green, or ripe state;
and it is surprising how many things are introduced
into the savoury dish.   One of the principal ingredients is the contents of the cocoa-nut, crushed with
its milk into a pulp.   Turmeric is grown, and largely
used.   The pods of the moringa tree enter into the
curry, while its scraped root is used by Europeans as
a substitute for horse-radish, which it strongly resembles in flavour.   The fresh chillies and capsicums
of the country are considered indispensable, while the
heart of the cocoa-nut tree, called cocoa-nut cabbage,
is another ingredient, though often used as a salad,
in which form it has a delicious nutty taste.

Under the name of *kachang* the Malays classify
the many varieties of beans, peas, and vetches.   These
they commonly eat parched; but, after the fashion of
our gardeners with the sea-kale, they often imitate the
Chinese plan, and grow some kinds in the dark, so as
to make them tender for mixing in curries.   We have
there, too, a creeper, whose name is not known.   It
grows very readily, and its leaf strongly resembles
spinach.

As might be supposed, all plants of the gourd
family flourish rapidly.   Water-melons come to great
perfection; cucumbers are plentiful; and the Malays
grow a large number of gourds, some of which are

edible, others useful for vessels for carrying water. Among other vegetables grown by the people are a kind of edible arum; sweet potatoes; and the bandicoi, which grows on a small'shrub, bearing a flower like a hibiscus. This, with a curious three-cornered vegetable, eight or ten inches long, is much appreciated. The Malays have also a great affection for onions.

The climate is, however, capable of producing, and does produce where the Chinese have settled, pulse, radishes, and a coarse lettuce. There is also no doubt that many kinds of familiar English vegetables might be grown, if care were taken to study the suitable time for planting, and to protect the tender shoots from the sun. Much has been attempted, though little has yet been done. In the higher parts of the country, on the slopes of the mountains, would be the most suitable spots. A few enterprising gentlemen have made attempts in the Settlements, and good English peas have been grown. Upon one occasion a cabbage was produced that would have been an ornament to a Covent Garden stall; but that wonderful cabbage had been tenderly nurtured in a flower-pot, and was its owner's anxious and almost only care; in Province Wellesley, however, asparagus has been grown with success.

Herbs flourish, mint growing well in the country, and there is a leaf with the flavour of sage; and when it is remembered that Perak runs from the low seashore swamps upward to the central hill-summits, abounding in fertile soil, and plentifully supplied with water, it is evident that, by management, the fruit or vegetable of most parts of the world might be produced with ease.

Advantage has been taken of this by the growers of the various commodities which are raised upon a large scale. Indigo has been tried by the Chinese settlers at Singapore with the most gratifying results. It thrives well, and its growth is apparently free from the many difficulties which attend its production in India. The juice is used by the Malays, who have probably learned its value in dyeing from the Hindoos.

Pepper is a plant natural to the Straits, and flourishes well, but it has the peculiarity of quickly exhausting the soil. The Chinese and Malays grow it readily, and it is a production that has a ready sale. Heat, moisture, and shade are indispensable to it ; and it may not be generally known that black and white pepper are, like black and green tea, the produce of the same plant.

Gambier is likewise largely grown in the Straits, and would flourish well in poorly-cultivated Perak. It is produced from a shrub, whose leaves are picked and boiled down into a syrup, poured into moulds, and then cut into cubes when dry. It is largely used by the Malays for masticating with their betel. As a drug, however, it is very valuable for tanning pur- poses, containing, as it does, some fifty per cent. of pure tannin. It is this drug which is used to give the nets and sails of our fishing-boats at home their cinnamon-brown colour. Cotton was tried in Singapore by General Cavenagh, and it grew with a fine long staple. It was merely an experiment in a garden, and the plants suffered from blight, but it is one of the productions for which the soil of Perak is eminently adapted.

To continue the experiments that have been made, sugar may be mentioned ; in fact, so successfully has the cane been grown that a company is reported to have just purchased ninety thousand acres of land in the country for a sugar plantation.

Coffee and Java are so well associated in most people's minds, that it will be no surprise to say that the berry has been successfully grown in the peninsula. Tea culture is in its infancy ; but it has been satisfactorily tried in the settlement bordering on Perak, namely, Province Wellesley, where the clove has also been grown. These have been but tentative matters, for, except by the Malays in their primitive manner, the soil of Perak, which offers itself for the cultivation of these valuable commodities, has hardly been broken, and is in fact a wilderness of fertility, waiting for the busy hand of man.

Another plant too would flourish well in Perak, namely, the tobacco, already grown in small quantities by the Malays ; and judges of the soil suited for this aromatic production assert, that if the planters who

have so successfully adventured in growing it just
across the Strait at Deli in Sumatra, had first seen the
land on the banks of the Perak, they would have
had by preference their plantations there. At the
present time the Deli cigars have found their way
into the English market, where they promise to be
formidable rivals of the well-known productions of
Manilla.

Cinchona, the tree from which quinine is obtained,
should also be tried, as a paying cultivation, for it has
succeeded admirably in Ceylon, India, and the neighbouring isle of Java. Most of these are growths that
may be looked upon as experiments—though such as
are almost bound to succeed. It is however only fair
to refer to a failure—namely, an attempt to reintroduce
that valuable spice the nutmeg. This has been tried
without much success at Penang and Singapore, and
no adequate reason can be assigned for the very
extensive failure of the plant about twenty years ago.
Perhaps Perak may be found the happy medium,
lying as it does between the two settlements.

Among the regular cultivations of the state, rice
must stand first, forming as it does the staple food of
the Malay. Wherever padi-fields are planted off the
banks of the rivers and drain-canals, the rice is grown
with very good results, while the waving fields of
sugar-cane and maize plainly show that the general
cultivation of these crops might be as well carried out
in Perak as in Province Wellesley in the north. Here

the sugar estates have for years past realised the most happy results.

The rice-growing is of two kinds—namely, the wet land and the dry land. The latter on the hill-sides is exclusively the native method; but for the wet growth the Malay is indebted to the Indians who settled in Sumatra, and from whom this mode of irrigating the fields and producing the rice spread through the peninsula. After the land is prepared, the grain is not sown after the fashion of corn in Europe, but in nurseries; and when the tender young plants are eight inches high, they are lifted and transplanted, after removing the tops, being placed in clusters of six or eight, pretty closely together, in the field ready for their reception, and in rows one foot apart.

The Malays are good agriculturists, but do little until they are obliged, being of a listless idle nature; and they suffer from the effects of one of our old policies—namely, that of discouraging rice cultivation, and letting them trust to the importation of this staple from places farther south.

The plough used is a primitive affair, drawn by buffaloes. It is a heavy pole, with a wooden fork to act as coulter, and a bar of wood inserted at an oblique angle by way of handle. The clods are broken by dragging over them a heavy beam, and the land is harrowed by means of another heavy beam full of spikes. The sowing in the nursery and planting out are generally performed by women, who, when the padi

is ready, cut it off about six inches below the ear.
This they do sometimes with a sickle, but generally
by means of an ingeniously-contrived little instrument, by whose action, aided by the fingers, the rice-
stalks are severed as if by a pair of scissors, leaving
the stems in the gatherers' hands. The husking of
the rice is contrived by means of a tin-bound pestle
and a mortar, and the woman's difficulty is to regulate
her blows so as not to crush the grain.   An ingenious
American machine has for some time been introduced
into the peninsula, consisting of a heavy shaft with
pegs or cogs, which alternately raise a series of pestles,
or stampers, which fall in as many mortars, and so
husk the grain. The Chinese also have established
primitive machines driven by water power.

Tapioca is largely cultivated in the peninsula, and
it would grow well in Perak, but at the present ruling
prices it would hardly be a paying adventure.   In
fact in forming plantations here, as in many other
parts of the world, the labour question is the great
difficulty. To meet this, however, there is the hope
that Coolie emigration will still be fostered by the
Indian government; especially as now every safe-
guard has been made for the protection of labourers,
and for their return to their homes; in fact, every
provision that could satisfy the most hypercritical on
such matters. The present Indian famine could not,
of course, have been foreseen; but had greater facilities been given for emigration from India, many of

those terrible deaths from starvation might have been averted, while the native states of the peninsula would have been correspondingly improved.

The flourishing growth of citronella and lemon-grass, from which essential oils are extracted, must not lack mention ; while the question of grass naturally suggests pasture-land, which is somewhat wanting, for this is no home of grazing cattle, like the park-like stretches of Australia. There is however a great variety of grasses in the peninsula. Capital sweet nutritious meadow-grass is grown at Penang and Singapore, upon which both horses and ponies thrive well; but the grass generally of the Settlements, except in Northern Perak, is not particularly good or fattening for cattle.

In connection with the clearing away of the jungle, and preparing the ground for cultivation, there are one or two curious points to consider. One is, that if the tall trees are cut down the brushwood should be left, or its place supplied with some other growth, otherwise miasma is likely to rise and produce fever. Secondly, the action of nature is so rapid that, in clearing away the trees and brush, or, as the Malays call it, *tabas-tabang,* no more should be cleared than is required for use, otherwise the *ladang* will run into *lallang.* In other words, the cleared but uncultivated land will be speedily overrun by a rank grass (*Gramen caricosum*) the roots of which are more expensive and difficult to clear away than the jungle that previously occupied the soil. This grass is so plentiful, and so overruns the country, growing in some places to a height of five feet, that it is a pity that it cannot be turned to some manufacturing account. It is said to make fair paper, but its success in this way is not yet publicly known. The Malays, however, use it for thatching, and cattle-bedding, and stuff their pillows with its flowers : here however its utility ends.

Like the inhabitants of Java, the Malays have a good notion of what vegetable productions are available for medicinal purposes. Unfortunately, too, their knowledge has extended strongly to poisons, and the Malay women have the credit of a great insight into those infusions which produce death.

Amongst the medicinal plants, the fresh roots of the male pomegranate is, as an infusion, a specific where a vermifuge is needed. For chest complaints, a jelly is made from a sea-weed called *agar-agar*. It is mixed with sugar, and not at all unpalatable; but the Malays probably owe the knowledge of this production to the Chinese immigrants, who bring with them no lack of medical knowledge : in fact their preparation of peppermint is an almost universal medicine, and invaluable in its properties.

One little shrub, called *tulvee,* which is in favour with the Indians for placing near the graves of the departed, has a black seed which when· mixed in water gives out a kind of white pulp. This is held in great esteem by the natives for its power in cooling the blood, and is often taken with lime-juice and sugar. Among the poisonous plants, the daturah is common in the peninsula ; and it has been remarked that when a person is under the effect of its poison, he constantly observes his fingers, and keeps passing his thumb over them in a most peculiar way.

In a district like Perak, however, where over the greater part of the land nature reigns supreme, these notes of the vegetable productions are necessarily very far from being complete ; they are, however, the result of observation, and show the reader how lush must be the growth of this tropic soil.

CHAPTER VIII.

SELF-PRESERVATION is so truly the first law of nature,
that it is only natural for a visitor to a far-off foreign
shore to eagerly inquire as to what noxious creatures
are there, and dwell especially upon the reptiles; for
the travellers' tales that have been brought home, respecting the acts and deeds of huge serpents, that
crush buffaloes in their folds and then swallow them,
have been as startling as those relating to the rapid
and fatal action of the poison of the smaller snakes.
Perak being a land of moist jungle, with large swamps
and lagoons, lying beneath a tropic sun, naturally
possesses its noxious reptiles; but as these creatures,
like almost all wild animals, hurry away from the step
of man, accidents are very rare.

When it is stated that boa-constrictors are said to
be found to the length of thirty feet, they might
reasonably be expected to be the most alarming of the
peninsula reptiles, but they are rarely seen, and are

for the most part dangerous to fowls. In fact, the writer shot one that had invaded his fowl-house in Labuan, and gorged itself to such an extent with poultry that, like the mouse of the fable, it could not crawl back by the hole through which it had entered. This creature was eighteen feet long, and nearly as thick as a man's leg. That pythons grow to exceptionally large size there can be no doubt, but twenty feet may be taken as the size of a well-grown specimen.

One of the keenest sportsmen in Singapore gives an account of a monster that he encountered; and also instances that the boa feeds occasionally on larger prey, which it can seize and crush. He had wounded a boar in the jungle, and was following its track with his dogs, when on penetrating farther into the forest, he found the dogs at bay, and advancing cautiously, prepared for another shot at the boar. To his surprise, however, he found that the dogs were baying a huge python, which had seized the boar, thrown its coils round the unfortunate beast, and was crushing it to death. A well-directed shot laid the reptile writhing on the ground, and it proved to be about thirty feet long : but such instances of extreme length are very rare.

There are some fifteen or sixteen different kinds of snakes — and many of them beautifully marked — known to the Malays, who however look upon them with the greatest unconcern, knowing from long experience that their nature is to crawl rapidly away

into the jungle.   They vary, from a little viper resembling an English adder, to the black cobra, which is
as much as five feet in length.   These cobras resemble
those of India in their spectacle markings, and the
peculiar manner in which they puff out the neck, and
rise up on the lower portion of the body; but, poisonous
as they are, the Indian convicts in the Settlements will
seize them by the tail with one hand, and draw them
rapidly through the other till the fingers grasp the
neck, when they allow them to twine round the arm.
There is one little serpent though, about eighteen
inches in length, and peculiar in its shape, as it is
equal in size from head to tail, these extreme points
being wonderfully alike.   This is believed by the
Malays to be extremely poisonous, and is more dreaded
than the black cobra ; but injuries from snakes are
very uncommon.   For the cure of snake-bites the
common people use a stone which, though not the
bezoar-stone, is said to possess the quality of adhering
to the wound and imbibing all the poison ; though a
European would probably prefer the application of
ammonia and strong internal doses of brandy or
whisky, to increase the action of the pulse, and arrest
the horrible stagnation which appears to be one of the
consequences of serpent venom in the blood.

The principal food of the smaller serpents is undoubtedly the frogs of the marshy parts.   These
reptiles abound, making a deafening noise after a
shower.   Their little green relative of the trees, with

his sucker-furnished feet, merely emits a faint pipe; but he is far more active than his ground companions, and is a pretty object amidst the leaves. Amongst the pests of the moist places of the jungle are the leeches; for these creatures, directly the earth trembles with the step of man or beast, stretch themselves out in savage hunger—or, it should be said, thirst—and by some means or another manage to make a lodgment upon the body of him who passes through the woods. Perhaps their presence is not at first felt, and they may not be discovered till the journey's end, when a bath reveals the little monsters gorged with their sanguinary repast. How they manage to get up a man's trousers-legs is a puzzle; and the only way to keep them at bay is to tie the trousers tightly round the ankle, place them inside the boots, and freely anoint the latter with lime-juice, which the little pests hold in especial abomination.

Tortoises are often seen in the swampy places; one of them being a curious reptile with a soft shell, a large snout, and very quick movement; scuttling away in a very different fashion to its shelly companion, who calmly pulls its head and legs inside its case, and waits until the danger that threatens is past. Their relatives the turtles abound off the coast, and especially about the Dinding Islands. One of the smaller isles is chosen by the turtles for the purpose of laying their eggs, and they come and go with the greatest regularity, a few Malays inhabiting

the place specially for the collection of this egg
harvest. In the neighbouring state of Quedah they
are so abundant that they are made a Government
monopoly. These eggs are about the size of those of a
bantam, but have a soft leathery skin, while the
contents have a peculiar astringent flavour; but they
are looked upon as a great delicacy. The turtles off
the shore are very sluggish in their movements, and
may at times be seen lying asleep on the calm surface
of the transparent water; when a clever swimmer will
approach cautiously, turn them back downwards, and
then float them ashore boat fashion; for when turned
they are as helpless at sea as on land.

Among lizards is the beautiful flying species, with
its curious extensive web, and one known in Perak as
the iguana, which it resembles; but it is only about
eighteen inches long, and it is commonly called a
blood-sucker, probably because it never sucks blood.
There are also numbers of smaller lizards, which are
very rapid in their movements, and the decided
enemies of the flies. In fact, one of the favourite
proverbs of the Malay is derived from the deliberate
manner in which the lizard seizes its prey. It answers
to our Latin *festina lente*, the hasten slowly of moralists'
pens. The great dangerous saurians are three, and
known to the Malays as the gouro, frog, and copper
species. These alligators abound in the rivers and
estuaries; and occasionally a death or serious injury
occurs through an incautious approach to a river-bank

where they are known to abound. Their favourite habitats are near the mouths of the rivers, especially the Jurumas and Bruas, on the coast.

These reptiles run up to twenty-five feet in length ; but are then heavy and sluggish of movement, and bear no comparison for dangerous qualities with those of twelve or fifteen feet in length, which are extremely powerful and rapid in swimming. It is no uncommon thing for the Malay boatmen to warn their passengers, when going up a river, not to hang their hands over the sides, as people often inadvertently do, to feel the cool fresh current pass between the fingers, for an alligator will often snap at the hand ; one sweep of the powerful tail sending the creature with a rush through the water.

An instance was known to the writer of a man being seized across the loins by one of these creatures, which tried to drag him into the river, but he had presence of mind enough to thrust his fingers into its eyes, when the agony caused the monster to quit its hold. Travellers with sporting proclivities have ample opportunities for a shot at them, as they lie basking on the mud in the mangrove swamps ; but it is a great rarity to get one, for they immediately rush for the river if wounded, and sink directly, while very often their scaly hide saves them from injury. They are not seen very far up the river, seeming to like an occasional visit to the brackish water, or even a cruise now and then out to sea.

G

The Malays have a stimulus offered them by
Government for the destruction of these reptiles, in the
shape of a reward of twelve dollars for every one
taken, even as fifty dollars are offered for the destruction of a tiger ; but without this premium they have
a deadly hatred for the dangerous creature, and are
very ingenious in their plans for its destruction. They
make a large hook, very ingeniously contrived, so that
it shall not be disgorged, and attach it carefully with
ligatures beneath the wing of a white fowl.   Experience has taught them that the alligator can break a
chain, and bite through an ordinary rope ; so they
fasten the hook to a rope composed of loose strands
made from the gamooty palm. Then, after securing
one end of the rope—which is of a pretty good length
—to a tree, they picket the fowl to a peg on the river
bank ; the whole process being like setting a bank-
runner for pike in an English stream. The alligator
generally takes the unfortunate bait, swallows it
whole, and returns to the river, to find that the loose
strands of palm-rope go between its teeth, and cannot
be bitten through ; and the end of the monster is that
it is ignominiously dragged from the river by a dozen
Malays, and despatched. This is fishing on a large
scale and to some purpose, for the alligators are a
dangerous pest.

The Malays are, however, famous fishermen ; their
amphibious life making them adepts in anything connected with river or sea.   And this is in nowise

surprising, when we remember that fish in some form
or another is one of the staples of their simple food.
Give a Malay fish, salt, rice, and the fruits he culti-
vates near his hut, and he is content, especially if he
can in addition obtain a little Java tobacco. If he
cannot, he is content with his own rough growth,
which he rolls up into a large cigarette in a piece of
palm-leaf sheath ; or else smokes with no little enjoyment out of a pipe made from the short joint of a
bamboo for bowl, and a stem composed of a thin shoot;
while, should he be at a loss for a light in the jungle,
he can obtain it by rubbing the sharp edge of one
piece of bamboo on a notch cut in another, the sharp
piece sawing through and the dust igniting inside.

Fish of infinite variety abound in the rivers and
pools of Perak ; and frequently, after heavy rains,
small drains and ditches that have been fishless are to
be found swarming with small kinds of five or six
inches in length, offering themselves for capture by
the boys and women. For not only is fishing an
occupation with the Malays, and a means of getting
their livelihood, but one of their favourite amusements ; and it is no uncommon thing to see an old lady,
venerable in years, come out of her hut, armed with
bamboo rod and line, and sit and fish for hours,
generally with pretty good success. Her take will
generally consist of what the people call the *ikan
sambilang*, or fish of nine, so called from the number
of barbs at its head. This fish abounds in the ponds

near the rice-fields, and in the running streams, and
is a big-headed fellow, something between a burbot
and a gudgeon. It is a great favourite, and adds a
relish to the frugal meal of the captors.

Fond as both sexes are of rod-fishing, the Malays
make frequent use in their rivers of the small seine or
drag-net, whose lower edge is loaded with weights to
keep it at the bottom. Their way of using it is much
the same as at home here in England, in dragging a
small river or pond. It is stretched across from side
to side of a river, and then cautiously drawn to the
bank, great care being needed to prevent the escape
of the fish. During the disturbances at Perak, while
the troops were quartered at Qualla Kungsa, the
Deputy-commissioner became an adept in the use of
the drag-net, catching some good bags of a kind of
perch, which formed a very agreeable variety to the
sameness of the up-country mess-table.

The cast-net is also known to the Malays, and this
they throw with great dexterity; but they are not
always so straightforward, from an English point of
view, in their fishing, for they not unfrequently poison
the fish in convenient places, in a very poacher-like
fashion, using the root of a creeping shrub called
toobah. This, like cocculus indicus, has the property
of drugging the fish, which eat it with avidity, and
then come to the surface, and are easily taken by
hand. This same root is largely used by the Chinese
for destroying insect life amongst their growing plants;

and after some effort, the writer has succeeded, through the kindness of Singapore friends, in getting it safely to the Botanic Gardens at Kew, where it is now flourishing.

The Perak streams most probably contain trout, and they abound in curious examples of fish life, some of which are remarkably brilliant in their colouring. One little fellow is of a brilliant scarlet, with a broad band of bright blue across its sides. Another is remarkable for its pugnacity; for if a couple confined in separate bottles or globes are brought near to one another, they commence with a severe examination, and end by setting up their dorsal fins, and butting at each other fiercely, like a couple of piscine rams. Perhaps the greatest curiosity of all, though, is the little shooting-fish, which, if kept in confinement in basin or tank, will sail round and round, firing a water shot every time, like a shell from a tiny cannon, at any unfortunate fly or ant that may be on the side of the fountain or basin, or upon an overhanging twig, and this with good aim, till the insect is brought down and swallowed. When three or four of these little creatures are in the same basin, they will fire in turn, one after the other, with singular regularity. They are prettily marked black-and-white fish, some three or four inches long, and principally found in Siam, but are not uncommon in the waters of the peninsula.

CHAPTER IX.

THE sea has its curious fish off the Malayan coast,
one of which, the ekan buntal or pillow-fish, is very
common. It is beaked somewhat like a parrot, and
has the power of inflating itself into a globular form
when alarmed or touched, an act which sets up all
over it a wonderful array of spines. It has, moreover, the peculiarity of being vocal, for when touched
it emits a sound something between a grunt and the
hoot of an owl. The Malays never eat it, but when
it is taken with other fish, they shake it out of the
net upon the sea-shore, where it may often be found
in all stages between life and death.

As in other parts of the world, it is to the sea that
the common people look for their best supply of fish
for food. Of those which are brought to the table of
the European resident in the Settlements, the principal
are the tungeree, the red mullet, and the pomfret—a
very delicious fish not unlike a turbot. There is also

the tongue-fish, which somewhat resembles our sole,
though very different in flavour. Prawns, shrimps,
crabs, and cray-fish are plentiful. Both rock and river
oysters may be had, but they are elongated in shell,
and not equal to our natives. The mussel, too, is not
unknown.

As a matter of course the fishing-grounds of Perak
are not developed, and thus during the investigation
of the country, little besides a kind of gray mullet
could be obtained ; but north and south in the settled
parts the waters teem with fish. Among other kinds,
a little smelt is brought in, a delicious yellow fish with
a silver stripe along its side ; a kind of skate ; sharks,
especially the hammer-headed, abound, and the smaller
kinds are caught and eaten, being frequently exposed
for sale. Salt fish is much eaten by the Malays, and
that caught and dried at Salangore, under Chinese
direction, is admirable as a relish, and quite as satis-
factory as the fish-roe of Siak, which is always obtain-
able in the markets. To the lovers of the durian—
that is, people who do not object to peculiar gaminess
of flavour—may be recommended for a relish, with
curry, the blachang of the Malays.

This favourite condiment is generally made by the
Malay fishermen on the sands, where, in a kind of bag,
they trample semi-putrefied shrimps and prawns into
a mass, salt it, and keep it. Tastes are various, and
this odorous compound is much in favour. These
fishers are fond of collecting shell-fish from the sands

after the tide has gone down, very much as it is done upon our own shores; facts which place the civilised and the uncivilised nations very closely together in this respect. In Perak they gather quantities of the little donax, and it is no uncommon thing to see a Malay down upon the sea-shore busy with a kind of hook and a bag or basket, going cautiously over the sand till his well-trained eye lights upon a peculiarly-shaped hole, when the barbed iron is thrust down and one of the familiar razor shells, or solens, is dragged out. In such waters as there are here, a few steps in the direction of oyster-culture must have abundant results. The pearl-oyster exists, but it is not now sought for. In bygone times, fully a century back, the Malays had the reputation of being great pearl-fishers; but now their pearls, some of which are very fine, are obtained from those of their nation who trade from the Moluccas. They make a curious assertion respecting this softly-lustrous gem, and that is, that if pearls are kept together in a box they will increase in number; a fact (?) this that might prove valuable to the possessor of a few good specimens.

Allusion has been made to the beauty of the submarine groves of coral, but the pen fails in any attempt to describe the wondrous scene spread out beneath him who gazes down through the limpid water in the neighbourhood of a coral reef. Zoophytes of endless graceful forms and lovely tints are glowing in these strange groves, where sea-anemones spread their life-destroying petals, and large medusæ, from a foot to eighteen inches in diameter, float or navigate slowly the clear depths below. The rainbow-like tints of these sting-armed creatures are glorious in the sunshine; and the beholder often pauses to ask himself why was all this beauty bestowed upon such lowly works of the Creator's hand. But ere the question has well been formed, other creatures of beauty glide by, in the shape of the brilliantly-marked fish which make these submarine groves their home. It is off these coral-bound reefs that sea-snakes may often be seen writhing through the water, many of them five and six feet in length. It might be imagined that the power of the sun, and the intensity of the light shed through the crystal waters, had something to do with the brilliancy of tint and strong contrasts of the scales of the fish. Stripes seem mostly the fashion, for many of them are of the perch family; and vivid yellows and scarlets are boldly contrasted with velvety blacks.

The Malays who live near the coast will frequently proceed for many miles out to sea, when bound on a fishing excursion. The canoe used is very small, and will contain two at the outside. It is navigated by means of a paddle and a matting sail; and the Malay, armed with his line, hooks, and bait—generally shrimps —goes off quite happy and content for his long trip. He usually protects his head with a circular hat made from the nipah-palm, and ornaments it with a shaving-brush-like tuft of the black fibres of the gamooty. This hat is parasol as well, and screens his head and shoulders from the vertical rays of the sun. In the stern of the little craft a grooved wooden upright is placed, for guiding the line; while, when great depths are fished, a small windlass is contrived for ease in getting it up.

At times the object of the Malay fisherman's attentions is that curious specimen of natural history, the skipjack (*caranx*); a long snipe-beaked fish, which may often be seen playing along the surface of the smooth water, darting out, and then bobbing along for forty or fifty yards upon its tail, hardly seeming to touch the surface as it propels itself along. The Malay will set sometimes capturing these strange fish, or their smaller relatives—the poopoot, with thirty or forty baits around his boat, at the end of float-furnished lines.

The people have a proverb relating to this fish— "Ikan todo lungar Singapora"—to the effect that some day or other it will force a landing on Singapore.

It is sometimes dangerous to bathers; an instance having occurred off the coast, in which one of these fish darted into a man's mouth, and it was with no little difficulty that it was withdrawn when the bather was brought ashore to a planter's estate.

Cockles are a favourite article of diet with the Malays. These little bivalves seem to have abounded on the west coast for ages. As was before intimated in the allusion to the geographical features of the country, these shells are to be seen in the Muda district, Province Wellesley, in enormous mounds, twenty to thirty feet in height. How they came there is a puzzle, and one which some competent geologist may perhaps unravel. The only theory that suggests itself to the writer, but far from satisfies him, is, that at some early date before the elevation of the country, these must have been points where the currents of river and sea met, and there swept up together the fish that were plentiful near the shore.

Mention of that singular relic of the Old-world crustaceans, the king-crab, must not be omitted. It is exceedingly like the picture of that curious fossil the *cephalaspis,* or buckler-head, and its shells are very common on the shore. It forms a part of the food of the Malays, but to a European it is rather an objectionable-looking creature, though not more so perhaps than the cuttle-fish, which are great favourites with the Chinese, for whose especial benefit they are often caught and dried.

Of the shells generally—sea, river, and land—the writer was unable to obtain any information, and his stay in Perak itself was too limited in duration to enable him to include them in his researches. This is the more to be regretted, as it is quite untried ground, where fine specimens could be obtained. A large selection made by the writer in the Straits and

Labuan, and rivers south of Perak, became merged in the collection of the late Mr. Cuming, of Gower Street.

Mention has been made of the manner in which the Malays use the ordinary drag and casting nets for the capture of fish, but they have a more wholesale way of obtaining their finny prey, by means of what may be looked upon as an extended fish-trap. This is the kaylong or fishing stakes, which are planted in the shore, so as to run out sometimes as far as half a mile. In fact, at the British settlements, these rows of stakes would become a dangerous interruption to navigation, were it not for the vigilance of the officials, whose duty it is to prevent their too great increase. Kaylongs have been in use from a very distant time, but whether invented by the Malays, who are one of the great fishing families of mankind, it is not easy to say.

There is no reason why it should not have been one of their customs from the earliest ages, and if it was, it is a strong proof of their being the people who migrated to Arabia and Africa, and were mentioned by Herodotus, as catching fish in "nets extended along the shoals upon the coast," "whose habitations were formed of the bones of the whale, and to whom fish rather than bread has ever been the staff of life." But though this may all be said to be true of the "Icthyophagi," it does not necessarily relate only to the Malays.

The kaylongs are made of hurdles composed of

strips of bamboo, some five feet long, fastened closely together with rattans, which are nearly as useful and strong as so much wire. These hurdles are attached to stout stakes driven at intervals into the sand or mud of the shore. The fish swim over these hurdles at high water, but as the tide recedes, their progress seaward is stopped by the water falling below the top of the bamboos, and they try to effect their escape by an opening left in the fence, but this only leads into a square enclosure in which a net is kept lowered. Over this enclosure a small covered shed is constructed, in which the men work who raise and lower the net.

At times these kaylongs, which are used in common by both Malays and Chinese settlers, are contrived so that pointed bamboos are arranged in the opening to the enclosure, so as to allow the entry of the fish, which on trying to escape are repelled by the points, just as they are in our own waters in the ordinary fish-pot or trap of wickerwork raised and lowered in the Thames weirs, to the puzzling of many a fat eel astir when the waters are up.

CHAPTER X.

ONE of the great pests of tropical lands which are well watered is undoubtedly that persevering little creature, the mosquito. It has puzzled every traveller, from time immemorial, how to account for the fact that, no matter how much energy he throws into his blows, he rarely can strike one; and at last, from being angrily aggressive, he assumes the passively defensive state, taking refuge behind mosquito-curtains, and leaving the virulent little insects to lay siege to his fortalice.

In passing, a few words must be said respecting the insects of Perak; and the mosquitoes may well stand first, from the way in which they insist upon making their presence known. They abound in the country, some of them being of very large size; but the most virulent is a small striped variety, banded with black and white.

Cicadas of the noisiest kind and grasshoppers are

plentiful enough in the plains, the latter being much sought for by the Malay youths for feeding their larks and quails. They catch them very readily by means of a little instrument of open rattan-work. This is formed something like a child's sea-side shovel, only larger, and is used with great dexterity by the boys, who are light and active in the extreme.

Scorpions are pretty abundant, and those unpleasant-looking creatures, the centipedes, some of which seem to possess pedal appendages enough to merit the term of thousand legs, while the ants are some of them enormous. One black kind is from one-and-a-half to two inches in length ; but these are not seen in large numbers together. There is the termes, or white ant, and the biting red ant, called by the Malays *krangga*. This little creature makes its nest between the leaves of trees, rolling them up and securing them with gluten, and is much dreaded, from the severity of its bite, which is as bad as a severe nip with a pair of forceps. It is fortunately not poisonous, but forms one of the principal supplies of that curious acid in use amongst photographers, and known as formic. Spiders naturally abound, and, judging from journeys through the country, the entomologist might collect many new species. Flies are also abundant. In fact, in this unexplored region there is open ground for lovers of every phase of natural history ; and the stag and rhinoceros beetles would alone form a collection. Every marshy place

is wonderful for its varieties of dragon-flies, flitting
about on their gauzy wings, and some of them are of
very great beauty, while the hornets are of immense
size, the largest the writer has seen up the eastern
archipelago.

But for brilliancy of colouring, the butterflies and
moths bear off the palm. Their colours are lovely,
and in the moist, sunny openings of the jungle, they
flap along on wings painted with the most refulgent
dyes. The capture of some is very difficult, from
their lofty flight ; but the merest tyro may net an
abundance of the beautiful moisture-loving specimens,
not excepting the great Atlas moth, which is found in
high perfection, many being nine and ten, and even
twelve, inches across their wings.

Leaf insects have often been described ; but
probably the custom existing here in the Malay
peninsula has not been noticed—namely, that of
keeping them in little cages, as curious specimens of
natural history. They are found about an inch-and-a-
half long, and are singular for their exact resemblance
to a leaf. Beautiful as these leaf insects are, they
bear no comparison to a remarkable species which
the writer has found haunting the trees of one kind
only. It is less than two inches in length, of a lovely
gray, liberally spotted with red. Its flight is the
most wonderful quality of the insect, for it goes from
tree to tree after the fashion of a bird. Attempts to
bring it to Europe have as yet failed, but, as far as

can be made out, it is an insect quite new to collectors, and peculiar to this part of the world.

Perhaps one of the most beautiful sights in Perak is a mangrove swamp on a soft, still, dark night, when the fireflies are out in myriads, flashing from leaf to leaf, and darting like brilliant sparks from tree to tree in showers of light. Every here and there they settle, and then seem disturbed, when the coruscations of tiny stars are perfectly wonderful. Every fly seems to send out its light in pulses or throbs, like the flashes from a signal lamp; and so great is the beauty of this scene that the lover of natural history would deem it alone worth a journey to the east to see.

There are plenty of destructive insects, one of the worst being the carpenter beetle, which is so industrious in its habits that it will riddle the beams of a building, if of wood that finds favour. Numerous accounts of its evil doings are given, the Government bungaloh at Malacca having suffered very severely. Doubtless, however, remedies for these insect pests could be found.

We were especially fortunate in our travels in Perak in not coming across a fly said to be peculiar to the peninsula. This insect is not unlike a cicada in form, but it has been furnished by nature with a long and sharp proboscis, with which it can inflict a wound that gives the most acute pain. On one occasion the writer was passing through the jungle at the foot of Mount Ophir in Malacca. The party was progressing in single file, and very slowly ; for the leader, a Malay, had to make use of his parang, or heavy wood-knife— which answers to the machête of the South American —to cut a way through the tangled undergrowth and rattans. Suddenly the foremost man uttered a cry of pain, and darted aside, a movement followed by the others in succession ; and before the Europeans of the party, who stood in the position of " ready," could ask the reason for this peculiar flank movement, three of the Malays who had been pierced by these insects were brought to us, with the proboscis apparently left in the wound. The remedy resembles that of our sailors, who, no matter what the injury, apply a little tobacco ; that of the Malays being a little of the lime formed from burnt shells, and carried about with them for chewing with their betel-nut and leaf. Efficacious it may have been, but, like the infallible nostrums for toothache, it evidently did not cure the pain instantaneously.

For students of entomology there are endless objects asking the collector's hand ; and though the writer is unable to call attention to many insects that might be considered peculiar to the State of Perak, so great is the extent of totally unexplored ground— tracts apparently never yet trodden by the foot of man—that doubtless a very valuable entomological collection might be made.

CHAPTER XI.

THIS is not the land of the wondrous birds of paradise,
whose brilliant plumes rise from beneath their wings,
and curve down like the waters of a golden fountain ;
but Perak possesses an avi-fauna of very great beauty,
and even a cursory survey of the country displays its
richness in this respect. For this is the home of the
glorious Argus pheasant, with its long extending tail
and largely-penned wings, each quill of which, with its
extremely broad web, is dotted with a row of eyes,
similar to those on the tail of the peacock. This
pheasant is rarely shot, on account of its nocturnal
habits ; even the practised hunter of the country only
shooting perhaps one or two in a long course of years.
It is, however, occasionally trapped ; but if taken alive,
soon pines and dies. The Malays call it " coo-ow," from
its peculiar shrill cry. It is unmistakable when heard
in the jungle solitudes by night, the writer often

H 2

recognising it, as the birds called one to the other in
the up-country when he was camping out.   This cry
is almost exactly the same as that of the jacoons—the
orang-utan, or wild hill-men of the country; the
reader being warned not to suppose that the huge
ape of Borneo is here meant, orang-utan being Malay
for wild man.   It seems probable that the jacoons have
adopted the call from the bird; while a remarkable
fact is that this cry—"coo-ay"—bears a wonderful
similarity to the "coo-ee" of the Australian savage.
The cry of the argus pheasant when once heard is
never forgotten, from its impressiveness in the still
night.   There has always been great difficulty in
bringing it to England alive; and this is probably
due to the fact that its habits have not been properly
studied, for it is essentially a night-bird, and if care
were not taken to afford it shelter, failure would
probably result.

There is another very handsome pheasant, namely,
the peacock, or ocellated, and also one resembling our
own, but with a short tail, in the forest in which the
jungle-cock abounds—a beautifully-feathered bird, the
probable ancestor of our game-cock.   The pugnacity
of this latter causes his ruin; for residents of shooting
proclivities, or even those who like an addition to
their table, take advantage of the bird's habits, and
picket an ordinary Malay game-fowl in their boat
when going up the streams.   The tame bird's challenge
soon rings out, and is answered, when jungle-cock

after jungle-cock is tempted out of the safe solitudes, and falls a victim to the gun.

Quails are pretty plentiful, and there is a variety of the plover and partridge. As to snipes, they abound in the low grounds, and a pretty good shot is sure of excellent sport. During the Duke of Edinburgh's visit to the Straits Settlements he made a tremendous bag in Province Wellesley, this being a sport for which no preparation in the way of beating or selecting warm corners could be made, His Royal Highness having to take his chance, as would any other sportsman—a fact which shows the abundance of the birds.

Peafowl form a magnificent addition to the birds of Perak. The male is not the ordinary peacock of Ceylon and Southern India, but the variety known as the Javanese; the principal differences being that it is a little smaller, that instead of rich blue, the neck is covered with green scale-like feathers, and that the crest is different in form; but the train is equally large and beautiful. Altogether it is a magnificent bird, and the flesh when eaten proves to be delicate in flavour and quite tender; for this there is the authority of Mr. Wallace.

This presence of the peacock in the peninsula, as already referred to, appears favourable to the theory that Solomon's vessels traded to the Eastern archipelago; and when it is taken into consideration what tremendous distances the praus of the present day

journey, the surprise is lessened. It may be argued
that Solomon's ships must necessarily have been small
and ill-made. So are the present-day praus, some of
which, however, are of seventy tons burden, and wholly
made without a scrap of iron, pegs and rattans taking
the place of bolts, while the sails are composed of
matting, and such a thing as a compass is unknown.
There is, however, one great argument in favour of the
supposition that Ophir was the present-day Ophir of
Malacca ; that argument is supplied by a consideration
of the language.

Prior to Pliny, in the first century, history does
very little to help us to a conclusion ; though the
important statement that apes and peacocks formed
part of the cargo of Solomon's ships, supports the
theory that the journey was made rather to India or
Malaya than to the east coast of Africa. To get over
the difficulty it has been sought to translate the
Hebrew word "tukyim" or "tuchim" (peacock) as representing a parrot ; and Crawfurd says that the Persian
word "tota" or "toti" (parrot) has a very near resemblance to the Hebrew word "tuchim ; " and he adds
that, as parrots can bear longer voyages than peacocks, it is more than probable that we have in this
the right interpretation of the word.

Dr. Kitto, too, says : "It is a question more of
geographical and historical than of biblical interest to
decide whether the "thukyim" (1 Kings x. 22) and
"thukyim" (2 Chronicles ix. 21) denote peacocks,

strictly so called, or some other species of animal or bird; for on the solution of the question in the affirmative depends the real direction of Solomon's fleet, *i.e.* whether, after passing the Straits of Bab-el-Mandeb, it proceeded along the east coast of Africa towards Sofala, or whether it turned eastward, ranging along the Arabian and Persian shores to the peninsula of India, and perhaps went onward to Ceylon, and penetrated to the great Australian, or even to the Spice Islands." Dr. Kitto believes that the rendering of "tukyim"—peacocks—is correct. There are, as known, only two species of true peafowl, namely, that common in India, which is the one familiar in England, and that just described as existing in Perak.

Now it is a singular fact that in the language of the Orang Benua, or wild men of the peninsula, the word for peacock, which in the modern Malay is "marrak," is in the aboriginal "chim marak;" and here we have the exact termination of the Hebrew "tuchim" in the language of the very people who must have lived in the peninsula and near Mount Ophir in the days of Solomon, namely, the Orang Benua, or men of the country. This name for a bird—"tchem" or "chim"—is mentioned in a report given only a short time since by Mr. Daly, who collected a number of common words from the wild people during a tour through Perak.

The Malays cultivate domestic fowls pretty extensively; principally, however, on account of their love

for cock-fighting. Their champions are evidently
the progenitors of the hard, close-feathered, high-
shouldered Malay cocks of our poultry-shows; but
these latter have been so bred to points by dealers and
fanciers that they are very different in appearance.
They have also a peculiar breed of fowl on the peninsula, which is remarkable for the manner in which its
feathers turn out the wrong way. Varieties of this
have been exhibited in England.

Both ducks and fowls are plentiful in Perak,
but not to the extent they might be; owing to the
indifference of the people, who look upon any branch
of industry as *soosa*, or trouble; much of which, however, is due to the uncertain tenure of the land, and
the oppression of their chiefs, who take tithe to an
alarming extent. The Chinese settlers, though, take
advantage of the nature of the country, and breed
ducks extensively, and their plan is singularly successful. The "Heathen Chinee" does not trust to
maternal solicitude, for the eggs are placed in sand or
husks of padi, and are then submitted to artificial heat;
and the difficulty here is to assimilate this heat to that
of nature. When hatched, the ducklings are fed with
prawns, bits of crab, and boiled rice; and being hardy
little things they are in a few days able to look out
for their own supplies, when they are turned into
small enclosures containing pools of shallow water, and
as they grow older are removed to more extensive
pasture-grounds. An old Chinaman generally acts

the part of mamma, and the way in which the little troops of ducklings know him and obey his call is very amusing. Hundreds may be seen in one enclosure, and the Chinese are often encountered followed by droves of the downy little things, which are being taken probably to new feeding-grounds.

Domestic pets are common amongst the Malays, who are very clever at catching birds by means of horse-hair nooses and springes—snipes being one of their favourite captures—and also by imitating their call. By this means doves and pigeons, some of them very beautiful, are readily taken ; the juice of the gutta or indiarubber tree being sometimes used as bird-lime, as before intimated. These doves are kept in bamboo cages. There are two varieties of the minah in Perak. This bird is said to be the best imitator of the human voice of any known, and hence it often enters into captivity. The Malay boys are exceedingly clever with the " sumpitan," or blow-pipe, and with this they are too apt to destroy the best songster of the peninsula —the Straits nightingale ; and they are also very apt at capturing the tiny little green and blue red-beaked love-bird—a small species of paroquet—which swarms in some of the forest trees. These, after capture, they imprison in an ingeniously-made cage, formed of strips of bamboo, arranged in a circle and bent over to a point, tied and furnished with a hook at the top ; a bamboo perch, and two short joints of bamboo for containing rice and water are secured within ; and the clever little construction, with a pair of prisoners, can be readily bought for coins representing twopence of our money.

One of their pets, which, like some of the doves, becomes very tame and fetches large prices, is a bird they call "baru-baru." It is of the size of a dove, but like a greenish-brown thrush, and speaks with great distinctness.

The ornithologist would find an ample field for his researches, the beauty of some of the birds being especially worthy of note, while their more sober-plumaged brethren are remarkable for their habits. On the rivers, wild ducks and teal are plentiful, while from the overhanging branches dart kingfishers of the most brilliant hues and of the largest size, such as make our pretty English specimen a quietly-painted dwarf in comparison. Several of these, however, are not fishers correctly speaking, as they live on insects. The beautifully-crested hoopoe is common in the forest, and so tame that it will readily approach the traveller, while its beauty will perhaps prevent its tameness from being "shocking" to him, as in the case of Alexander Selkirk, according to the poet. Every here and there magnificent toucans, with their apparently cumbrous but cellular bills and gorgeously-painted gorgets, are to be seen hopping from twig to twig, while literally abounding, and making the jungle echo with their shrieks, the long fork-tailed collared paroquets flutter amongst the trees. These are very

beautiful birds, and with their delicate green feathers
and brilliant coral-tinted beaks, form conspicuous
objects in the jungle.

Those brilliant little gems the humming-birds are
not absent in the open sunny glades, where flowers
open their tempting petals ; while those almost equally
beautiful objects of nature, peculiar to the Eastern
archipelago, the sun-birds, with their scaly plumage
of gorgeous metallic hues, are as frequent in their
search for the honey of the blossoms. On some of the
forest trees the nests of what are there called tailor-
birds—probably the sociable grosbeak—are seen, deli-
cately woven out of grass and cocoa-nut fibre, hanging
from the boughs and forming a very curious feature in
the scenery. While speaking of nests, the limestone
caves of the coasts must not be forgotten. These
caves are the resort of the bird's-nest swallow, whose
peculiar glutinous nursery is sought for in the most
dangerous places by the Malays, who obtain it by
means of bamboo ladders. Their idea is that the
gluten which hardens into the nest is obtained from
the sea-foam ; and probably some kind of seaweed
does afford them the material, which by a natural
process, similar to the production of beeswax, is first
formed and then built up into their nests. It is of
course well known that these nests are regularly
harvested, and form an object of trade with the
Chinese, for their bird's-nest soup.

Apparently so many distorted relatives of the

toucans are the hornbills, which, in spite of the
monstrous proportions of their bill with its large upper
story, are wonderfully active birds, and use their
apparently clumsy beak with great dexterity in seeking
fruit.   Two or three varieties, one being very large,
are found here.   The writer has not seen their nesting,
but it is so remarkable that Mr. Wallace's account
thereof is well worthy of note.   It seems that the nest
is formed in some large hollow of a tree, and at the
time of incubation the male bird plasters up the
entrance hole with clay, merely leaving an orifice
sufficiently large for the hen bird to be fed; and this
attention to his mate, and afterwards to her one
offspring—which is at first a great gelatinous-looking
creature, a shapeless featherless lump, as big as a
pigeon—is scrupulously performed.

One very pretty little object is the grass-bird,
which seems to stand on the top of a thin feathery
stalk by a swamp, but which all the time is balancing
itself by means of the rapid motion of its wings.
The buffalo-bird, with its wattle like a minah, is
common, and hangs about the large bovine quadrupeds
in search of food, as the starling does at home; which
is also strongly called to mind by the constant presence
of the familiar old chirping sparrow in his black cravat,
whose note is for all the world the same as may be
heard at early morn in a London square.   There is
the little Java sparrow too, with its drab-speckled
feathers and tiny reddish beak; while in nearly all

marshy ground, many varieties are seen in flocks of
the so-called padi-bird, with here and there, in the
water-holes and swamps, the little dusky moorhen, and
very fine herons watching for the small fish, with cranes
and rails; while especially in Perak and Quedah there
is found a wading-bird, said to be common in Egypt
and Palestine—perhaps the "porphyrion" of Kitto.   It
has a hard crimson shield upon its forehead and
flesh-coloured legs; the head, neck, and sides are of
turquoise blue, shading off into a dark but brilliant
indigo.   The natives tame it with ease; and among
other places, the writer has frequently seen it stalking
about the gardens of the Hon. Mr. Whampoa, one of
the principal Chinese residents at Singapore.

The padi-birds are netted by thousands and eaten
by the Chinese as a delicacy; for, as at home, the birds
flock together at certain seasons in search of food.
One very pretty instance of this is at the time when
the waringhan tree, already mentioned for its beautiful
clustering blossoms, is covered with red berries.
These form an attraction to thousands of tiny birds,
which at daybreak seem to keep the tree in a perpetual
twitter, as they busily flit from spray to spray.   These
small birds of the jungle are not without their enemies,
for there is a pretty plentiful supply of hawks to check
their increase.   These are for the most part very similar
to the ordinary sparrowhawk of England; while in
turn they have an enemy that attacks them bravely,
in the shape of a bird of the crow family; with long

racket-shaped produced feathers in its tail. It is a
handsome bird, of an intense black.

Very commonly at evening a bird familiar at
home is seen in the shape of the night-jar, which,
after sitting for some time motionless on a branch,
after the fashion of its kind, like a lump of feathers,
sweeps round the tree in an easily-performed circle
and returns to its perch with one of the beautiful
moths or beetles of the jungle. Similar to this bird
in marking, with its brown-mottled feathers, is the
ordinary owl of the peninsula; a bird which again
recalls home by its familiar aspect. By day the
hollow trees resound with the busy hammer of the
woodpecker, which also seems to belong to Old
England instead of this tropic shore, so simple
and quiet is its plumage and familiar its well-known
sound.

The eagles of the country have been alluded to,
but not the vultures, which are of a very familiar type.
They are encountered on the river-banks in Perak, of
very large size, with enormous claws, and are evidently
birds of great power. On one occasion the writer
came upon a group that had been attracted by the
body of a dead buffalo, which after being carried down
the stream had been washed ashore. The birds were
feasting on the carrion, while, from time to time, one
of those singular animals—the pangolins, or scaly
ant-eaters, was making a run at them, the animal

evidently resenting the intrusion of the vultures, who interfered with his feast of carrion-flies. As for the vultures, they took but little notice of the aggressor, merely moving a little aside, and then resuming with bill and claws their disgusting banquet.

CHAPTER XII.

THE buffaloes mentioned in the last chapter are a
large heavy kind of ox, domesticated by the Malays.
There are two varieties, called the white and black;
but the former is more of a pink tint. They are used
by their owners both as draught cattle and as beasts
of burden. In the rice-fields it is a common thing to
see them yoked, and drawing the clumsy plough to
prepare the soil, a rattan cord through their noses
being the general way of leading them. When
attached to one of the long, narrow, roughly-made
country carts, they can draw very heavy loads; but
in this task they are rarely yoked in pairs, on account
of the narrowness of the roads and the width of 'the
buffaloes' horns, the points of which are more than
four feet from tip to tip.

When used as a beast of burden, the buffalo's load
is arranged as a pack, placed in a pair of rattan
panniers on either side of the great animal's back.

This is the custom in the more unfrequented parts, where a track for a cart is seldom seen. The buffalo has tremendous strength, and is very enduring, though exceedingly slow, and the animal is much petted and caressed by its Malay owner, great care being taken to keep it clean ; though, like our domestic friend the pig, nothing delights a buffalo more than a good roll and wallow in one of the mud-pools by the padi-fields. When drawing burdens the buffaloes are often un-yoked to bathe in the rivers and streams they pass, while an awning is stretched to shield them from the power of the sun ; and to protect them from those pests the mosquitoes, a fire is lit by night, of which the great beasts are sagacious enough to take full advantage, for they always go to leeward, so that the smoke may blow all over their backs and sides. No doubt the rolling in the mud-holes is an instinctive proceeding, so that the mud may cake over them, and thus form an effectual armour against the flies.

The great strength of the buffalo renders it a for-midable adversary to the tiger, and its encounters with this beast when wild or in the forest paths have doubtless been the origin of one of the principal sports of the Malay—the buffalo and tiger fight, of which an account will be given in a succeeding chapter. Gentle in the extreme with their owners, and greatly attached to their young, which at times they will carry from place to place on their back, buffaloes seem to have the same dislike to anything white that our English

I

bulls are said to have for that which is red; and this
makes an encounter with them, when grazing in a
herd at a distance from a village, rather an unpleasant
thing for a European.   For at the sight of a white
face they lay back their horns, raise their muzzles,
and make ready for an attack with wonderful rapidity,
the whole herd charging in a way that would startle a
square of infantry.   With the Malays, on the contrary, the word of command, or a pull at the cord from
a boy, is quite sufficient to ensure obedience, though
instances have been known of a native being gored
from maltreatment of some unusually ferocious beast.

The natives seldom use the milk of the buffalo,
though it is doubtful whether it does not at times find
its way into the milk of the ordinary domestic cow
which is supplied in the Settlements to the European
residents—these cows, like draught bullocks, being imported ; and it is a fact worthy of note that the troop
cattle, principally bulls from Quedah, used during the
progress of the little army through Perak in the disturbances, suffered a great deal from foot-and-mouth
disease, the remedy used being turmeric and salt.

The flesh of the buffalo is very unpalatable and
tough to a European, but the Malays have a great
liking for it, and consider the flesh of the black to be
preferable to that of the pink variety.   Upon the
occasion of some special festival, it is customary to
kill a buffalo, when pretty well the whole of a village
will take part in the proceedings.   So valuable is this

beast to a Malay that their code of laws contains special references to it, and the forfeitures to be made for losing or killing a borrowed buffalo, or for being the possessor of one that is vicious, and has done injury to personal property. Theft of a buffalo is a serious crime. Petty thefts amongst the Malays are rare, though it is no uncommon thing for the inhabitants of one village to make a raid upon the dwellers in another who are weaker, and carry off their herds—a form of cattle-lifting which, with several other points to be afterwards mentioned, links them singularly with the northern clans of old. As for the lower-class Chinese that have settled in the states, they are most expert thieves, and will steal cattle whenever they have a chance.

There is a story told of one gentleman of the pigtail who, while suffering imprisonment under the native Government, was condoled with by his friends on account of the severe sentence inflicted upon him, for, according to his own account, merely picking up a piece of string, which he thought might prove to be useful. It turned out, however, that the piece of string was the nose-cord of a buffalo, and that it was attached to the animal, with which Ah Sin had walked off bodily.

There are droves of these buffaloes wild in the country, and also a variety of the family more resembling our own ox, but they are not often encountered ; neither are the troops of wild elephants, which are in the more remote fastnesses of the jungle. The supply of these huge beasts, though, that has been obtained by the native chiefs, is derived from the forests. A full account of the capture is unnecessary, as it has been given so often in works of travel. Suffice it that the great quadruped is taken much after the same fashion as in Ceylon and Siam, namely, by driving it into a strong enclosure of bamboos, and then stabling it with a steady old elephant, to which it is attached by stout ropes of rattan. The supply of food is made very meagre for a month, but kindness is tried as well as coercion, the animal being petted and fed with stems of the plantain, sugar-cane, with other succulent dainties, and cakes. Elephants are pro-verbially fond of bathing and syringing themselves with water from their trunks, so the wild animal is allowed to go down to the river after a few days, but of course strongly secured to his tame companion. Then begins a struggle for freedom, but it results in the tired beast giving in and going back quietly to his old bonds in the stable, where he is once more securely fastened.

This process is kept up, with the addition of a man occasionally getting upon his back and walking upon him, till the elephant submits to the mind, and owns by his passive obedience that he is conquered; though he cannot be thoroughly trusted for perhaps two years, during which time he is frequently troublesome, and requires the society of the female to keep him in

11 6 1

PERAK ELEPHANTS.

order. After this an elephant is considered safe for
any mahout to manage. These mahouts are very
often men of good position. They sit, as in India,
upon the animal's neck, with its great flap-ears acting
as a protection, and drive by means of a sharp iron
rod provided with a hook—an instrument that is sometimes used in the case of a restive elephant with
terrible effect.

Every elephant has his own familiar name, and the
mahout has its history quite by heart; and while
fondling and talking to the animal, will frequently
remind it of the various striking episodes in its life.

The howdahs, as shown in the engraving, are very
different from those of India, being really nothing
more than panniers of rattan, over which sometimes a
tilt is stretched on canes. Raw hides are placed
beneath the howdah, to keep it from fretting the
elephant's back, and it is then secured by bands of
rattan, which are formed into girths passing behind the
animal's shoulders and before his hind legs ; and the
howdah is further kept in position by a rope round
the chest, and one in the form of a crupper. The
basket is then pretty well filled with leaves, over
which a cover is placed, and the rider mounts to his
very uneasy position ; for elephant-riding, though not
so bad as camel-riding, has a tendency towards shaking
the body all to pieces, and aches and pains in the
joints are frequent after the first trials. Not that the
animal is to blame, for he generally goes at about the

rate of two miles an hour, and will at the word of command snap off an interposing tree the thickness of a man's leg as easily as if it were a twig.

Elephants here are not the monstrous beasts found in some parts of the world, those of ten feet high being exceptionally large. Their principal disease seems to be a kind of leprosy, which shows itself in the ears.

They are the chief beasts of burden of the country, and will walk away comfortably with half a ton of tin ; but where the load is of a bulky nature, from four to six hundred weight is considered sufficient. They are naturally the property of the Sultan and his chiefs, and elephants are looked upon as part of the Sultan's regalia, fifty being reckoned in his regal list.

The well-known white, or as it should be called flesh-coloured, elephant is very rare, but is not, like its darker brethren, held in much veneration by the Malays. All elephants are petted and caressed and considered of great value ; but their treatment is very different to that received in the neighbouring country of Siam, where those belonging to the king are objects of the greatest dignity, each having its own following of royal attendants. In fact the white elephant, which Dr. Finlayson looks upon as being an albino of its family, is believed by the Siamese, who speak of it as an animal " so noble, so docile, and so strong," to be animated by the illustrious soul that formerly occupied the body of some prince—an idea due to the fact that these people being Buddhists, believe in the doctrine of the transmigration of souls.

It is related that one Siamese prince despatched three elephants as presents to the grandsons of the then king of France, a nation with whom the Siamese have long held intercourse. As the animals were going he whispered to them : " Go, depart cheerfully ; you will be slaves, indeed ; but you will be so to three of the greatest princes of the world, whose service is as moderate as it is glorious." After this address the elephants were hoisted into the ship, and because they bowed themselves to go under the deck, the Siamese cried out with admiration of their sagacity.

A curious trait of the elephant is worthy of notice. When not observed, the great animal will go to a cocoa-nut tree, and, to obtain the nuts and young blossoms, place his head against the trunk, and then commencing a swaying movement, throw the whole weight of the body against the tree over and over again, till it comes down with a crash, leaving the coveted treasures at his feet.

The rhinoceros is occasionally seen, and two varieties are believed to exist. They are very shy, and at the approach of man rush off through the jungle ; being very different to their relatives in Africa, one kind of which charges directly he perceives man or horse, even a hut or a fire being an object upon which he will vent his fury. The natives tell of a beast that they call the *kooda-ayer*, or water-horse, by some supposed to be a hippopotamus; but it is evidently either a rhinoceros or one of the larger tapirs, which are found in the marshy places, calmly browsing on the herbage by means of their prehensile upper lip, waiting, like the rhinoceros, for the time in the future when the gun of the sportsman shall disturb their rest.

There is plenty of game for the hunter who does penetrate the jungles, splendid deer of very large size being common. Some of these approach the elk in magnitude, and among them are the sambre, the spotted-deer, hog-deer, and the chevrotin or palandok. Wild-boars are not at all uncommon—not the progenitors of the pigs of the Settlements, for their presence is due to the Chinese—the Malay, from his religion, rejecting pork. The boars are both large and fierce, one poor fellow—a convict employed on the road—dying of the injuries he received from one of these beasts up in Province Wellesley. His dog was baying at something in the jungle, and, on entering the forest, he found that the animal was holding a wild-boar in check. The latter set upon him at once, ripping him terribly, the beast being afterwards shot by the European overseer of the works. These boars' tusks are very large and white; and taking advantage of their peculiar curve, a Chinese goldsmith in Penang joins the root and point with a chain, letters the ivory, and forms of them very handsome decanter labels. That these boars have other enemies besides man has been shown in the attack of the boa-constrictor.

There is only one representative of the bear, in the person of that peculiar little black animal familiar to most visitors to the Zoological Gardens. It is a smooth-coated little fellow, black, with a patch of white on the throat, and, from its cleverness in raising itself upon its hind legs, and curious actions, has a great resemblance to a short thick-set monkey. They are pretty common in Perak, but quite harmless, save to the young cocoa-nut plantations, amidst which they create great havoc.

Otters are common, though not, of course, the English variety; the polecat family is pretty well represented; squirrels may be seen amongst the trees, as well as those curious little animals the bats. Of these there are several varieties, the fruit-bats being the most worthy of note. These, which are commonly known as flying-foxes, visit the peninsula during the fruit season in enormous flocks, coming from the direction of Sumatra, and settle and destroy the fruit to an enormous extent. They are of the size of a large rat, and their wings have a spread of from two to three feet, while in the larger variety, which is equally destructive, the stretch of the wings from tip to tip has been known to be over five feet. Specimens as large as this are at the present time in the museums. Java and Sumatra are the principal homes of these creatures, but they find their

way to Perak, as if led by some strange instinct to a
place where fruit abounds.   They come with a slow
steady flight, in a straight line, and devour indis-
criminately every kind of fruit that comes in their
way.   They are however easily shot, and their destruction is a boon to the place.

For Perak is a land where it is necessary to com-
bine the use of the gun with research and travel, since
at any time the journey may be interrupted by some
fierce beast of the feline kind, as there is the tiger-cat
and the black leopard—a magnificent beast, whose
coat is jetty in one light, but displays the peculiar
spots in another.   Taken altogether, it is in its wild
state one of the most beautiful creatures of the
jungle.

An amusing incident occurred at the time of the
Duke of Edinburgh's visit to the peninsula, with a
black leopard, which had been captured and was kept
in a cage, roaming slowly up and down, or crouching,
with that far-off look, which seems to see the native
wilds through the impertinent gazers who disturb the
privacy of the noble beast.   A medical officer present
had been talking of the power of the human eye over
the untamed animal, and went up to the cage to prove
it by fixing the dilating eye of the savage beast with
his own.

The leopard bore the stare for some little time
with gathering anger, and then, without the slightest
warning, made one fierce bound at the gentleman

with the magnetic eyes.   There was a growl, a dash,
an ejaculation, and the officer staggered back, with his
cap torn off, and his cheek laid open by the animal's
claws, the peak of the cap having saved the beast-
quelling eyes.

But *the* animal *par excellence* of Perak and other
parts of the peninsula is undoubtedly the Malay tiger,
fine specimens of which are in the gardens of the
Zoological Society, as are also others of the black
leopard, which were sent direct from the Malay
peninsula, and presented to the society by Sir Harry
St. George Ord, late governor of the Straits Settlements.   The Malay tiger is rather smaller than that
of Bengal, and displays more white in its under
parts ; in fact, it thoroughly answers, save in size, to
that graphically-described beast the moollah of Captain Lawson's New Guinea—a book of travels of
which the critics have expressed strong doubts, as its
wonders do somewhat trench on the narratives of our
older navigators of the world.

The Malay tiger is a fierce and terrible beast, and
exaggerated stories are told of its appetite in the
island of Singapore, where those that frequent the
jungle are said to have eaten a man per diem all the
year round.   There has been terrible loss of life in the
island, but this is very far beyond the mark.   There
are no doubt many in Perak, and their lairs are frequently seen ; but from the country being so thinly
populated, few people are killed.   It is, however, one of

the misfortunes of a place, that the tiger takes to haunting new settlements, lying in wait for or stalking the
unfortunate coolies stooping and picking the gambier
leaves, upon whom it springs, after waiting hours for
its opportunity. In almost every case the first blow,
which is almost always on the back of the neck,
seems to be fatal, the power of the paw being
enormous. There is good work here in Perak, undoubtedly, for the sportsman's rifle ; but to seek the
tiger in the dense forests would be almost suicidal,
the beast that is being tracked in the dusky
twilight of the jungle being probably watching his
would-be destroyer unseen. One plan frequently
adopted is to place some animal for a bait, and then
to sit in a tree and wait all night for the tiger's
coming—a plan that rarely succeeds, and consequently the governmental fifty-dollars reward is not
very often earned. Fortunately, the increase of this
beast is kept down by the love of the male tiger for
his own offspring as food. He devours them whenever he has an opportunity, for he is wide in his
choice of dainties, and will put up with buffalo when
he cannot obtain man, crushing in the thick skull of
this animal with one blow if he can take it unawares,
and avoid impalement upon its formidable horns.

The Malays make pitfalls for the tiger, funnel-
shaped holes of fifteen feet deep, right in its track,
knowing full well that it will return by the way it
has gone. If this were merely covered with sticks

and leaves, the tiger would be suspicious, try it, and go another way ; therefore the Malay cuts down a tree, so that it falls across that side of the hole by which his enemy will approach, and then hides the opening with leaves and boughs. The fall of a tree in the forest is so common a thing that the tiger's suspicion is not excited. A tree has fallen across its path—*voilà tout.* It plants its fore-paws on the trunk, draws up its hind-legs, and leaps lightly down—crash through the frail covering into the pitfall, where it is approached with sublime respect, the Malays hardly daring to go near enough to give the *coup de grâce* to the dreaded beast.

Another way, as the cookery-books say over a fresh recipe to dress the joint previously dealt with : The Malays, on finding the track of a tiger, very ingeniously hang a heavy balk of timber across the path from the projecting bough of a tree. The string which suspends the beam is attached to a cleverly-made trigger, and the trigger again to a noose, which is arranged right in the animal's track. The result is as may be anticipated : if the tiger's mind be occupied with how to provide for the next repast, an unguarded foot is placed in the noose, the string is drawn tight, the trigger is touched, the beam falls, and the tiger lies paralysed, with a broken back, awaiting his destroyers' spears.

The Malays are equally clever in capturing the monkey, by means of a noose through which the active little thing puts its hand, and draws the string

tight. In fact, the noose is a favourite plan with the
inhabitants of the peninsula and the isles adjacent.
Mr. Wallace mentions how cleverly the natives of
Waigiou, near New Guinea, noose the birds of paradise; and allusion has already been made to the way
in which the argus pheasant is taken, and "springes,"
not "to catch woodcocks" but snipe, are made.

Of those curious little creatures monkeys there
are many kinds; but, as far as the writer can tell, no
apes, such as the mias or orang-utan of Borneo, and
the wa-wa of Java, a tailless animal something like
the agile gibbon. The most rare is one of a milk-
white colour. Only two specimens have come under
the writer's notice during a long residence in these
parts; and it may after all be, as Dr. Finlayson says
of the white elephant of Siam, only an albino. It is a
small monkey, only about eighteen inches high, and
very peculiar.

One large short-tailed monkey is a great favourite
with the people of Perak. To its master it is very
tame and greatly attached, acting as his protector in
a journey through the woods, from campong to campong, and being ready to attack any aggressor, even
as a dog would in England. It is a large strongly-
built animal, standing as high as an ordinary dining-
table, and possesses large canine teeth, with which it
will seize its enemy by the back of the neck, and hold
on so tightly that it is hard to shake it off.

The Malay being too sedate, dignified, and often

too idle to climb a tree himself, trains this monkey to pick cocoa-nuts for him. The writer has frequently seen one with a string attached to it run up a tree with the greatest activity and seize a nut. A pull of the string shows the monkey that this is the wrong fruit ; and by constant guidance with the string, the little parody of humanity readily distinguishes the particular object it is to obtain, and at once seizing it with its hands, begins to screw it round and round, till the footstalk gives way, and the heavy nut with its thick husk of fibre falls with a thud to the ground.

This anecdote savours so of "the travellers' tale," that it may be well to repeat in all sincerity that it is a fact, and that the practice is common.

Several of the smaller kinds are easily tamed when captured by the Malays, though it must be said that some of the larger species are very vicious, one that was given to an English sailor proving too wild to keep. It is amusing to see them in the jungle, apparently watching the intruders, and peering round from the far side of branches. Troops of them may be seen on the sands at the mouths of the rivers when going up, their object being to search for the shell-fish which abound, and which seem to be a favourite delicacy to the simian palate.

The loris, one of their near relatives, is pretty common : but to be brief, the fauna of Perak is an extensive one, and embraces many animals that have

been passed unnoticed, among others the musang and
the porcupine, which can be often found in a suitable
habitat.

Of the more domestic animals, that most useful of
creatures the horse is not found in Perak, neither has
it been naturalised anywhere else in the peninsula,
though found in Burmah, Pegu, and Siam, as well as
in Sumatra, Java, Borneo, and several other of the
islands of the Archipelago.   One variety imported is
really a spirited pony, but probably from there being
no extensive plains suitable for their increase, even
this diminutive form of the horse has found no
dwelling-place in the interior.

The goat is domesticated by the Malays, as it is
everywhere by people of their faith, Mahomet having
attached a special blessing to the possession of this
animal. The attempts made at Malacca and Singapore
to introduce sheep resulted in failure.   They could
only be kept by placing them at night upon a plank
flooring raised above the earth, and by feeding them
with imported hay.   Neither the pasture at Malacca
nor in the island seemed to suit them.   But there is
the possibility that the pasture of Perak might prove
better, and attempts should be made to acclimatise the
Indian breed ; or perhaps that of the Chinese might
prove more hardy, for as the country becomes more
opened out and cultivated, there is no reason why
sheep should not thrive as well as the goat. The
advantage to settlers would be no trifle, as will be seen

when it is stated that good mutton, at Singapore, costs about half-a-crown a pound.

Rabbits have been essayed, but they soon fell a prey to the musangs or wild-cats, and this will probably be for some time their fate, these fierce little animals catching them quite close up to the houses; and even in the suburbs of Singapore rabbits and pigeons have to be carefully secured, or their indefatigable enemy will find them out and destroy them without mercy.

CHAPTER XIII.

THE inhabitants of Perak are of several races. The
bulk of the population, which is excessively small and
scattered for so fine a country—one which cannot
show even a village of any great size—consists of the
Malays ; the Batta Barak, Rawa, Mandeling, and
Korinchi—people of Sumatra ; the Bugis ; and lastly,
the wild tribes of the interior. There are of course
the few European settlers, and a certain number of
Chinese, whose skilled labour in mining, agriculture,
and artifice is a valuable acquisition to the country.

The Bugis are evidently a distinct race from the
Malays, and come originally from the southern part of
the island of Celebes. They compare most favourably
with the Malays proper, being intelligent, courageous,
and enterprising ; and though very similar to them in
appearance, they speak a different language. The
Malays fear and respect them above all the other races
of the Archipelago ; and among them are to be found

the principal native traders and merchants ; but their influence has greatly dwindled since the time when they had the principal amount of the trade in their hands.

The Bugis at one time made a strong movement westward, and overran Quedah and several other portions of the peninsula ; but at the present date there are but few of them actually established in the country, their habits being wandering and unsettled, as they seem to have been of old. When the conversion of the different races to Islamism took place, these people were the last to go over to Mahomet, and probably are held now amongst the most strict of his followers. The character given to the Bugis is not always of the best, for he has been termed a beggar, treacherous, given to stealing, braver than a Malay, but not possessing the other's good points, being one who will lay his plans to obtain revenge on the offending party.

The Bugis race has kept itself very distinct from the people amongst whom it dwells, but occasionally inter-marriages take place. One of the most important of late has been that of the well-known Bugis chief of Perak, Nakoda Trong, who led to the hymeneal altar one of the Perak ladies of distinction, Inche Maida, or Princess Maida. Their portraits are given in the accompanying engraving, with the female attendants. This princess has her home at the station high up the Perak river at Qualla Kungsa ; and she won the good-

will of many of the Europeans engaged in quelling the
disturbances, by her singular hospitality, and also by
the ready aid she has always given to the British
officers since the country has been under our protection.
Inche Maida's lord and protector was however found
somewhat wanting at the time of the disturbances, his
Bugis nature and unsettled habits coming uppermost,
with the result that he found an imperative call for
absenting himself on business, leaving his lady to the
wars, while he sought for more peaceful regions and
the protection of his noble self away from Perak.

Among the settlers named, the Korinchi are
immigrants from the interior of the island of Sumatra.
They are Malays in manners and language ; but giving
themselves the credit of being a purer race of Mahomedans, they hold aloof from the ordinary Malay, and
dress always in white garments. Greatly resembling
the Perak Malays, they are more industrious, with the
natural result that they live. in better style, and
surround themselves with more comforts than those
amongst whom they dwell. They write the Malay
language in a peculiar character of their own, one
which Mr. Crawfurd is of opinion was the original
character of the Malay people, and generally used
before the adoption of the Arabic, which is now in
common use.

These Korinchi people are peaceable, and were
found to be quite willing to assist the British in
making roads and felling jungle ; but, with the

customary dignity of the Malay race, objected to being employed as coolies in carrying weights, or, as they expressed it, being treated as beasts of burden, their idea of the creature man being rather higher than amongst the busy nations of the West.

The Rawa and Mandeling people are also immigrants from Sumatra, not far from the particular district of the Batta Barak tribe, who inhabit a portion of the eastern coast of the island in the same latitude as the state of Salangore, across to which state of the peninsula many of them have also migrated. In their own country they are principally fishermen.; but the progressive instinct which has sent them to seek pastures new renders them more amenable to the advance of civilisation, and ready to clear the jungle, cut down trees, plant, and generally prepare the land for a better state of things. The Mandeling people are said to be a branch of the Batta of the interior of Sumatra, a tribe who have enjoyed the unenviable reputation of being eaters of human flesh, and the most fierce and warlike people of the land.

This cannibalistic charge was repeated many years later by Mr. Anderson, viz. in 1823, and though denied by many, was subsequently distinctly proved. Whether the custom still exists the writer is unable to say, but it is still mentioned ; and if at an end, the discontinuance of the practice is of very recent date. Sir Stamford Raffles's remarks, in which he quotes

Dr. Leyden's opinion, are worth repeating.   He says,
in 1823 :

The Batta language, which I regard as the most ancient language
of Sumatra, is used by the Batta tribes, who chiefly occupy the
centre of that island.   The singularity of their manner, and particularly the horrid custom of anthropophagy, practised by a nation
in other respects more civilised than the Malays by whom they are
surrounded, has attracted the attention of Europeans from the time
of the earliest voyagers to our own times, but no very satisfac-
tory account has ever been given of them as a nation.   The
best description of them is certainly given by Marsden, in his
History of Sumatra ; but even that is very imperfect and superficial, and at variance in some respects with the information I
received from individuals of the nation.   Marsden confines their
cannibalism to two cases—that of persons condemned for crimes,
and that of prisoners of war; but they themselves declare that
they frequently eat their own relations, when aged and infirm ;
and that not so much to gratify their appetite, as to perform a religious ceremony.   Thus, when a man becomes infirm and weary of
the world, he is said to invite his own children to eat him, in the
season when salt and limes are cheapest.   He then ascends a tree,
round which his friends and offspring assemble, and, as they shake
the tree, join in a funeral dirge, the import of which is : " The
season is come, the fruit is ripe, and it must descend."   The
victim descends, and those that are nearest and dearest to him
deprive him of life, and devour his remains in a solemn banquet.
This account is certainly more likely to excite incredulity than the
account of Marsden ; but it is the account of some of the Battas
themselves, as well as that of the Malays in their vicinity.

The Malays of Perak, like those of Malacca, are
doubtless descendants of that parent stock which in
bygone times migrated from the district of Menang
Kabau, in the island of Sumatra ; and by all good
Malays this is looked upon as the original seat of their
race.   The whole of the traditions of the people tend to

show that this was their origin; and even at the present day a stranger coming among them from Mcnang Kabau brings with him, so to speak, a pass which ensures him the respect and veneration of all Malays.

Physically, they have broad flat features, the nose wide, and dilated at the nostrils; cheek-bones high,. and eyes placed as in the European, and in no case even slightly oblique, as some writers have said in trying to classify them with the Mongolian or Tartar races. In fact, it has been asserted that if a Malay were dressed in Chinese costume, he could not be distinguished from a Chinaman. This is a grave error, for the Malay of the peninsula is never found with the oblique eyes peculiar to the Mongolian race. The Malay's forehead is slightly prominent; the hair of the head lank, coarse, and universally black; but very slight trace of beard; the mouth large, with the upper lip slightly lifted; complexion of a dark yellowish brown. Their arms are long, chests broad, and their lower limbs strong and muscular; they are, as a rule, below the middle height, but, on the whole, sturdy formidable-looking fellows.

Amongst some of the chiefs there is an evident trace of Arab descent; and this was particularly noticeable in the Laksamana of Perak, who was perhaps the most clever and intriguing of the native chiefs of Perak during and preceding the late *émeute*, not even excepting the Muntri, who in his intriguing ways frequently descended to the low cunning of the Kling, or native of Southern India, whose blood to some extent was said to course in his veins.

The Malay women compare very unfavourably with their lords in a European's eyes, for they seem, with very rare exceptions, coarse, plain, and wanting in the charms nature generally bestows on the softer sex. When quite young, however, they occasionally possess good looks, as may be seen by the illustration showing Inche Maida's attendants, which gives a fair idea of the better-class young girls among the Malays.

Marriages are made at a very early age, in consequence of the rapid approach of maturity, though extreme longevity is not uncommon ; and when, as is customary amongst the poor, polygamy is not practised, the average number of a man's children is from three to four, large families being rarely, if ever, known.   Polygamy, however, which is authorised by the Mahomedan faith, is largely practised by the more wealthy of its followers ; and it has brought about its customary train of evils in Perak, in the shape of slavery in some of its worst forms, and a gradual depopulation of a country already far too thinly inhabited.

The wild tribes of the interior of Perak form a very interesting subject for consideration.   They may be roughly divided into two classes : the Aborigines and the Oriental Negroes; or the "Orang Benua" and Samangs of the Malays.   The words Orang Benua

literally mean "men of the country;" and these people
have been variously styled Jacoons, Basisi, or Sakai,
with other terms from the localities or rivers upon
which they are found. Sakai is the name generally
given to them by the Perak Malay, though sometimes
they may be called Orang Laut—sea-gipsies, or men of
the sea; and Orang Bukit—men of the hill, or hill-
tribes.

There can be no doubt that these people are the
aboriginal Malays, such as the present ruling race
were before their partial civilisation and conversion to
Islam. For though they have a peculiar dialect and
idiom of their own, their language is essentially of
Malay origin. In appearance they greatly resemble
the Malays; but are much shorter in stature;
and, like most rude nations, very little addicted to
injuring their figures by the adoption of tight and
inconvenient clothing. They trade a little with
the superior race; and by means of barter obtain
sometimes the sarong, or national kilt of these people,
and the sapu tangang, or kerchief, for the head, which
they wear in the same way, excepting that the women
leave the bosom uncovered—save when, imitating the
more civilised of their sex, they throw a small cloth
over their shoulders.

The kris, or native dagger, and parang, or knife,
they obtain from the villages; but for their weapon of
offence they use the "sumpitan," or blow-pipe, whose
tiny darts they send through the tube to a long

distance, with great precision and with considerable
force. By means of these tiny arrows they kill birds
and other animals, which, with wild fruit and roots,
form the staple of their food supply.

In Sumatra, on the contrary, according to Mr.
Marsden, these people do not hold any intimate communication with their more civilised neighbours, who
when anxious to obtain honey, wax, or other products
of the forest from them, place clothes and tobacco in
some part of the jungle they are known to visit, and
after a certain time, on going they find their offering
removed, and the products of the forest of greater value
laid in the place.

The sumpitan is formed out of a piece of bamboo;
and the arrows are in some cases poisoned at the tips,
the other end being furnished with a tuft of cotton or
similar growth, which tightly fits the hollow of the
cane, so that a strong puff from the lungs has more
effect upon the dart. When at rest these people will
stand on one leg, resting with the foot of the other
leg against their knee, and the hand grasping the blow-
pipe for a support, just as the Australian blacks rest
upon their spear. Some of these sumpitans are very
neatly made and ornamented, while the arrows used
are both plain and barbed.

The engraving, taken from a photograph of a group
of these people, gives a good idea of their peculiar
characteristics. In this some two or three are seen
with the " limbing," or spear. This is not common

WILD TRIBES OF PERAK, OR "SAKAIS."

with them, but when possessed has been obtained from the Malays. The photograph was one taken by the late Resident, Mr. J. W. W. Birch, who to his many other qualifications added those of being an excellent naturalist and a clever photographer.

Efforts are being made to civilise these people, dating from some years ago, when a French missionary of the name of Borrie went into the jungle of Malacca, and seeking out the Jacoons, as they are there called, found them migrating from spot to spot, as food was plentiful or scarce. Selecting a suitable place he made signs to them, and in their presence planted seeds and tapioca slips, encouraging them to watch what he was doing. Some little time after, on their return to the same spot, he pointed out to them the rooting and growing of the seeds and slips; and in this way, by the exercise of great patience, combined with kindness, he induced them to begin tilling the ground for themselves.

The writer visited the home of this pioneer of civilisation; and it was impossible to avoid lending admiration to the devotion of M. Borrie to his work. From his labour of love he had apparently lost all thought of the outer world. The French mission has also already extended its work to Perak, where it has erected a little church on the very confines of the jungle, and is eagerly pursuing its self-inflicted task amongst the half-civilised Malays of the state.

It was whilst visiting the lonely home of the

French missionaries, that the writer was a witness to
the wonderful skill of the Jacoons with the sumpitan,
their aim being almost unerring, and the weapon
deadly in its effects.

The class of wild people known by the Malays as
Samangs, have been called by Europeans Oriental or
Asiatic Negroes—Negro Malayan people ; and, when
compared with those who inhabit the Philippine
Islands, Negritoes, Aetas, or Little Negroes. Some
recent geographers taking the Malayan word Papua,
literally "curly," have given this name to New Guinea,
and dubbed the inhabitants of this great island with
those of Fiji and others in the Pacific, Papuans,
with whom they class the Samangs of Perak and other
portions of the Malay peninsula.

The writer's knowledge of the so-called Papuans is
not of that thoroughly personal description to enable
him to speak with decision on the subject, and he
can only judge from the accounts given by others ;
but the Samangs, who range from the Nicobar group,
through the Malay peninsula—though, singularly
enough, not found in the island of Sumatra—cannot
be classed with the race of small squat negroes of the
Andamans and Philippines, as described by Crawfurd
and other writers.

For these Samangs differ widely from the little
aborigines—the Sakai, or Jacoons, of Perak—being of
about the same size as the Malay ; are in complexion
of a dark brown, more than black, with flat nose, thick

lips, large mouth, and hair not lank and black like the Malay, nor woolly like the Ethiopian negro, but long and in tufts.

Baron Maclay, the Russian traveller, with whom the writer is personally acquainted, has been recently making a careful study of the habits and features of these people, and will doubtless soon issue an opinion worthy of all respect; but according to the information now possessed, it seems correct to place the Samang with the class called by Dr. Pickering Malayised negroes, and the same which will be subsequently referred to in the chapter on the ancient history of the people, as being found on the island of Madagascar.

It seems only reasonable to suppose that in the constant intercourse which took place in early times between the Arabs and maritime Malays, and between these latter and the people on the island of Madagascar, people of this class were conveyed by the Malays to their own country; and that, not being a maritime people, and strangers to the land, they retreated towards the interior, even as the new Malay colonists from Sumatra drove back also with them the aboriginal inhabitants, the Orang Benua, or Sakai, who were originally dwellers on the coast.

To return to the Malays of Perak : it may not be uninteresting to say a few words respecting their diseases. Like most people who live a simple natural life, they are comparatively free from the ailments of

civilisation ; but disease is by no means rare. That
scourge of Eastern lands, leprosy, is not often seen ;
but occasionally a Malay may be encountered whose
hands and feet are covered with white spots, though
these are said not to be contagious. That terrible
swelling of the leg known as elephantiasis, is sometimes to be seen ; and in cases of this kind the
Malays seem to look upon the afflicted person with a
kind of awe. In fact, in the interior, the people
looked upon an individual thus afflicted as invulnerable, and blindly followed his advice in matters
appertaining to war.

The ordinary blood diseases and fevers are known ;
and among them the small-pox, from which they
suffer a good deal, but look upon the European custom
of vaccination as opposed to a sincere religious faith—
being in fact an endeavour to frustrate the ends of Pro-
vidence in sending disease. By judicious explanations
though, and management on the part of the medical
officers of the Government, the prejudice has to a great
extent been overcome.

Dysentery, one of the complaints that affect Europeans, is not general ; but the inhabitants suffer a
great deal from entozoa, for which nature seems to
have prepared a specific in the male pomegranate tree.
Rheumatism, too, is common, and called by them "wind
in the joints ;" their remedy for it being beating and
kneading till the pain has gone. Many of these simple
remedies are very efficacious ; and the knowledge pos-

sessed by the natives of plants and roots is not unworthy of respect. Pressed leaves are applied to their cutaneous eruptions ; and though dirty in their homes, the Malays have a good idea of the sanitary value of cleanliness, the bath being daily used; while enclosures of mats and bamboo are contrived at the ends of their boats for bathing-places as shown in one of the engravings, the sign that such a place is temporarily occupied being given by hanging the sarong, or skirt, over the outside.

Far as these people are removed from civilisation, they are fully awake to the effects of bhang, an intoxicating liquor prepared from hemp ; to destroy which they chew betel-nut, which is said to counteract the effects of an overdose, even as amongst Europeans chlorodyne is said to remove the intoxication produced by an over-indulgence in stimulants. The Malays being an intensely nervous race this may be so ; in fact, so highly strung are they, that in some instances they have a singularly wild way of mimicking any movement made to them, and if it is continued it seems to have the effect of working them up into a complete state of frenzy. To these peculiarities further allusion will be made when treating of the strange madness known as amok, or, as it has been commonly called, "running a muck."

CHAPTER XIV.

PROBABLY in no country is the custom of keeping
to the national costume more thoroughly adhered to
than amongst the Malays. Civilisation has naturally
introduced many articles of clothing; but no matter
how many of these are adopted, the Malay, from the
greatest sultan of the peninsula down to the poorest
inhabitant of a squalid campong on the banks of a
stream, always wears the sarong, which literally means
a case or envelope.

This is an oblong cloth, from two to four feet in
width, and some two yards long. The ends are
sewn together, and there, in its simplest form, is a
skirt or kilt, which is worn by men and women alike
—on the men reaching to just below the knees, on the
women to the ankles. The men tighten it round the
waist by two or three ingenious twists, thus forming
with it a skirt and belt at one and the same time, in
which they carry the kris, or native dagger, tighten-
ing or loosening the band at pleasure. The women

wear one that is wider, and secure it close up under
the armpits so that it covers the breasts, throwing
another over their heads as a veil and to cover the
shoulders; and when abroad and they meet men, they
extend this upper sarong by holding their hands at a
distance on either side of the head, so as to form with
the garment a long narrow slit, covering the face and
forehead in such a way that the eyes alone are visible
to the stranger's gaze.

This ingenious and very simple form of yashmak,
as it would be called amongst the followers of the
Prophet in Turkey, is of course used in accordance
with Mussulman traditions.

The sarong greatly resembles the tartan of our
own Highlanders, inasmuch as it is invariably a check,
and generally of gay colours, very tastefully woven by
native hands. They are manufactured at many places
in the peninsula, and in Java, Sumatra, and Borneo.
Those from Tringanu and Johore are held in great
esteem, while the cotton sarongs from the Celebes
fetch high prices. The best are of silk from China,
dyed before it is brought over, though the Malays are
very ingenious in the use of dyes; but there is an
intermediate quality, of silk and cotton combined;
while the sarong of the lower classes is of simple
cotton. It is singular that a check should be adopted
by these people for their national robe, one which
really answers to the Scotch plaid scarf, and is often

L

worn in precisely the same way, as in many respects
they resemble our Highlanders in their clannish or
tribal habits, and thoroughly chieftain-like ways of
dealing with their fellows.

The extremely simple garb of the Sakai or
aborigines, and the Samangs or negro Malays has
been already alluded to, as likewise has that of the
Sumatra tribes, who adhere to white. The particular
dress of the Bugis may be gathered from that of
Nakoda Trong, in the engraving. The trousers are
of calico, frequently ornamented with open work at
the base, and over this is worn the sarong, kilt fashion.
This, with the Bugis, is invariably of cotton, and after
protecting the loins by day, is opened out and becomes
a sheet at night. The jacket, worn loose to the figure,
is called a *baju*; it is made with long sleeves, and
generally of white but sometimes of coloured cotton :
in the latter case the pattern is the check to which
the Malay is so partial. The headdress is a handkerchief nattily tied on, and this kerchief is common to
the Bugis and Malay of Perak ; but with the former it
is mostly of a larger size.

The Malay chieftain, while adhering to the sarong—
which is a garment most suitable to the climate, very
convenient, and giving great freedom to the limbs—is
very fond of adopting European costumes. Sultan
Abdullah ordered a magnificent uniform from England,
something between that of a field-marshal and a
hussar colonel's, of which, with its little engineer

busby, he was very proud; though, as will be seen from the group of which he forms the centre, it is doubtful whether he looked so well as the chiefs of his court, who stood on either side when they were photographed by the writer.

The general Malay costume is very similar to that described as worn by the Bugis. It consists of an inner vest, having a collar to button tight round the neck, and the baju or jacket, often of light-coloured dimity, for undress; trousers worn loose and long, or what are now often preferred, a loose pair of short drawers, made of cotton or silk. In the case of a chief, these trousers or drawers are of richly-patterned yellow silk, and often very handsome. Next comes the sarong, which, by the way, is sometimes made to do duty as a scarf by both sexes, who are as tasty in their manipulation of this robe as a Spanish lady in Seville.

As an example of the tribal nature of the costume, the inhabitants of many places wear distinctive-patterned sarongs; and though this is not evident to Europeans unacquainted with the peculiarities of the people, a Malay will readily tell from what part a stranger comes by a glance at his dress. Speaking generally, however, a Malay's costume in Perak may be said to consist of the loose trousers, baju or jacket —which is made of any kind of material to suit the fancy—and the sarong.

The chiefs have taken a great fancy of late to a natty and very effective little skull-cap, of a military

L 2

shape, and the use of this has extended amongst the
better classes of the people.   It is generally of black
and white, and greatly resembles that in favour
amongst the Klings, or natives of Southern India, from
whom it was probably adopted.   But while the Kling
delights in making it of gorgeous colours, with which
he ornaments his wife and everything appertaining to
him, the Malay keeps to modest sober tints; and a
chief will occasionally wear one formed out of a kind
of reed, and have a text from the Koran embroidered
on the front.

The national headdress however of the Perak
Malay is the handkerchief, which is stiffened and tied
with a peculiar twist round the head.   When on a
journey, and expecting to be exposed to the weather,
it is not uncommon for the *battek* or skull-cap to be
worn inside the handkerchief, both being arranged in
no ungraceful manner, for the Malay has a very good
idea of attending to his personal appearance.   Mr.
Crawfurd is of opinion that the Malay took the idea
of his kerchief as worn upon the head from India; but
it is far more probable that, like the sarong, it had its
origin far enough back, with the original tribes who
came from Menang Kabow, and who are, as has been
intimated, looked up to by the better-class Malays,
as the ancestors from whom they trace descent.

Another form of headdress often worn is that
which has been already alluded to as used by the
Malay fishermen for protection from the sun.   It is

also worn by the peasants, and, in its umbrella-shape and cane-work head-frame, greatly resembles that with which we are familiar in pictures of the people of China and Siam.

Where the Malays have associated much with Europeans, and have adopted our ordinary costume, they are much given to the short military patrol jacket, and cover their feet with our socks, and not only the ordinary, but the patent-leather shoe; though they have not yet adopted our chimney-pot hat. Still the sarong is retained; and in these cases it never looks incongruous; for, startling as the statement may seem, a gracefully put on sarong, either with our ordinary dress, or even a military uniform, has not only an admirably picturesque effect, but it is invaluable to the European; and those who have worn it day and night in these latitudes will, from the better health they have enjoyed, have learned to respect the Malays for their experience-bought knowledge of what is most suited for their climate. In this question of dress, as well as in more weighty matters, the Malays of the peninsula have good reason to feel grateful to the Maharajah of Johore, who has set an admirable example in adopting the sensible customs of the Europeans, to the rejection of those unfitted for the climate and absurd.

The Malay wears his hair cut short, or shaved, presenting a striking contrast to the Chinaman, with his tail plaited with silken threads, and coaxed down to

touch his heels. The face is little adorned by nature
with hair, and is generally denuded of what little
appears, except in the case of the chiefs, who retain a
thinly-cut moustache that sometimes reminds one of
Albert Smith's description of that worn by a young
gentleman of his acquaintance, whose eyebrows seemed
to have slipped down on to his upper lip.

The hair of the women, however, is long and luxuriant, and is kept beautifully clean by means of the
juice of lemon and vegetables, which with the soap-
nut makes a good lather, and is either worn over the
crown of the head, or twisted up at the back in the
universal mode that was perhaps established in the
days of our mother Eve. Through this knot, which is
often so jetty and massive that it resembles the chig-
non of modern European society, are thrust pins—very
often of gold ; and on festive days jasmine, chumpaka, and other sweet-smelling flowers are introduced
in a coquettish and very tasteful manner. These pins
or bodkins are called *chuchu kundei*, and, like the
other gold ornaments that are mentioned, are very frequently tinged of a rich red hue, probably caused by
burning in a charcoal fire ; and seen against the jetty
hair, they have an excellent effect, though only second
to the flowers.

The ordinary dress of a Malay woman is, amongst
the more prosperous, an inner garment of white cotton
cloth, covering the breasts, and hanging down to the
hips. Over this is the sarong, held up at the waist

by a twist, as in the case of the men, and falling in graceful folds to the ankles, but further supported by a belt or zone of silver or gold, or of embroidered cloth, and ornamented in front—where an English lady would wear a buckle—by a large oval plate called a *pinding*. This is about the size of the oval mount to a photographic cabinet portrait, and is either of silver or gold; while, in the case of ladies about the little native palm-palace courts, it is frequently studded with precious stones, and beautifully chased by the native goldsmiths. Over all this is worn a long loose dressing-gown style of garment, called the *kabaya*. This robe falls to the middle of the leg, and is fastened down the front with circular brooches known by the Malays as *krosong*.

Very frequently the sarong and kabaya are the only garments; and when going to bathe—a matter of daily custom amongst the Malay women of Perak and other parts of the country—the sarong is perhaps alone worn; and it is in these instances that it is neatly and decorously held up close beneath the arm-pits by an ingenious tuck in the folds, the part hanging over the breast being called *panchong*. Simple as the Malay woman's costume is, it is far from unbecoming; and it possesses this advantage, one which will be held in esteem by every paterfamilias in our empire—namely, it never is out of fashion, so as to cause the outcry so cleverly satirised by Mr. Butler—"Nothing to wear."

One necessary part of the female attire has how-

ever been omitted—necessary or unnecessary, as the
case may be—namely the *salendang*, which is a very
pretty graceful sash, made of cotton or silk of the
most delicate texture. This is worn over the shoulder
or waist, according to the taste of the wearer; frequently after the fashion that an English lady wears
her Shetland shawl.

Except when walking, and likely to meet strangers,
or when liable to be exposed to the sun, the head is
seldom covered; and then it is that the second sarong
is thrown over the head, and drawn out, leaving a
narrow slit for the eyes. It is worthy of remark that
the less bountiful nature has been to the Malay
woman in the matter of beauty of feature, the narrower
she contrives that the slit shall be—a work of supererro-
gation, that, it is to be presumed, is not confined to
the Malays, since strange use is sometimes made in
European countries of a veil or fan.

The covering of the feet is generally omitted by
the women, though they in nowise resemble the
Chinese in smallness, nor those of European ladies in
beauty; but Malays are very clever in embroidering
slippers in gold tinsel, and these, like those of the
Turks, are worn by the higher-class ladies just over
the toes. By way of protection in walking, they
sometimes wear a kind of clog, which is made of
a light white wood; and this is not held on by strap,
toe-piece, or leather covering, but by the simple insertion of a peg on the top, so arranged that it passes

between the toes, and so holds the clog on in what seems to be a very precarious and uncomfortable manner.

The umbrella, or sunshade, is the property of the nobler sex, and is generally of some gay colour ; while amongst the chiefs it will be of rich silk, and often richly fringed and worked in gold. The use of these protections from the torrid rays is probably borrowed from the Siamese, who are great in umbrellas, many of them being of a very gorgeous kind.

Both male and female wear rings—the fore and little fingers being the most in favour for displaying the ornaments ; but the greatest piece of dandyism observable amongst the Malay gentlemen in the way of decoration—quite equalling the ladies' custom of using henna to their nails—is in the custom of displaying the status as a man who never works. The custom is that of wearing the finger-nail long. In one instance, that of Kooloop Mahomed, a relative of the Princess of Perak, the fore-nail of the left hand had been allowed to grow till it was about two inches long. It was carefully tended and kept clean ; while to preserve it from dangers, its owner wore it in a sheath, something like a stiffened elongated finger-stall. Whether this custom has been derived from the Chinese, who have long nails, it is impossible to say, but such a talon always speaks for itself, and says to the world at large : " This gentleman never toils."

Amongst the little points of personal ornamenta-

tion adopted by the Malay women are the wearing of
earrings, or ear-jewels, with swivels, necklaces, and
armlets or bangles. Some of these are very beautifully
worked in silver and gold like the pinding, the goldsmiths having no mean idea of finish in their
art. Less admirable however are their practices of
rouging—a custom confined to married ladies alone—
and using antimony after the fashion of kohl, to
darken the eyelids, and give a lustrous look to the
eyes. But after all, these customs are infinitely
preferable to those of the Hindoos, who give a ghastly
yellow tinge to their faces, by the use of a powder
composed of turmeric.

A glance at the engravings will give a very good
idea of the dress, both of male and female, amongst the
Malays, and at the same time it will be seen how fond
they are of introducing a little variety, even while
adhering to the formal custom of the country in which
they dwell.

CHAPTER XV.

THE villages of Perak, which take the place of towns,
are, as has been intimated, nearly all situated on the
various rivers. They are mostly of very little importance, but as in the opening out of the country
they may rise to the dignity of busy commercial
emporiums, and as reference to them is made in these
pages, it is necessary to give their names. They consist of Chigagala, Kotah Lamah, Korinchi, Saiyong,
Boyah, Sengang, Blanja, Campong Syang, Botah,
Pulo Tiga, Passir Sala, Kotah Lumat, Durian Sabatang,
Batu Rabit, and Kotastia, on the Perak river, with
Kinta and several smaller villages on the river of that
name ; Thai-peng and Kamunting have already been
referred to in the Laroot or tin district, but there is
also in this district the village of Bukit Ganting, the
residence of the Muntri of Perak. Near the Bruas
river is the village of Chindrong Klubi; and on the
Kurow river is another village named Mandring

Semboh.   Qualla Kungsa, so often alluded to, has
become of importance as the military station of
the British Government.

The custom of polygamy seems partly to blame
for the state of these villages and the surrounding
country, bringing about, as it has done, a gradual
depopulation, misery amongst the people, with slavery,
and a variety of other abominations ; while no doubt
many have fallen victims to smallpox, fevers, and
other diseases for which these people have no remedy,
but being fatalists, leave them to fate to perform
the cure.

Doubtless many years ago there was a great drain
on the male population, who went across to Sumatra
to re-people Acheen, which has been a very hotbed of
wars for some time past ; but under a wise and good
régime, with the people assured of personal safety and
protection for their property, Perak would have occupied a very different position as to population to that
at present shown.   This question of inhabitants in an
uncivilised country is always one that is difficult to
decide.   There are no adequate means of judging
where the villages are scattered in all directions, many
being in out-of-the-way spots, perhaps untrodden by
a European foot.   In fact there is no doubt that the
chiefs themselves are in utter ignorance of the numbers
of the settled, wandering, and floating population of
their district.   That of Perak has been variously
estimated at from thirty thousand to eighty thousand,

with five or six thousand to represent the wild tribes.

To make an approximation of the numbers by reckoning from the houses and villages on the river-banks, would naturally give a very unsatisfactory and doubtful result; but after pretty well traversing the country in all directions, the impression made on the writer's mind is that the lower estimate would be about correct. Mr. Birch, however, the late Resident, a man who had seen more of the country than any European, and who had been up every river in the interior, was of opinion that the higher number was correct.

Mr. Birch's opinion may be accepted as reliable; but it must be taken into consideration that during the disturbances of 1875–76, there most probably was a very extensive emigration across the mountains, to the states of the east coast; and if this proves to have been the case, there is every prospect of a strong return current as the country becomes, as it is becoming, more settled. This is greatly to be hoped for, since the return of the people to their old homes will add materially to the prosperity of the country.

Though many of the Malays reside in the interior, and on the pathways or tracks through the jungle between the different rivers, the bulk of the population chose the banks of the rivers themselves for setting up their homes, for many reasons: one of the principal being that as a maritime people and given to boating, here was to a certain extent their habitual life at hand;

though probably, fear of the tribes whose land they had invaded, had something to do with the choice of dwelling of the first settlers of the country. Consequently the Perak Malays have come to be known as the tribe of such and such a river, instead of being reckoned as dwellers in a province or district of the country.

It has already been stated that the rivers are the chief highways to the sea, and hence they became the means by which the people obtained the supplies brought into the country—such as salt, salt-fish, and the simple necessaries on which they depend for support; while a current of trade set in the other direction, tin and rice being sent out in exchange. This river system has made it very convenient for the chiefs of the country to obtain their dues; for no sampan or prau goes up or down the river without being squeezed by the followers of the chief, whose boats are ready at the campong at which the lord resides. One is strongly reminded of the robber chieftains, or barons of the Rhine, in the case of the Perak and its tributaries; though here the enforced tribute has been exacted in a far milder way.

Another reason, doubtless, for the choice of the banks of a stream for residence is the fact that the Malays, who migrated from Sumatra, became, as they drove back the Aborigines into the interior, accustomed to till the ground for the cultivation of rice, their staple food. For rice is now extensively grown, as it has been cultivated more and more with the progress of civilisation. This grain, in its many varieties, cultivated on both wet and dry ground, is coming more and more into fashion with the people, especially the dry ground, or mad padi, which yields a crop in the shortest time.

It is, to one who studies the manners and customs of the Malays, curious to see how habits approximate in different countries. One sees the scarecrows and plans laid to keep off the birds at home, and on going thousands of miles away to the clearings in the jungle of the far East one meets with them again. That ubiquitous bird the sparrow, has been mentioned as amongst the birds of the country, and as he will grub up and devour the peas at home in a suburban garden, so he makes himself, with other mischievous bird-bandits, busy here. The consequence is that the rice-fields are made grotesque by means of long strings which radiate from little bamboo huts in the centre of the fields. To these strings are attached bells, dolls, feathers, rags, anything light and striking, and seated in the hut is a little Malay boy or girl, whose sole costume is a red chintz or cotton bib, which just covers the chest, while the child's duty is to play spider, and agitate the webs that emanate from this centre, though not to attract, but to drive the birds away. Miniature windmills, too, are set up to spin round and rattle in the breeze ; but the sparrows of Perak are as impudent as those elsewhere, and often treat these plans with contempt.

Allusion has already been made to the harvesting,
which is here a time of rejoicing, as at home ; but it
has not been said that prejudice necessitates the
cutting of the rice stalks one by one, while the
valuable straw is destroyed and burnt, its ashes being
about the only manure that superstition allows the
Malay to apply to his land.

Situated as it is, with the river flowing before it,
the appearance of a Malay village amongst its palms
and other fruit trees is exceedingly picturesque, the
graceful aspect of the waving trees, with their beautiful columnar trunks, and feathery fronds, shading
the quaint bamboo palm-thatched structures, being
pleasing in the extreme.   There is but little attention
paid to order ; but the houses are placed here and there
according to the taste and convenience of the owner,
who readily plants cocoa-nut trees around, though he
has to wait about seven years for their fruiting.
When there are so many houses that a double row
occupies the river-bank, a line of communication exists
between them that does not deserve the title of road,
for the Malay never thinks of constructing anything
of this kind, but leaves as much as possible to Dame
Nature.   In this case the houses are built, and as the
people walk to and fro the path comes of itself.

Below the houses—as may be seen in the illustration, which gives a very good general impression of an
ordinary Malay village—posts are driven into the soil,
and upon these small sheds are erected, which serve as

bathing-places, and are extensively used by both men and women, and it is upon the palm-thatch of these places that the sarong is thrown as a sign of occupation. In fact, it is a rare thing to go up or down a river without seeing someone bathing, for the Malays of both sexes are very fond of the water; but great care has to be taken on account of the alligators, which are in places exceedingly numerous. After a bath the all-important sarong frequently occupies the place of a towel; and amongst the better classes cosmetiques are used to rub the body, which at other times, if not sufficiently lithe and pliable at the joints, is made to undergo a kind of shampooing or kneading, the joints being folded, the limbs stretched and pulled, and the knuckles carefully cracked; but this is gene-rally when the Malay is ailing, or suffering from " wind in the joints."

The residence of the Malay is invariably built upon posts, some of which are close to and over the water, though there are no floating bamboo raft-houses as in Siam. The floor is from four to six feet above the ground; in fact, in the jungle, houses may be found built upon the natural posts formed by the growing trees, the floor, which is reached by a ladder, being fifteen, twenty, or even thirty feet from the ground. This is for protection from wild beasts, cases having been known of that formidable cat, the tiger, entering a hut and bearing its occupant away.

The Malay who desires to have a comfortable

M

home literally builds two houses or huts—one at the back of the other—separately roofed, but with a way of communication to join them and form one shelter. The front house is the place for general reception ; while the back, which is shut off by a doorway and curtain, is the exclusive home of the women and children. Again, behind this, there is a kind of shed or lean-to, in which the ordinary domestic arrangements, such as cooking and preparing food, are carried on.

The ground-floor, if it may be so called—that is to say the space between the supporting posts—is the general receptacle of all the dirt and refuse of the family ; and so wanting in sanitary arrangements, and so idle is the Malay peasant, that sooner than construct drains, or clear away this rubbish, he will allow it to lie and fester, so that it very frequently brings on ailments which a due attention to cleanliness would have warded off.

Palm and bamboo are the chief village building materials, though in the Settlements good houses are constructed of bricks, for which there is plenty of excellent clay, while lime made from the limestone coral that abounds is easily procurable. It is mostly prepared by the Chinese, who build up a kiln of alternate layers of coral and timber, and after the requisite burning, a ready sale is found.

The uprights of a house and its sides having been constructed of bamboo or palm by the Malay of a campong, he makes the flooring either of bamboo, or, what is preferable, the nibong palm, which can readily be split into laths. This flooring is elastic, and not unpleasant to bare feet; and upon it the people, who sit upon the floor, are in the habit of spreading mats, which form their seats by day and beds by night. The sides of a house of the lower class are either made of the bark of trees or of split reeds; but in the better-class houses the walls are of far more elaborate work, being sometimes composed of planks which are laboriously cut from the serayah tree, though more often of a kind of mat which is in very general use. These mats are called *kadjangs*, and are made of the leaves of a kind of palm, carefully dried in the sun, and then literally stitched together with the universal rattan; for the Malay is most apt in the way in which he utilises the abundant materials that nature has placed to his hand.

Windows are not forgotten, and these are placed at a height suitable to the convenience of a gazer seated upon the floor; and in the better-class houses they are provided with a mat shutter, and a great deal of tasty work is visible in their framing. But, just as in our own land, there are very careless builders; and in some of the poorer houses, the supports being held together with rattans instead of nails, these former work loose, and at last the whole house goes over bodily right out of the perpendicular.

In such a case it might be supposed that, with

M 2

abundant materials in the jungle, the Malay would at
once proceed to rebuild. He does nothing of the
kind; but evidently content with feeling that the slip
has tightened the rattan lashings of his home, he ac-
commodates himself to the new circumstances, and to
the want of the horizontal in his dwelling, and goes on
perfectly happy in the feeling that he is after all not
called upon to take the trouble to rebuild his hut. In
fact, there seems to be a belief that it is unlucky to
pull down the old dilapidated dwelling, which stands
till it falls; and the Malay strongly reminds one, in
his home arrangements, of the Irish cotter, who could
not get at the roof of his house to mend it when
it was wet, while when it was dry it did not need
repair.

The universal roofing of a Perak house is *attap*
stretched over bamboo rafters and ridge-poles. This
attap is the dried leaf of the nipah-palm, doubled over
a small stick of bamboo or nibong. The pieces of
attap for roofing are generally about four feet in
length, and are bound on to the rafters with rattans';
series overlapping series, and forming a splendid rain-
proof thatch. Like all thatches, however, the attap
will show tender places in time; when the Malays,
instead of re-covering the whole roof, ingeniously introduce new leaves in the bad spots; for when driven
to take measures, they are adepts at saving themselves
trouble. Where extra protection seems to be needed,
it is not uncommon for palm-leaves to be laid along

the ridge of a roof over the pole, the leaflets being tightly plaited in and out; these efforts to obtain a waterproof roof being very necessary in a land where at times the rains are exceedingly heavy.

The attap makes a very cool and pleasant roofing material, and is used extensively by the Europeans of the Settlements, in place of slates or tiles for their dwellings; the former having to be brought from England at great cost and risk of breakage, while the latter are not easily procurable of good quality; those of Malacca however are the best. The objections to the attap-thatch are its inflammability and want of lasting qualities, since it has to be renewed every three or four years. It is still however used over the European barracks, and for the roofs of many of the residences in the Settlements.

The best European residence in Perak is one that was built by the Assistant-resident in Laroot—a house to which allusion was made as overlooking the tin mines of Thai-peng. In this case adze-squared timber was used; some portions of the verandah, rails, doors, and flooring, being actually planed—a wonderful novelty in Perak; while—greater novelty still—some of the timbers were painted; but a great part of this was done by means of Chinese labour, which is far more costly and finished than that of the Malay.

At the same time, it must be granted, that the Malays are very ingenious in the construction of their

houses, a great part of the work being done with a tool
which they call a *biliong*. It is made of iron, and is
so constructed that it can be shifted in its rattan
socket, and becomes either adze or hatchet at the
workman's pleasure. Still, for any particular or neat
joiners' work, the Europeans are mostly dependent on
the Chinese, who have erected nearly all the handsome
dwellings in the British Settlements north and south
of Perak ; though a large share of praise is due to the
admirable application of convict labour. These convicts, mostly from India, were employed generally in
the construction of our roads, and in building the
Government House, that handsome structure the
cathedral at Singapore, and other public buildings
both at Penang and Malacca ; but transportation to
the Straits Settlements has ceased for many years,
and India now sends her convicts to the Andaman
Islands.

CHAPTER XVI.

THE Malay, when put to the test, and compelled by
necessity to work for his own benefit, is by no
means slow in protecting himself from the elements.
After a weary heating walk through the jungle, and
securing his return journey by blazing or marking
the trees with his parang, he does not think of lying
down upon the ground to rest, but rapidly fits up a
few posts, and a floor upon them, a yard above the
level, places a palm-leaf roof over the structure, and
then protects his loins from the wind as he lies down,
by means of a few palm-leaves.

But it is in the building of a chief's house that
the best efforts are put forth; and very picturesque
are some of the efforts in this way, with their neat
thatching, matted windows, and elegantly-woven
sides, gracefully shadowed by the beautiful growth
of palms; though there are irreverent Englishmen
found ready to make comparisons between these
jungle palaces and the barns of their native land.

A house of this kind will be decorated by the sides being formed of matting composed of split reeds, woven into a neat check pattern, red and white; while other parts are of strips of bamboo neatly interlaced. An elegant lattice-work is often introduced with admirable effect, and various little efforts are made to embellish a building that is thoroughly in keeping with the jungle scene. Such a place will be protected by surrounding it with a stout fence of split bamboo; the best example of this being at the home of the Muntri of Laroot, at Bukit Gantang, which is perhaps one of the best-built places in Perak. At times these fences are so strong that they will throw off a musket-ball; and those not acquainted with the country, who have come across these *pagars*, as they are called, have taken them for the stockades used by the Malays in time of war. Sometimes these fences are merely placed round the base of a house itself, thus enclosing the open part between the posts through which an enemy could otherwise make his way. A necessary precaution; for it is said that at times, where revenge is sought, a Malay will wait till his enemy is at rest, and then, having obtained a knowledge of where he sleeps, will go beneath the house and pass his kris between the palm-strip flooring into the recumbent body—the mat which forms the unfortunate person's only bed being no protection against the keenly-pointed blade.

The residence of the Princess of Perak at Qualla

168

Kungsa gives—as will be seen in the illustration, from a photograph taken by the author during the Governor's progress—a very full idea of a Malay noble's residence. The house to the left is really the kitchen, while that on the right is, as far as its principal apartment is concerned, fitted up with a bed which occupies about two-thirds of the room, greatly resembling in the matter of size the Bed of Ware. This house, with the whole of the campong adjoining, was placed by Inche Maida at the disposal of the British during the disturbances, and formed the head-quarters of the general commanding and the com-missioner with the contingent of troops from India.

Inche Maida's principal apartment boasted little furniture; but the bed possessed a coverlid of red calico with an ornamental border, and curtains meant as a protection from the mosquitoes, but of a texture stout enough to set at naught the attack of a swarm of locusts. Down the centre extended a long pillow, or "Dutch wife," ornamented at either end with gold brocade embroidery, the work of the princess's own fingers; while round pillows similarly worked finished off the head of the bed. Upon the intro-duction taking place between general and princess, the lady claimed the former as her guest, and with all the pride of an English country dame of the last century over her well-filled ticks, drew his attention to the bed, which had been, she said, prepared regard-less of expense; but the general was so simple in his

tastes that he preferred to make his resting-place of a
camp-cot.

There are Malay chiefs though, who, having been
more in contact with European civilisation, follow our
example not only in dress but in the construction of
their dwellings.   One instance of this is found in
Rajah Bot, ruler of Lookoot in the Soonghy Ujong
territory near Malacca, who has supplied himself with
a house precisely similar to that which would be built
by a European ; while ascending higher in the scale
of improvement we have the palace of the ruler of
Johore, at Johore Bahru or New Johore, which has
been built somewhat on the model of our own
Government House at Singapore, the Balei or Hall
of Audience being altogether unique in its exquisite
taste and elegance.   Lookoot and Johore have, however, been for many years on the borders of European
civilisation.   Going north though, we have the Rajah
of Quedah making similar advances ; the impulse
being doubtless given by our settlements in Penang
and Province Wellesley.   This latter chief has gone
so far as to have the grounds about his palace tastefully laid out with gravelled paths, flower-beds,
shrubberies, fish-ponds, and various other adjuncts
of a wealthy person's garden at home.

In such a house as that of the Princess of Perak
the bedding is formed only of mats ; one of these and
the sarong for cover being all that a Malay in this hot
climate seems to need.   The apartments are divided

by curtains, and a tasty effect is produced by the use of hangings of dimity or chintz upon the walls; the ceilings of rough thatch and bamboo being covered with the same material of various patterns. But the Malay ladies, as in the case of Inche Maida and her coverlid and pillows, are very clever in embroidering on frames, producing very pretty effects with silk and gold threads or tinsel, which they are fond of working in patterns on red and white cloth.

The various objects that take attention about the poorer houses of a campong are very interesting. On approaching a hut, with its ladder-like flight of steps to the door, close by will be seen the small enclosed shed or granary, with sides of bark, in which the Malay stores his rice for the family during the season. Inside the hut, and swinging from a rafter of the ceiling, is that universal adjunct to a married home— the cradle, with its little dusky occupant fast asleep. A couple of children of larger growth, nude save the chintz bib hanging from their necks, have taken a peep at the strangers and bounded away; or probably the mother has been encountered carrying one, walking with a firm, elastic swing, with the child sitting astride upon one of her shoulders. These brown-skinned little fellows are not without education; for where there are native schools, antiquity asserts itself, and they are seen, as we have read of them in the old geographical works dealing with Arabia, seated upon the floor before boards covered

with sand, upon which they are taught to trace the
Arabic characters with the points of their fingers.
The way up to the house has been along a narrow
track, for the Malays never walk abreast, but always
in single file, and so silent is the place that but for
the tops of the huts it might be imagined that no
trace of habitation was near.

About the houses the tamed pets of the Malays
may be noticed—doves, minahs, or parrots, with
occasionally a monkey; but as a rule the huts alone
are seen, the natives avoiding the sight of a stranger,
more often than not from fear. Very frequently,
however, an offering in the way of hospitality is laid
where the stranger can find it, this being a cocoa-nut
fresh and green; though where the people are not so shy,
the fruit is fetched for the traveller by one of the Malays,
who, if he be unprovided with one of the monkeys
to screw off the stalk, will himself take a band, make of
it a sling which embraces the tree and his body, and
then proceed to climb one of his fruit-trees for the
refreshing nut. This he does by hanging back against
the sling and pressing his feet against the leaf knots
in the bark, shifting his band and his feet alternately,
and gaining about twenty inches at a time as he
ascends; of course grasping the tree stem tightly with
his hands the while, till he reaches the crown of great
leaves, when, selecting a suitable nut, it is lopped
off by a blow from his parang or knife, and falls to
the ground.

At times, however, the Malay cuts little steps for his toes in the sides of the trees, and climbs them in this manner. When this fresh green cocoa-nut is opened for the visitor with the parang, its contents are not the hard white nut to which we are accustomed, but a grateful sub-acid water, very refreshing after a journey through the forest.

This cocoa-nut is one of the most valuable of the Malay's home fruits, and it is used at different periods on its journey to ripeness. At one time it is soft and white inside, and can be eaten with a spoon; while when the nut grows hard it is either boiled for its oil or rasped and steeped, and its milky juice used in a variety of ways for cooking.

The common people have two ways of performing this rasping process, not being at all deficient in culinary utensils. One way is to pass the nut rapidly over an iron implement, shaped like a military spur, the other is by rubbing on a sort of coarse wire brush, whose bristles are short pieces of wire stuck in a small neatly-formed board.

This rasped cocoa-nut enters largely into their food preparations, and is particularly palatable, especially in curries, which can never be tasted in perfection except in the east, on account of the absence of fresh cocoa-nuts and other ingredients.

Mutton is generally unknown, but beef, in the form of buffalo flesh, is much in favour with the Malays, who use it when on journeys, after cutting it in strips,

which are dried in the sun ; the intense heat acting
upon the meat too rapidly to allow of decomposition
taking place, and prepared in this way it is very
tender and good.   Fish is of course largely eaten, for
a Malay never loses an opportunity of catching those
of river and sea ; but he would think it a sin to cut
or crimp it when alive, and carefully puts it to death
before it is prepared for food.   Salt fish is largely
consumed, and brought from long distances into the
interior, with large quantities of sun-made salt.

The Malay has a very good appreciation of
poultry, both for his amusement and eating ; hence
the familiar crow of the cock is often heard about
the campongs.   These people are even discriminating
in their choice of them for food, but choose those
which would be rejected by every good English
housewife, who is particular to pick out clean, white-
legged Dorkings, while the Malay epicure prefers his
poultry with black joints, considering them far better
and more tender.

It may be interesting to the reader to have the
description of Malay mixtures or sambals for eating
with curry, as it will doubtless seem more appetising
than the blachang or fish condiment, already described
as being composed of putrescent shrimps mashed up
in the sun.   For the mixtures to eat with his curry,
which is always of a very simple kind, the Malay
takes dried prawns, cut cucumber—sliced in cocoa-nut
milk, chillies ground up into a pulp, yam carefully

cooked and chopped small, the balimbing fruit cut into pieces, mangoes occasionally, chutnies of various kinds, and green ginger shredded small with vinegar. These mixtures are served up on saucers, and eaten with the curry, as we English at home eat pickles, and salad from those handy gibbous-moon plates which are seen ˙ at some highly-civilised tables. And it is not only amongst the Malays that this custom obtains, for the Chinese and Japanese have trays especially designed for their sambals or sweetmeats. These trays are circular, and have the appearance of a large Pope Joan board, only that the divisions are saucers to contain the mixtures.

In India the curries themselves are made hot with chillies, but the Malay makes his curry of very simple materials, with a great deal of cocoa-nut milk therein. Very often the dish is entirely vegetable, and the hot spices are mixed in the sambal or condiment which is eaten therewith. Taking it for granted that the native knows best what is suited for the digestion in his climate, this custom is freely followed by the European residents, who add the curry mixture to their breakfast and dinner as a rule.

But it is with their staple food—rice—that the Malays, whose right hands are cunning in culinary preparations, contrive their greatest variety of dishes. It is eaten dry or parched; plain boiled, after being washed by these particular people in six or seven different waters; made into cakes with scraped

cocoa-nut and sugar, and then neatly arranged in a
scrap of cocoa-nut leaf, which is pinned together with
one of the native pins—that is to say, a tiny skewer
of bamboo.   Plantain-leaves too are great favourites
for food purposes, and are often used as dishes from
which the native eats his rice; and it is needless
to say that such nature-supplied dishes are never
washed, but renewed from the garden for the morrow's meal; while should a convenient fire for cooking
be required, nature has supplied a stove and fuel
ready to hand, which will go on burning at a
powerful red heat for many days.   This unpatented
stove is the mound of the white ant, which contains
in itself all the necessaries for this sustained com-
bustion, supplying a want and at the same time
getting rid of a noxious pest; as an antidote to
which the Malays use one kind of wood-oil, or
this product in combination with arsenic and sugar
of lead.

CHAPTER XVII.

A PEOPLE who are fond of condiments to flavour
their simple preparations of rice, and who are enormous eaters of fruit, may very naturally be supposed
to have a taste for sweets, and this is the case. One
of their favourite dishes is a sort of syllabub, composed of sago, which the palm yields them in abundance, boiled down with sugar, and covered with
cocoa-nut milk. This is known as *booboor*. These
are but a few of the culinary preparations of the
Malay, who has in addition his sugar-cane, of which
he is inordinately fond—eating it largely raw, and
taking lengths of it, to peel off the silicious skin,
and then cut it in convenient pieces for chewing;
maize, and the rice, and abundant fruits and vegetables—onions among the latter being great favourites;
while by way of luxury the use of tobacco is not at all
uncommon.

N

As a rule the Malay prefers Javanese tobacco, but failing this he uses his own coarse preparation of the leaf, grown in his own patch of garden, with very little trouble.   He makes no hubble-bubble pipe as a rule—though these are occasionally constructed out of the native tin—but contents himself with one rapidly extemporised out of a cutting of bamboo for bowl, and a shoot of the same for stem.   More frequently, however, .he goes to nature in her simplest form to aid him in what some people would call his very bad habit. Turning to his universal friend, the palm, he obtains from it a supply of cigarette papers ; in other words, he takes the *roko*, or outer sheath of the palm-leaf, or else the thin sheath of the plantain, or pisang, rolls in it a little tobacco, forming rather a large cigarette, and smokes in peace.   In fact, in no part of the world has nature furnished man with so many means to his hand for supplying his simple wants ; and even when these simple wants grow into those of a more luxurious kind, the forest still seems to provide a never-failing store, only asking to be sought for by those who need.

For opium - smoking the Malay is doubtless indebted to the nations farther east.   It is not greatly practised by the poorer Malays, but it is a luxury too frequently indulged in by the chiefs, to the great detriment of their health and mental vigour.   This, of course, is from the excess of use ; for there are authorities of great experience who tell of the practice of smoking opium being carried on to an extreme old age without deleterious effects. There is no doubt, however, that when a man becomes a slave to the habit, decrepitude, loss of appetite, and a miserable early death result. The Chinaman is the greatest consumer of the drug in the peninsula, and in the Settlements either smokes at home, or goes to one or other of the opium-houses.

The process of smoking opium has often been described—perhaps never more vigorously than by the late Mr. Charles Dickens—but it is so peculiar a practice that it may bear repetition. The opium as used by the smoker has been purified from the coarse, heavy, dank-smelling gum of commerce, roughly prepared from the poppies grown for the purpose, and when ready resembles thick treacle in consistency. This is placed ready to the chief's hand, and he then reclines upon his mat and takes his opium-pipe, which is generally of thin cane, with a metallic bowl. A tray with a lamp and a little fork form part of the paraphernalia. Upon this fork a little bit of opium is twisted up and applied to the pipe, which in turn is held to the flame of the lamp, and the little point or fork is used to keep up the supply of opium, clear the pipe, and generally, so to speak, stoke or poke the tiny fire, so that it receives a sufficient supply of oxygen. This kind of smoking is quite a serious matter, and takes as much time as a Turkish bath, the smoker having to sink into a state of lethargy, enjoy his dreams, and lie passive till he wakes. In fact, it

is a kind of intoxication, during which he who
indulges sinks into a state that should only be allow-
able to calm the anguish of a terrible disease.   Then
it would be a valuable medical aid, but as an indul-
gence, it is degrading to mankind, and sensual in the
extreme.

The habit of betel-chewing is not much to be commended, but it is universal, and seems not to be injurious
to those who practise it.   In fact, betel-chewing is so
national a custom with the Malay that he will actually
reckon time by the space occupied in the consumption
of a "quid ;" the term is vulgar, but too appropriate
not to be used.   For instance, a Malay visits you on
business, and sitting down he will not commence the
object of his mission until such a time has elapsed as
he considers that the chewing of his betel should take.
During this interval he is most probably squatted
upon his heels, looking remarkably absurd, with his
mouth distended, his eyes half-closed, unable almost
to speak save in monosyllables or grunts.   There are
exceptions, however, many Malays holding the betel
between the upper lip and teeth, and conversing pretty
freely.

Both sexes indulge in this habit, which is commenced at a very early age ; and extends from the
lowest, who carry their supply in a bag, to the Sultan;
in whose regalia there are a certain number of betel-
boxes, some of the choicest make.   Its use, to quote
the quaint saying, is probably "as old as the hills."

In looking back into ancient chronicles, it is found that according to Salmasius, even in the first century, betel formed an article of commerce, and was sent from the Golden Chersonese for lovers of the drug in Arabia and Persia, and that as a compound it was sold in the markets of those countries under the name given to it by the Greeks of *Mala-bathron—bathron* being the name for the betel, or areca palm, or the betel of Mala or Ta-Mala. No doubt it was known to the Arabs long before this period, and it is worthy of note that the Arabic name *Tambal* has some resemblance to Ta-Mala. In fact, as the ingredients of the mixture as used have always been produced in the Malay peninsula in the highest perfection, and the habit of chewing it is more prevalent there than probably among any people on the face of the globe, it may not be unreasonable to draw from the above a further proof of the extremely early acquaintance of the nations of the more Western lands with the Ta-Mala, Tanah Malai, or Land of the Malays, which has previously been suggested as the notable Ophir of Solomon.

This betel is a curious mixture, being composed of several ingredients, according to the taste or quality of the person using it. Generally, however, it is the leaves of the sirih, a creeping plant, that is trained up a stick, and much cultivated in gardens. It is probably one of the pepper family ; and its leaves are gathered, tied in little bundles of fifteen or twenty,

and sold at the bazaars or little shops of the
villages.   The second component is the nut of the
areca-palm, or betel-nut, which grows in clusters on
the tree, and somewhat resembles a nutmeg, with a
yellowish fibrous coating.   These nuts are also sold by
the dealers ; and for the convenience of the purchaser a
quaint-looking instrument, like a combination of nut-
crackers and scissors, is kept at hand, to enable the
chewer to break up the nut into small pieces.   Next,
there is a fine kind of lime, formed by burning sea-
shells, and kept like a paste in a brass box about the
size of that used for tooth-powder at home, while the
more luxurious use gambier, sold in strips or cakes of
a gum somewhat like jujube—this to give astringency
—and a clove—which, by the way, is an expensive
luxury in these parts.

The betel-chewer, thus provided, takes a sirih leaf
from his bag, smears a little lime upon it from his
box, places a scrap of areca-nut upon the lime, rolls
and folds the leaf up into a neat little packet, and
transfers it to his mouth, where after a little mastication the saliva begins to assume a vermilion hue,
and the custom for which our sailors have become
famous is in full force.   Where, however, it is a rajah
who is chewing betel, he uses a spittoon, frequently
shaped like a handsome chalice, and of pure gold.
In such a case the chief has a regular tray before him,
bearing the spittoon and lime-box, and another for
betel, full of compartments containing spices as well.

His wives, stationed behind him, are employed beating up the components, to save trouble in mastication; and, using a curiously-elongated pestle and mortar of brass, they beat nut, leaf, and gum into a red paste, which is presented to the rajah on a bright copper spatula, which he draws across his tongue, chews, and is supremely happy.

This brass pestle and mortar are also used by old people whose dentition has become imperfect or worn out. The flavour of the betel-nut, if tested by a European, is very pungent, aromatic, and astringent; and one essay is generally sufficient to decide the experimentalist that betel-chewing is not a practice or vice that it is worth while to contract, even though it is sedative, and probably intoxicating to a certain extent. The effect is to stain the teeth of a dark red, in some cases almost black, and seen in a young girl this is to a European anything but pleasant; but the Malays believe it to be a great addition to a person's appearance. They consider it to be a sign of refinement, and say that it is only monkeys and other animals who should glory in the possession of white teeth—a saying by no means complimentary to the European residents of the place. This betel-chewing seems however to possess one good quality—namely, that of preserving the teeth; for that racking pain of civilised life, the toothache, is rarely heard of in Perak or the neighbouring states.

The following quaint description of betel-chewing

amongst the neighbours of the Malays of Perak, the
Siamese, though bearing somewhat the nature of a
repetition, is worthy of notice from showing how
thoroughly similar was the custom in the past to
that of the present day. The account was written
by De la Loubere, the French envoy, nearly two
hundred years ago.

The *Areca*, which the Siameses do call *Plou*, is a kind of great
acorn, which yet wants that wooden cup wherein our acorn grows.
When this fruit is yet tender, it has at the center or heart a
greyish substance, which is as soft as pap. As it drys it waxes
yellower and harder, and the soft substance it has at the heart
grows hard too. It is always very bitter and savory. After
having cut it into four parts with a knife, they take a piece every
time and chew it with a leaf resembling ivy, called *Betel* by the
Europeans which are at the Indies, and *Mak* by the Siameses. They
wrap it up to put it the more easily into the mouth, and do put on
each a small quantity of lime made of cockle-shells, and redded
by I know not what art. For this reason the *Indians* do always
carry this sort of lime in a very little china dish, for they put so
little on every leaf that they consume not much in a day, altho'
they incessantly make use of the *Areca* and the *Betel*. The *Areca*
whilst tender wholly consumes in the mouth, but the dry always
leaves some remains.

The sensible effect of this acorn and this leaf is to excite much
spitting, if they care not to swallow the juice ; but it is good to
spit out the two or three first mouthfuls at least, to avoid swallow-
ing the lime. The other less sensible effects, but which are not
doubted in the *Indies*, are to carry from the gums, perhaps by
reason of the lime, whatever may prejudice them ; and to fortifie
the stomach, either by reason of the juice, that is swallowed at
pleasure, and which may have this quality, or by reason of the
superfluous moistures which they discharge by spitting. Thus have
I never found any person at Siam with a stinking breath, which
may be an effect of their natural sobriety. Now as the *Areca*

and *Betel* do cause a red spittle independently on the red lime which is mix'd therewith, so they leave a vermilion tincture on the lips and teeth. It passes over the lips, but by little and little it thickens on the teeth till they become black; so that persons that delight in neatness do blacken their teeth, by reason that otherwise the spittle of the *Areca* and *Betel*, mix'd with the natural whiteness of the teeth, causes an unpleasant effect, which is remarked in the common people. I shall transiently declare that the vermilion lips, which the Siameses saw in the pictures of our ladies which we had carried to this country, made them to say that we must needs have in France better *Betel* than theirs. To blacken their teeth they do thereon put some pieces of very sowre lemon, which they hold on their jaws or lips for an hour or more. They report that this softens the teeth a little. They afterwards rub them with a juice, which proceeds either from a certain root or from the *Coco* when they are burnt, and so the operation is performed.

Betel-chewing, combined with the ordinances of Mahomet, probably accounts for the fact that the Malays are not much given to drinking to excess. There are, however, intoxicating drinks in the country, one of which, known as *samshoo*, is prepared by fermenting rice, and is chiefly used by the Chinese settlers, the native having ready to his hand the toddy of the palm. This is obtained by simply climbing the tree and tapping it in a particular place, just among the great fresh leaves, when the sap or juice exudes, and runs pretty copiously into the little earthen jars which the Malay ties beneath. When the juice first runs from the tree it is sweet and perfectly innocent as a beverage, but if left a short time, the heat of the sun produces fermentation, and an intoxicating drink is the result.

Arak, as it is called, is an intoxicating spirit evidently produced by distillation, which is, however, practised to a very small extent in Perak, though the Malays know the still, or alembic, whose use they were probably taught by the Arabs. They call it *kukusan*, from a word which signifies smoke or steam. That distillation is not more practised is explained by the ease with which fermented liquor can be obtained, nature's process with the palm-juice being thoroughly appreciated by one who looks upon matters requiring effort as *soosa*—trouble.

Domestic implements are not very abundant in Perak, but the people seem to have all their simple wants demand. The popular plate or dish has already been mentioned as growing on the palm-tree, some of whose leaves make a covering to be envied, being a spear-blade ten feet long by as much as four feet in its greatest width. To the palm, or pisang, they go for leaves for wrappers ; palm-sheaths form cases instead of paper for parcels, or they are cleverly skewered together with splints of bamboo, and become buckets that will hold water ; or better still, a thick bamboo, three or four feet long, is a very convenient water vessel, and is often seen standing up against a hut. Buckets are also made from the outer bark or skin of the plantain, across which a stick is tied, and a rope attached for drawing up water from the river for drinking or bathing purposes ; for the natives do not as a rule dig wells, and it is a matter of custom to wash the feet after a journey before entering a house.

Iron vessels are not plentiful, but many families have a kind of pan which they use in their cooking, while the half shell of a cocoa-nut, with a stick passed through two holes near the edge, forms a capital ladle. The cleverness of the women at embroidery has been mentioned ; they are also adepts at netting, while the men can scheme a basket or cage out of a few rattans and a bit or two of bamboo in a very short time. In this way they will twist together a cage big enough to carry a wild cat, monkey, or the largest bird, and all made and tied with freshly-gathered rattans.

If the Malay requires a light for his house he has but to procure a cymba shell, laying in it a wick formed of fibrous wood or pith, filling the shell with oil from cocoa-nut or palm, and he has a lamp of antique pattern and graceful shape. If, on the contrary, the light is to illumine the way through the jungle, or to keep off troublesome beasts, a rough torch is readily made of the leaves of the cocoa-nut tree tied together; but the better kind are formed of a resinous product known as *dammar*. This is placed between palm leaves, and burns fiercely with a capital light ; while for temporary purposes an extempore cresset is often made by fixing an entire cocoa-nut husk on the top of a bamboo pole, and filling the opening with dammar.

This dammar, which is the general Malayan name for resin, is dug out of the forests by the Malays, and

seems to be the fossilised juices of former growths of
the jungle, probably palms, and is of infinite value to
a people who use no coal.   A peculiar kind of this
resin has been lately discovered in Borneo.   It is
opaque-white, but where broken freshly the fracture is
of a beautiful translucent blue, but soon grows opaque
on being exposed to the air.   Like the dammar of the
Malay, it burns very readily, and is the more remarkable from being the fossil production of a land where
the coniferæ or pine family are almost unknown.   This
curious production, which might almost be looked
upon as a white amber, is now undergoing tests in
the laboratory of the School of Mines, Jermyn Street;
but at the period of writing this work, has not yet
been pronounced upon by the chemist who is investigating its qualities.

Not only are mats woven for the sides of their
houses, but very fine ones are often made for ornamental purposes. Though not especially tidy about their
dwellings, the Malay nations have that most domestic
of utensils, a broom, which is made from the midribs
of cocoa-nut leaves tied to a bamboo handle; while
among other articles will be found bamboo baskets,
and, if the people are very fortunate, a china basin
and a spoon.   At a rajah's house it is no unusual
thing to find a complete tea-set, of which the owner is
very proud, but invariably follows the Chinese fashion
of preferring an earthenware teapot to one of other
material.

Metal finds its way, though, into some of the domestic utensils, the metal generally being the native tin, of which they construct ewers and water-bottles. As to gold, the work of some of the better articles is very beautiful, notably the gold and silver flowers presented as tribute to the King of Siam. These are some eighteen inches high, and exquisitely worked in filigree.

CHAPTER XVIII.

ALLUSION has been made before to the similarity of
habit amongst peoples in far-distant parts of the world.
In any county court in our agricultural districts the
judge's pest is the ever-recurring case of the tallyman,
who summons ten or even twenty labourers for small
debts, caused by their wives running up accounts with
these travelling drapers and tea-men in their absence.
Precisely similar cases take place in Perak, where,
however, there are neither tallymen nor county
courts. But the place of the former is taken by the
ubiquitous Chinaman, who, in the most adventurous
manner, goes off into the interior with his wares,
consisting principally of calicoes, chintzes, and sarongs,
borne upon the ends of a bamboo, while in one hand
he carries a rattle-drum to announce his coming; this
latter being a tiny instrument formed out of three or
four inches of hollow bamboo, covered at the ends
with python skin, and pierced through the centre

with a stick which serves as a handle. The percussion is caused by means of a pea at the end of a string attached to the middle of the bamboo, which the Chinaman twists rapidly backwards and forwards by means of the handle as he enters a campong, when the pea strikes first one and then the other end of the drum.

This signal has its effect upon the Malay women, whose husbands are away at work in the fields, and the pedlar's visit is welcomed as readily as that of his prototype in England. Then comes the taking of credit followed by the day of reckoning, when furious quarrels arise; the husband not unfrequently resenting the demand for payment with his kris, to the serious injury of the heathen pedlar, who is sometimes murdered in the up country, for the sake of the money he has collected in his adventurous rounds.

These sarongs, by the way, are always presenting themselves under fresh auspices: one of the most peculiar uses to which they are put is that of slinging one upon a bamboo, after placing therein the body of an injured or slain man, and the bamboo being lifted on the shoulders of a couple of Malays, the sufferer is borne away in this extemporised litter with ease.

Debt is a serious thing in a land like Perak, where bankruptcy is not exactly paid for with a pound of flesh, as in the days of Shylock, but with the whole nine or ten stone which form the bankrupt's body, and this too often becomes the creditor's property for life, the unfortunate debtor's wife and children succeeding to the bondage in their turn.

The Bugis may sell himself to another Bugis, if he is indebted to him, and he can at any time redeem himself if he can raise the purchase-money; but this is not the case with the Malay, who becomes a slave indeed, and has no way out of his state of bondage. If a debt cannot be paid, the Malay is handed over at once; and failing himself, his child or some other relative has to take the place, though exceptions are made by which the security of the debt depends on the life of the person alone.

The debtor lives with the family of his creditor, to whose benefit the work done is applied, and even Chinese in the Settlements obtain the labour of their debtors in this way. In fact, the strict manner of defraying debts is a remarkable trait in the customs of the Malays, who are very punctilious in paying their dues. Damage done by cattle or elephants is appraised and paid for, their code of laws containing forfeits for these matters; while, if the damage be nocturnal, and arising from neglect in confining buffaloes, the penalty is particularly severe.

This custom of debt-slavery exists to a great extent, and seems, says Mr. Davidson, her Majesty's Resident at Salangore, "to have arisen from the abuse of an old practice in Malay countries. It is contrary to the Mahomedan religion for a person born in a Mahomedan country, and brought up in that faith, to be a slave, though the reduction to slavery of the Battak people, and those who do not profess the Mahomedan faith, seems nowhere prohibited by the laws of that faith."

Revolting as slavery is to the feelings of an Englishman, and eminently un-Christian as it is, we must remember that it is a peculiar soil in which it has grown, and not deal with it from our own vantage-ground; for the slavery of Perak is an institution of the country. That it is a custom at times terribly abused there can be no doubt; but, on the whole, the *régime* under which the slave lives is mild and not disadvantageous. Among the evils of slavery, the power of the Sultan or chiefs to seize upon the person of any one to whom they take a fancy, will be treated of in a future chapter, in connection with the Government of the country. There are, however, other evils, which it is to be hoped have been greatly exaggerated by those who narrate the matters as facts. For instance, it is asserted that the Sakais, or Jacoons, are literally hunted down, captured, sold, and made slaves; and the late Mr. Birch states that from his experience these people were far worse treated than others of their class; since they were badly clothed and fed, and made to work excessively hard; while they were considered as debt-slaves on account of the money that had been expended upon them. It might be considered that these people, accustomed to a wild life, would readily escape to the woods; but they have little chance of

getting away, and the penalties are too heavy, the
least being severe ill-usage, perhaps death; for if a
Malay killed one of these slaves, it would excite no
attention amongst the owner's people.

Instances of this slave-hunting are not at all
uncommon, as recorded by the various Residents;
one of whom specially notifies Perak as the scene
of these outrages. The Sakai women seem to have
been frequently hunted down like wild beasts,
becoming with their children slaves through generation after generation. Not that this practice is
approved of by the Malays, who speak very strongly
in reprehension of the cruel act; and in one case
that is recorded, where fourteen of the wild people
were caught and carried off in chains, attempts were
made to discover the offenders and set the Sakais
free—though doubtless this was on the action taken
by the British Resident.

Instances are given of death being inflicted for
these attempts at flight, and even for far more
trivial offences; whilst one, special in its atrocity,
is reported from Salangore. In this case three debt-
slaves, two girls and a boy, all under twenty years of
age, fled from their master, and took refuge at a place
some two miles down the river. They were, however,
caught, brought back, and the boy was at once taken
to a field and put to death by a thrust from a kris.
As, however, it was not the custom to kris or stab
girls, these two poor creatures were told by the Rajah's

wife that she was going to bathe, and they were ordered to accompany her to the river. This was only a short distance from the house; and upon their reaching a log lying in the water, one girl was seized and held, while a follower of the Rajah's wife caught the other by the hair, thrust her into the water, and held her head down beneath the surface with his foot until she was dead. The other was then seized in the same manner and drowned; the poor girls' bodies being afterwards left upon the muddy river's bank, exposed to the attacks of the alligators, until such time as the relations might come and remove them. These were slaves of the Sultan of Salangore, and were killed by order of the Rajah, his second son; and upon the Sultan expressing anger at the deed, the Rajah generously presented the relatives with winding-sheets for the bodies of the dead. Only a short time subsequent, another son of the same Sultan krissed one of his debt-slaves, not for an actual offence, but for threatening to become a thief.

One very general way of getting in debt amongst the Malays is through gambling. By an infatuated love of play, a man gets so in debt that he gives himself up, with perhaps wife and children, to his successful opponent; and then, so far from being cured of his mania, he is seized with an insatiable desire to free himself by the same practice, and gambles to raise the money to buy himself from his owner. How often he is successful may be readily surmised. In

fact, it is almost beyond credence to see how extensive is the range of debt caused by gambling, and
how frequently a Malay will pledge self or child to
his creditor by way of payment.

In addition, there are in Perak many intricate
points in connection with the system which make it
excessively hard for those innocent of complicity in
the incurring of the debt.   For instance, the con-
traction of a debt by a married man binds his wife
and children ; and, what is more, those children who
may afterwards be born to him.   Again, if an un-
married man or woman be in debt, and afterwards
marry, the husband or wife so taken becomes part of
the bond, and the children who result from the marriage are in like evil state.   Their destiny is to work,
often under hard usage, for the creditor, who must
repay himself many times over for his original loss;
and this must be a great temptation to the Malays to
keep up the system, though they frankly own that it
is wrong, and contrary to the laws of the Prophet.

One curious fact in connection with this custom,
as showing how thoroughly secured a creditor is,
deserves mention.   In cases where a child is placed
with a creditor as a security for a debt, and this
child dies, another is supplied in its place ; and in
the case of a Rajah, the whole family may be taken
into his house.

In spite of the objectionable nature of this custom,
and its opposition to progress amongst the people, it

would be extremely injudicious to try and put a stop to it at once, as it is like dealing with a man's property to ask him to give up that which produces him his daily supplies, or in some cases represents capital that he has lost. Rigid measures of suppression would be ill-advised and out of place; for the course to be taken should be one which would tend to soften and modify by degrees the arduous_ character of the native laws by influence and persuasion, when the example set by the higher classes would presumably result in the customs falling slowly into disuse. This has been the case in the states where British influence has been for some time at work; and there can be no doubt that, time being given, it would prove to be so here.

Somewhere about 1820, when Sir Stamford Raffles was trying to reform the Mengiring system at Bencoolen in Sumatra, he laid down certain rules which were admirably adapted to the purpose in view; for they afforded the greatest relief to the debtor consistent with the just claims of the creditor. These regulations are quoted in Moor's "Notices of the Indian Archipelago," and are well worthy of repetition here.

Any person who had fallen into the condition of a slave, or was liable to it from inability to pay the amount of his debt, might redeem himself by entering into a voluntary contract, with any person who should agree to pay the amount, to serve for a specified period of time proportionate to the sum paid; such sum being considered as an advance to be liquidated by a certain definite service to be rendered by the debtor. Thus, in lieu of absolute and unlimited slavery, will be substituted a system of free and voluntary contract, by which the debtor or slave enters at once into all the privileges of freedom, subject only to the fulfilment of an equitable contract, at the same time that the interest of the creditor is fully secured.

Similar regulations would be most appropriate for Perak, but would of course be only applicable to that slavery which is due solely to debt.

It is much to be desired that in Perak and other native states, now more closely under the wing of British protection, steps should be taken to abolish by degrees this system of debt-slavery, through which the improvement of the country is greatly retarded, and all general efforts to increase the industry and commerce are blighted in the offset. When once the native rulers are taught that a way out of the pernicious system can be found, and without prejudice to the creditor, there is no doubt that they will gladly forsake what they know to be contrary to the Mahomedan law; and the oppressive regulations will give place to a milder and more civilised code.

Other existent forms—comprising the slavery about the palace; that of the Battak people, who have been regularly bought and brought over; and also that of the people and girls of the country—will not be so easy to eradicate, and must be left to the influence which time and the spread of civilisation will bring about.

To turn for a few minutes, before concluding this subject, to the oppressive way—it may be said the barbarous way—in which debt-slavery acts, let the following be given by way of illustration. The reader must be asked to suppose what would be the opinion of Englishmen upon a case at home, were it possible, in which a labourer who was in debt to the amount of five-and-thirty shillings, being unable to pay the sum, should be seized by his creditor, with his wife, both thus becoming bond-servants or slaves, unable to free themselves, or their children to come, from their position. And yet such things have occurred amongst the Malays. One of the latest travellers through Perak, the Hon. W. Adamson, quotes a case in which a man and his wife became slaves for a debt of seven dollars. Endless are the hardships of these poor people, whose children become hereditary bond-servants; and though, as a rule, their treatment is good, yet the iniquity of the system is monstrous, and leads amongst the women to a degradation that lowers the whole tone of the country. The misfortune is that, until the upper classes of the Malays grow more enlightened, the position cannot be altered; Sultan and chiefs setting the example of being the hardest taskmasters, and feeling it, under the present *régime*, to be to their interest to maintain the status of the slave; while one of the greatest difficulties the British Residents have had to deal with has been the settling of disputes, when, urged by some faint echo in their wretched souls of the knowledge of England's persistence on every man's freedom, some unfortunate

or another has fled to Her Majesty's representatives
for protection from a cruel master.

Every visitor to the state joins in condemning
the practice; but to each in turn the feeling is
brought home that nothing can be done by a sudden
change. Our position in the country is only that of
protectors and advisers; and stern persistence would
only result in embittering the chiefs, without im-
proving the condition of the slave. It is an old ulcer
on a beautiful land, and must take time for its cure.
Wherever the beneficent light of civilisation has begun
to shine, there the position of the bondsmen has
rapidly improved, as in the states of Johore, Salangore,
and Quedah. Perak is comparatively new ground;
but even here our Residents have made improvements,
such as have vastly benefited the lower orders. In
short, the good seed has been sown, and in time a
better state of things will brighten the face of the
land.

200'

PERAK CHIEFS AND ATTENDANTS.

CHAPTER XIX.

The Malay character—Dealings with chiefs—Mr. Muntinghe at Palembang.

PERHAPS in no people is a more singular combination of qualities found than in the Malay. In his general character in Perak, or other parts, where his intercourse with the European or Chinese has been infrequent, he can be described only by a knowledge of his internal disposition, and by the associations by which he has been surrounded since he first emerged from what was little better than barbarism. Naturally he is dull, heavy, and listless, fond of a life of slothful ease, and takes a good deal of coaxing to make an effort for the improvement of his state, or to do anything conducing to his profit or advantage—even, it may be said, to his amusement. But when once roused—and sometimes a very slight thing will be sufficient—his energy is remarkable, and the dogged determination he will throw into the pursuit of his object is surprising, bringing out, as it does, so different a phase of character that he seems to have a new existence.

With such a disposition, upon which was grafted the various ideas brought about by intercourse with the Arabs, and the subsequent adoption of the religion of Mahomet, the natural result was an increased indolence and listlessness of character, and incapacity for steady labour. In fact, the Malays gradually imbibed much of the careless lawless nature of the Arabs of the desert ; and the adventurous spirit of the marauder whose hand is against every man, broke out in the various acts of piracy for which the Malay has so long been famed. These dangerous forays were quite in keeping with the clannish habits of the Malay, while, being now by religion made fatalists, they grew careless of exposing their lives, since the future was secure.

They recognise however no such thing as caste, like the Hindoos ; though so tribal are they in their tendencies, that when the Viceroy of Salangore, himself a Quedah man, sent for some of his people to come and support him during a petty war in Klang, the Malays of the country looked down upon these newcomers as aliens and strangers, not belonging to this tribe, and nicknamed them Orang-Quedah, or men of Quedah, as they do to this day. This strong feudal pride, arising from their principle of tribal associations under chiefs—a practice common to both Arab and Malay races—with its natural independence of spirit and love of liberty, makes it at all times a difficult task to render them tractable under coercion, though capable, under a patriarchal sway, of readily yielding an implicit and cheerful obedience. The obstinacy, however, and determination of the Malay, make him at times strongly to resemble the spoiled child, who will destroy all rather than give up a single point.

Their sense of power, which, under the influence of higher civilisation is a fine trait in their character, renders them, in a less civilised state, morbidly sensitive to slight or insult. In fact, one of their proverbs says : " A wound may heal, but will always leave a scar." Acting upon this, a Malay rarely forgets an offence against him, but nurses it in his bosom until opportunity arrives for revenge ; and as his idea is that the insult must be washed out in blood, and as likewise he always carries the familiar kris, fatal cases of retaliation are not uncommon.

In demeanour among themselves, and towards the European, the Malays are at all times courteous ; while with one who speaks their language and understands and respects their manners and customs, they are extremely social and friendly ; but, from their own staid and retiring ways, they very quickly lose respect for anyone who is boisterous in his mirth, impulsive and rude in his habits, and otherwise displays a thoughtless disposition such as is so foreign to their own nature. For a Malay, as a rule, speaks slowly, giving to every word a distinct emphasis, while he is utterly unable to take a joke, or to view it in the light in which it has been intended.

In their own social life they are fond of their
wives and children, and live, as a rule, in great
unity ; petty thefts amongst themselves being almost
unknown. They hesitate a good deal about displaying their worldly possessions, but this is chiefly
from a dread of exciting the cupidity of the chiefs,
by whom, in so many instances, they are hardly
oppressed.

So courteous are the Malay chiefs by nature, that
in the places where they have not yet come under
European influence, they will apparently acquiesce in
any measure that may be proposed by saying, *Baik
tuan*, or, " Very good, sir." This expression must not,
however, be always taken to mean that the chief agrees
with the views expressed by the speaker, though there is
much in the way of the delivery of the words ; but more
often they may be taken to mean that the views of the
speaker shall receive due consideration. At the same
time, there is the probability that this may be a polite
way of giving an acquiescent reply for the moment,
but with no ulterior idea of following out the wishes
expressed.

Chiefs of this stamp, of whom there are many in
Perak and in the native states, possess great capabilities for dissembling, and very rarely show in their
features that which is passing in their minds ; so that
the carrying out of any act of revenge that may have
been determined on, is often reserved for a fitting opportunity, the victim, in the meantime, not having the

slightest suspicion of that which has been planned against his life.

In political interviews with such chiefs it is always well to keep to the point under discussion, and to force them to follow your example. The subject should be approached with perfect good temper and gentleness of manner, but with a firm determination to carry the point, *coûte qui coûte*; the opponent being made to understand this more from the speaker's manner than from the words expressed ; and as difficulties are advanced from their point of view, they should be assured that all these have been thought of and duly considered from sources of information which the speaker possesses, but which are naturally beyond the reach of the chiefs. All doubt or hesitation in such meetings may be looked upon as almost invariably fatal to success.

Again, in all intercourse with this class of Malay chief—and here let it be clearly understood that a marked distinction is drawn between this class and those with whom we have been brought in contact, more especially in Johore, Quedah, Tringanu, and other places—the examples of the past should not be lost sight of, some of which are unfortunately only too fresh in our memories, both as regards the peninsula and Sumatra.

A Malay has a great idea of his own dignity as a man, his love of, and belief in liberty, causing him to resent what he looks upon as insolence or overbearing treatment, and it is at such times as this that he displays his most dangerous traits. Left to himself, like the poisonous snake of the jungle, he will avoid the coming footstep and pass on; but arrest him, and try to force him to your will, and he strikes. A good example of this peculiarity of character was shown in a case which occurred some years back on the frontiers of Malacca, where a European official was passing along a path followed by a policeman. Meeting a Malay peasant, the man passed on without salaaming the official. The latter, indignant at what he looked upon as a want of respect, angrily spoke to the ryot, asking him how he dared to pass without saluting. The Malay calmly replied that he did not know the official, who then sharply laid his hand upon the offender's shoulder. In an instant the man's kris flashed in the air, and a deadly thrust was delivered, but fortunately the blade fell to the ground, and the blow, given like lightning, was delivered with the handle alone. But for this incident in his resentment at what he looked upon as an insult, the Malay would have killed the European, who was however saved from further attack by the policeman seizing the offender.

Moor also, in his "Notices," as far back as 1824, gives us an instance of failure in dealing with this people which occurred to Mr. Muntinghe, who was a member of council, at Palembang, in Sumatra, during the British and Netherlands administration of Java.

Before proceeding to Palembang, as commissioner of the Javanese settlement, Mr. Muntinghe dwelt with much complacency and self-conviction on the idea that he should, in less than twelve months, establish the revenue system there as firmly as it had been done in Java; and that then it could soon be extended to all Pulo Percha, or Sumatra. He was cautioned against this plan by Mr. Raffles, afterwards Sir Stamford Raffles, who said that it was unsuitable to the place and people; but Mr. Muntinghe, perhaps from a want of practical or intimate knowledge of the people, and not persuaded that such a diversity of character existed between the Javanese and the Malays, held to his determination, and was rather strengthened in his private plan, and lured on by the chiefs, as usual, into a belief that all his wishes might be gratified and accomplished. The attack on the fort and the Residency, the precipitate flight of Mr. Muntinghe from Palembang, and the subversion of all his measures, were the work of a single day.

The wise Grecian legislator of old said: "I gave to the Athenians, not the best laws, but those most fit for them;" and the notice ends with the very just remark: "It should not be necessary in the nineteenth century to write laws with blood."

The most advanced of the chiefs in European civilisation is the Maharajah of Johore, a gentleman who has, while retaining his native state, adopted our English manners and customs almost in their entirety, and where they are mingled with those of Malaya, far from having a barbaric effect, they are on the whole pleasing. His *Istana*, or palace, at Johore is a handsome building, admirably furnished; the drawing-room, with piano for the use of English visitors, being perfect in its appointments. The Europeans of the Settlements are frequently his guests; and in every possible way his efforts seem to be directed towards making them feel that they are being entertained by an English in place of an Eastern prince.

A good deal of this is due no doubt to the effect of a visit to England some years back; where during his stay an amusing illustration of our ignorance of the qualities and state of Eastern chiefs, was afforded in the way in which the late Sir Roderick Murchison introduced the present Maharajah at a meeting of the Royal Geographical Society.

It was while a speech was being made by Sir Roderick that a paper was passed to him as a reminder of the coming of the distinguished visitor, when he remarked: "Ladies and gentlemen, I had almost omitted to mention to you that we are honoured here this evening by the presence of an eminently intelligent Eastern prince—the Jinny-gong of Tohore."

A whisper immediately passed on to him by way of correction, and referring once more to the paper he exclaimed: "I beg your pardon, ladies and gentle-men—the Tumongong of Johore." Then to the giver of the paper pettishly: "Your T's and J's are all alike."

The Maharajah, always celebrated for his hospitality, gave the Duke of Edinburgh a very notable reception on the visit of His Royal Highness to the Straits Settlements. Here the mingling of Eastern pomp and European customs was very remarkable; for while carriages of British construction, and servants in liveries of the royal Malay colours, green and rich yellow, were in attendance, a grand effect was produced by the Maharajah's state barges, which were painted and manned for the occasion in a very striking manner. Each barge was rowed by sixty or seventy men, all wearing silk jackets of a brilliant hue. One barge would be painted bright blue, the jackets of its rowers being to match; another was of a bright green; another yellow, and so on. Open house was kept and sports were arranged; the whole forming an event in the history of the peninsula which is recalled with pleasure by the natives to this day.

Upon another occasion, the Maharajah entertained a departing Governor and his lady at a banquet at the *Istana*, or palace, when the *menus* were printed on pieces of rich yellow satin bordered with green silk lace. As an example of the style in which an Eastern prince who adopts our customs can give a dinner, it may not be out of place to print here *in extenso* the contents of the bill of fare, in spite of the peculiarity of the Malay language. It is unnecessary to give a

P

translation in full, and the reader will surmise that
Tim signifies soup, *Ikan* fish, and so on. *Sambals*
have already been described ; while amongst the
Manissan, or sweets, plum-pudding and custard are
sufficiently English to need no interpreter. Suffice
it that the list contains all the delicacies to be procured in the Straits, not omitting *Dodol Baku* (ices),
Ananas, Susu, and Limau.

SANTAPAN.

TIM.

Panggang pringi dungan badam.
Sayur kerchachan.

IKAN.

Rendang Tengiri.
Merah kwah anchovy.
Dainblang kwah tritep.

IDANGKAN.

Opo etek dungan kanah.
Rendang chinchang Plentong.
Burong pati chindawan busote.
Panchur sarak tritep.
Rusuk daging biri-biri.
Sumbret panggang pringi.

PAHHAR.

Tanggang kalkun isi truffe.
Ayam blanda rubus di Jawa.
Daging biri-biri di panggang.
Kambing rubus pati santan.
Lumbo golie.
Leda sapi dalam belda.

SAYUR.

Kintang. Loba mera. Kachang hijau.
Sulo di France. Bunga kobis. Jagong muda.

Goulai di Johore. *Goulai Santan.*
Singapore Curry. *Madras Curry.*
Sayur Kechambak.

SAMBAL.

Serai. Tumis blachang.
Asam. Tumis kuchai.
Trubo. Tumis hudang.
Telor di rendang. Tumis blimbing.
Seronding.

MANISSAN.

Limping dungan limau China.
Plum-pudding.
Buahulu dungan custard.
Serikaya.
Pengannan buah-buah.

Belda Susu. Belda Sirop.

Jubun rendang. Keju.
Plampong di Whampoa.

Halwa buah Kring. Halwa Chayir.

DODOL BAKU.

Ananas. Susu. Limau.

Courteous, religious, social and hospitable, gentle
in his ways when calm, and his passions not roused,
the Malay, when angry or under excitement, is reck-

less and bloodthirsty in the extreme. He may, in fact, be described as volcanic : presenting to the eye all that is goodly and fair, while beneath the surface a fire is always smouldering, ready to burst forth without warning, and spread ruin and destruction around. There can be no doubt that by nature the Malay is of an extremely nervous temperament ; and in several ways this is made known to the Europeans with whom he comes in contact. For instance, under certain circumstances that peculiar nervous affection already alluded to, is seen, where a man's will appears completely under the influence of those he meets, and he seems bound to imitate every gesticulation or movement that is made ; but the affection or mania that makes these people a terror and a danger to their fellows, is that known as *Amok*.

" Running a-muck," as it is popularly called, is so common that the term has been adopted among our own quaint sayings to apply to any person who is reckless or wild in his doings ; but probably the extent to which this practice obtains is not known to the reader. Even while this work has been passing through the press, Rajah Mansur, one of the sons of Yusuf, the present ruler of Perak, during a strange fit of excitement, drew his kris and rushed off, striking right and left, killing six and severely wounding two persons, and finally making his escape into the jungle. In the illustration which is given of the Sultan and his two sons, the one upon his left is the

young man in question. He was only about twenty
years old.

Even in European countries, example amongst
people with overstrung or disorganised nerves seems
to be contagious, and the sufferers apparently feel
compelled to perform acts that would, while in sound
health, be repugnant to every disposition of their
nature; and among the Malays this custom of Amok
has unfortunately grown to be national, and is looked
for just as the Japanese performs the *hari-kari*
as a termination to his career. In this latter case,
however, the unfortunate is content with destroying
his own life, while the Malay may be the cause of
death or severe injury to twenty or thirty people
before he is literally hunted down and destroyed, like
a mad dog.

Physiologists attribute this uncontrollable fury to
disease—in fact, to a kind of monomania induced by
disorder of the digestive organs; but there are occasions when the practice is made subservient to the will,
and a Malay will "run amok" to gratify revenge, or,
as if for a forlorn hope, adopt it in the little wars of
the people, rushing amongst the enemy and killing
right and left. In fact, it will be seen that on the
occasion of the murder of Mr. Birch, the cry of
"Amok, amok!" was raised, and a savage rush was
made by all present, who seemed to be animated with
but one desire—to kill. The Malay, speaking of
Amok, says : " My eyes got dark and I ran on." In

other words, he says he was blind with fury : or he
will attribute the seizure to vertigo.

In the Settlements the first warning of such an
event is given by the cry of " Amok, amok ! " when
there is a rush, and people fly right and left to shelter;
for the runner makes no distinction between friend
and foe ; his eyes are indeed dark, and he is blind to
everything but the intense desire to kill all he can
before he renders up his own wretched life.   Shrieks,
cries of warning, the rush of feet, people trampling
over each other in their hurry to escape, and the eager
excited eyes of the Malays, as each man's hand goes
to the twisted band of his sarong to draw forth the
deadly kris.   For, as the runner's desire is now to kill
all he can, that of the peaceable is to slay him before
he can do much mischief.

The cry goes on far in advance of the madman,
and the Sikh police clutch their weapons, the Europeans seize gun or revolver, and every eye is strained,
every nerve attent for the coming peril.

"Amok, amok ! " followed by a wild shriek or two
and a groan, as the madman rushes on, striking here
and there, taking people at a disadvantage, and
marking his course with bleeding victims, while his
pursuers gather in numbers, the Malays among them
growing as madly excited as the runner they pursue.

The object nowadays is to take the man alive, to
try him by our laws, and punish him for murder; and
to further these ends, the police in the Settlements

are provided with a huge short-pronged pitchfork, to catch the madman by the throat, and pin him to a wall when he is driven to bay.

But this is not yet, and he runs on in his fury, driving his kris into one fleeing unfortunate's back, leaping over his body, avoiding a thrust made by an opponent, and returning it with deadly effect. Or it may be that he is gashed with cuts, and bleeding from the stabs he has received himself. Shots are fired at him, some taking effect; more, from the hurry, missing the flying maniac, who still runs on, marking his course with his own blood and that of fresh victims, his strength in his exaltation being prodigious, and wonderfully enduring, so that he is a match for two or three of his fellows ; and so he goes on and on, till he falls from some shot, or sinks from exhaustion, to be despatched by the ready krisses carried by every Malay.

But there are times when, cut off and hemmed in, the Amok runner stands at bay in some house, or against a wall, glaring with bloodshot eyes, dripping with blood, and holding out his stained kris, he defies anyone to approach. Now it is that the police of the Settlements bring into use the great fork mentioned, deftly thrusting at him till he is caught by the throat, pinned to the wall, and held there by the strength of two powerful arms, when his kris is wrested from his gory hand, he is quickly pinioned, and if he does not die of his wounds he is tried and

executed by the English or native laws.   For in such
a case the man has become far more dangerous than
the fiercest tiger that could haunt the jungle, and by
all verdicts his fate is sealed.

Some years ago at an "amok" in Singapore, the
Malay was pursued to, and took refuge in, the canal,
where, as he would not surrender, he was fired upon
while cunningly diving to avoid the shots, and it was
some time before he was wounded and secured.

If, however, the madman can force his way through
the people who hem him in, he may possibly continue
his course and escape to the jungle, as in the case
of Sultan Yusuf's son; but, generally speaking, the
fate of the Amok runner is a violent death, few
being reserved for trial.   Various have been the
opinions given upon this subject.   There have not
been wanting writers who have attributed the custom
to the use of opium and its effects upon the system ;
but there can be no doubt that the Amok had its
origin in the deed of some desperate Malay ; that
tradition handed it down to his highly-sensitive suc-
cessors, and the example was followed and continues
to be followed as the right thing to do, by those who
are excited to frenzy by apprehension, or some injury
that they regard as deadly, and to be washed out in
blood.   In fact, Newbold says that he has seen letters
in which, alluding to the desire to revenge an insult,
Malays make use of the following expression: " I
ardently long for his blood to clean my face blackened

with charcoal ;" or, " to wash out the pollution of the hog's flesh with which he has smeared me."　.

In these last words we have thoroughly the feeling of the Mussulman expressed, and his deadly hatred to the pollution of a touch from the flesh of the pig—a pollution that was often made the excuse for the terrible rising in India, where it was spread abroad that the cartridges the natives had to use were greased with the fat of the hog.

CHAPTER XX.

IN a people of so highly nervous a temperament, and of so morbid a disposition, it is not surprising that superstition should be strongly mingled with their religious tenets. For instance, they have a thorough belief in the efficacy of charms and amulets; and this is not only seen amongst the lower orders, but exists even in the chiefs. Rajah Abbas, who suffered from that loathsome disease elephantiasis, had recourse to charms for its cure. Amulets in the shape of written words are often worn, or even placed about a house. But a very favourite charm or preventive of disease is the tiger-claw, which the Malay is very fond of wearing—very sensibly too if he looked upon it as for the prevention of injury from these fierce beasts, and the practice of wearing the claws became universal. They examine horoscopes, and study the stars, so as to obtain a propitious day for some adventure or plan; and from their connection with the Indians they have doubtless acquired their belief in the existence of many orders of celestial beings.

Some of their beliefs approach the superstitions of the lowest savages in the scale; and it is a constant matter to find them making offerings to some spirit or another by way of propitiation. When a European wishes to penetrate some unexplored portion of mountain or jungle, he is met with opposition, for the simple-minded native sees the horrible in the unknown; and the would-be explorer is begged not to enter the domains held by evil spirits, who may withhold rain, send storms or diseases, or in some way show their displeasure at the sanctity of their homes being invaded. So dangerous are these spirits of the woods considered, that in the jungle campongs, high up amongst the trees, pieces of wood are carefully prepared, and hung up in a way that causes them to give forth plaintive musical sounds, similar to those of an Æolian harp, or the stretched wires of the electric telegraph when the wind blows through them—the traveller often being startled by the mournful notes. These are supposed to keep off the goblins, and make them leave the campong dwellers in peace.

Mines have always been supposed in Europe to hold their special spirit or demon from the earliest times, but it seems singular that the superstition should exist in such an out-of-the-way part of the world as Perak. And yet it is so with the tin-miners, who make offerings to propitiate the good spirit who presides. Mr. Daly gives an interesting account of this propitiation of spirits in his late journey down the Perak river, where, before the passage of the dangerous rapid, Jeram Pangang, at the entrance to which is a large boulder, called by the Malays "Berala Bujok," which literally means "the idol to be propitiated," everyone is expected to make an offering and ask permission to pass. Upon the occasion in question the pilot stood up and made a speech to the rock, asking for leave to go down the rapid in safety, as there was a white man on board, and if anything happened to him it would be the cause of much trouble to the people. This being ended, bananas and betel-nuts, combined with a biscuit, supposed to be the white man's offering, were thrown upon the rock, and then the passage was commenced.

The idol upon this occasion must have been dissatisfied with the value or extent of the offerings; for when the bamboo raft upon which the traveller was journeying came to the worst part it telescoped, the great bamboos snapped like matches from the force of the water, and went floating down the stream. This rapid is a source of great terror to the natives, who tell a number of stories concerning the mishaps that have occurred there; and when joked about them in this instance, replied in all seriousness that Berala Bujok was angry at the offer of the biscuit, and because a white man had descended the river.

The objects held in reverence are innumerable:

the tiger, the cow, the monkey, and even the
waringhan-tree, are all revered or feared, as the
case may be. There are demons who utter cries in
the woods and haunt burial-grounds; spirits who can
be domesticated, and if fed with their owner's blood
can be utilised for purposes of revenge; demon hunts-
men, who have their own dogs; witches, who leave
their human bodies by night to feast on the above
sanguinary diet; and spirits of the storms and winds;
and one Rajah is stated to have krissed a woman with
his own hand, and without a word of inquiry, for
being suspected of creating, and having in her possession, a "Pulong," a name that the Malays give to a
horrible phantasy of theirs, a sort of "bottle-imp,"
which they believe can be let loose and made to take
demoniacal possession of the enemies of its creator.
The doctrine of metempsychosis has obtained some
little hold upon the Malays, who consequently hesitate
to slay the tiger, lest his body should be the tenement
of some human being. In fact, they believe that,
after the fashion of the wehr-wolf of German romance,
certain people have the power of occupying the body
of the tiger by night, and transforming themselves at
pleasure. So great is considered the power and intelligence of this beast, that the Malay will reluctantly
mention its name in the jungle, lest evil should
befall him; and if asked if a tiger is nigh, will probably give his answer in the faintest whisper, and
with trembling voice.

Their little observances for the procuring of good luck are many, and extend even to the most trivial acts : for instance, a betel-chewer will almost invariably spit to the left; and this superstitious feeling, combined with idleness, has something to do with the reluctance of a Malay to repair an injured house—in fact, even when he builds a new one the old is left standing.

As a body, the Malays follow very strictly the religion they profess—Islamism ; and, whether they have performed the pilgrimage to Mecca or not, many keep regularly the Ramadhan : but, as may be seen from the foregoing, they mix their religion up with the traditionary customs and superstitions ; this naturally being chiefly amongst the poorer classes. One very favourite theory is that certain persons can render themselves invulnerable through the agency of spirits. Several such instances have been mentioned in Perak, notably in the case of a man called Rajah Abbas, previously alluded to as trying to charm away elephantiasis. It is related of one pretender to this invulnerability, that an officer put him to the proof, and exposed the silly belief to the surrounding crowd by pricking the Achilles-like skin of the man's arm with the point of his sword. The invulnerable man's blood flowed, and it was nearly followed by that of the officer ; for the pretender vowed revenge, and had to be kept at a distance to prevent him from making a savage attack.

The ordinary diseases and epidemics are supposed to be driven away, either by conciliating the spirits with offerings, or else by the practice of affixing cages and palm-leaves to trees in the neighbourhood of the dwellings or campongs. The ignorant seem always to believe strongly in those yet more ignorant than themselves; hence we have the Malays attaching great faith to the supernatural powers of the aborigines, and trusting frequently to their knowledge of herbs and simples in cases of disease. Both in Perak, and beyond our frontier in Malacca, the writer has known the people to have a great veneration for the Sakais, or Jacoons, and Mr. Swettenham, who has travelled much among them, and is well acquainted with the habits of the Malays, says that in Ilim, a part of the country between Perak and Salangore, the common people frequently consult them and ask their advice on important matters.

Those curious freaks of nature, Albinos, are found amongst the Malays; and where they exist they are looked upon by the people with a kind of superstitious awe. One of these men was seen by an English party at the village of Kotah Lamah; and Newbold speaks of one as having been in 1838 the chief of Jellabu, near Malacca. He was a descendant of a prince from Menang Kabau, and was looked upon with the gretaest reverence by the superstitious Malays, on account of his having white or very light blue eyes and jet black hair. Dr. Pickering, too, speaks of one having been

seen amongst the Malays in one of the islands of the
Polynesian group : but their occurrence is particularly
rare.

Beliefs as to their origin are remarkably curious,
and the geographical notions of the common people are
very strange.   One is that the world is surrounded
by mountains, which they call by the name of "Kāf."
The following is the idea of the Creation taken from
their own literature :

> From the Supreme Being first emanated light towards chaos;
> this light diffusing itself became the vast ocean.   From the bosom
> of the waters thick vapour and foam ascended.   The earth and sea
> were then formed each of seven tiers.   The earth rested on the
> surface of the water from east to west.   God, in order to render
> steadfast the foundations of the world, which vibrated tremulously
> with the motion of the watery expanse, girt it round with an
> adamantine chain, viz. the stupendous mountains of Caucasus, the
> wondrous region of genii and aerial spirits.   Beyond these limits is
> spread out a vast plain, the sand and earth of which are of gold
> and musk, the stones rubies and emeralds, the vegetation of odori-
> ferous flowers. . . . From the range of Caucasus all the mountains
> of the earth have their origin as pillars, to support and strengthen
> the terrestrial framework.

With regard to the particular form of Islam embraced by the Malays, it will naturally be inferred,
when it is remembered that their intercourse with the
Arabs dates from a very early period, and was very
extensive, while that with the Persians was narrowed
in its limits to the meetings with them in trade at
Engrah on the Persian Gulf, that they would embrace
that followed by the Arabs in the purest form; and

accordingly we find them to be chiefly belonging to the sect of Shafeites, with here and there, in Perak and Quedah, Hanefites and Hunbalites, but also the orthodox sect, or Sonnites. The so-called sect of Ali is rarely met with amongst the Malays; but they may exist, though not to the writer's knowledge. ·

According to Yule's "Marco Polo," a Malay chronicle of Acheen dates the accession of the first Mahomedan king of that state—the nearest point of Sumatra to India and Arabia—in the year answering to A.D. 1205; and this is the earliest conversion among the Malays on record. It is extremely doubtful, however, whether there were kings of Acheen in 1205, or for centuries after: and it is therefore open to question whether this date applies to any real event or not.

The dates of the conversion of the Malays to their present religion are variously given, however; but Crawfurd, who is perhaps the best authority, follows pretty closely the above idea, and puts the conversion of the Acheenese at 1206 of our era, the Malacca Malays at 1276, and the Javanese at 1478; while the general conversion of the people of Celebes did not take place till the arrival of the Portuguese in their midst, or about 1510. This progress of conversion took several centuries to accomplish, and was not effected by the Arabs in the same rapid way as that of the natives of Western and Central Asia; for the Malays were too numerous and powerful

Q

in those days to be subdued and overcome by these people.

The ultimate aim of every good Moslem is to make the pilgrimage to Mecca ; and accordingly every year a very numerous concourse of Malays proceed from the various states of the peninsula on this religious errand. When the pilgrim returns to his own country he is privileged to wear the Arab costume, and to be styled by his fellows *Tuan haji*. Unfortunately, however, the influence he now possesses is not always employed to benefit his fellow-country-men, but often for intriguing to his own advantage, so as to recoup himself and family for the outlay to which he has been put in his long and weary journey to the west. A very recent writer on these Malay hajis speaks of them as making the voyage "in order on their return to be ordained as priests, when they may wear turbans, and will commence a life of idleness—doing nothing, except, perhaps, inciting the populace to revolt or to make *amok*, and living like leeches on the toil of their fellow-men."

In Perak these people have been found to be at the root of every system of oppression ; and, if not the actual instigators of the assassination of the late Resident, they at least stimulated the worst characters in the place to open rebellion ; and finding themselves supported by the recognised chiefs of their religion, the rebels were the less punctilious in carrying out their lawless designs.

It must be owned, however, that the pilgrimage is an arduous task; and some years ago the ships in which the voyage was made were in so terrible a condition, from overcrowding, that the interference of our Government became a necessity. Now, however, the pilgrim is able to make the voyage across to Jeddah in comparative comfort; and it is only when he arrives in port that the real hardships of the journey commence. Some of the pilgrims succumb to these hardships, but they meet death with the calm stoicism of the fatalist; and when the news of a death reaches friends and relatives at home, the end is looked upon as a glorious one, and using their proverbial expression which accepts it as inevitable, they are at once contented and resigned.

Amongst their religious practices the Malays are in the habit of indulging in relic-worship, which takes the form of a visit to the tomb of some revered person on particular days of the year. They wear a kind of rosary of beads for telling, and are very particular about the month of fasting, which, like the Arab Ramadhan, is in the ninth Mahomedan month of the year. So punctilious are they as Mahomedans, that it was only with difficulty that the writer could obtain their consent to sit for their photographs, though after a time less objection was made. One Rajah, however, and one of the more civilised, absolutely refused. This was the Rajah of Quedah.

In their religious observances they are very par-

ticular, and at the proper times the sight of the
Malay at prayer is very common; his carpet, or that
which answers the purpose, is spread, and the pros-
tration follows with the seven members of the body
which touch the ground—namely, the forehead, the
palms of the two hands, the knees, and the feet.
When speaking of the Portuguese, or the people of
mixed European and Malay blood, it is worthy of note
that they call them *Nasarini*, the origin being most
probably the old term Nazarene.

It will not be out of place here, in the face of late
discussions on the belief in, and implied support given
by the Moslems of the East to, the Sultan of Turkey,
to say that, though the Malays believe in Istamboul,
or Roum, as the centre of their faith, and look upon
the Sultan as the chief temporal sovereign, with
Constantinople as the principal seat of Mahomedan
government, they are very little influenced by what
may happen in the fortunes of that country.   Mecca
is to them the Holy City, and the Koran, as expounded
by Arab teachers, supplies them with their rule and
practice of faith; and, come what may in the future,
they are never likely to be moved to any religious
war against the Christians on account of the neglect
by us of the welfare of Turkey, in leaving her to
pursue her own line of policy in opposition to the
propositions of the great Powers of Europe.

When a village or campong grows to any size—
that is to say increases to over forty houses—it is

GENERAL ASPECT OF A MALAY VILLAGE ON A RIVER BANK.

considered to be of sufficient importance to need
officers, and the religious welfare of the place is
better provided for. It will be seen from these
points how little deserving of the title of savages
the Malays are, and how misinformed are they who
have been in the habit of looking upon them as merely
a bloodthirsty set of pirates, infesting a marshy coast.
When, as above stated, the village has so increased,
the usual Malay officers are selected. These include
the *Punghulu,* or head-man; the *Mata-mata,* a kind
of policeman; and a *Billal* and *Khateeb,* or preacher.
A mosque is also formally built and instituted, and
the welfare of the people is then considered to be
properly cared for.

In the engraving giving the general aspect of a
Malay village on a river-bank, the mosque will be
seen occupying a central position. In this case the
building was carefully finished, the finial of the roof
being one solid mass of coral-rock elaborately cut. As
funds flow in, improvements are made; one of the
most important being a large tank, built of masonry,
kept filled with water, to enable the faithful to perform the proper legal and religious ablution before
entering the house of prayer. On the outer verandah
of the mosque a large instrument somewhat resembling a drum is placed; and this is struck by the
muezzin, and gives out sonorous tones at the appointed
time of prayer, both before and after he gives the
customary call to the faithful to attend. This drum

is a hollowed cone of wood, made sonorous by having stretched over it a head formed of buffalo-hide. Where a minaret has been erected, as in Malacca, a gong is used in place of the drum, but this latter is in common use.

CHAPTER XXI.

Religious ceremonies—Sacrifices—Teeth filing—Marriage—Wedding
feasts—Funerals—Salutation—Polygamy—The kris.

THE children of the Malays are received into the
world quite in religious form, prayer being said, and
the *Azan,* or Allah Akbar, pronounced by the father
with his lips to the tender infant's ear. On the
seventh day the head is shaved; and later on the old
religious ceremony, common to all Mahomedans and
the Jews from the time of Abraham, is performed.
The children have a name bestowed upon them at
their birth, but this is allowed to lapse when later on
their regular name is given. Allusion to their edu-
cational instruction has already been made.

It is at their religious ceremonies, such as births
and weddings, that buffaloes are sacrificed; and at
the particular feasts, as with the Jews, the animal
must be, according to Newbold, "without blemish or
disease; its fore and hind leg bones must not be
broken after death, nor the spine; neither are the
horns to be used for common purposes." The animal
to be sacrificed is bound as to its legs, thrown down,

its head fastened, water is poured upon it, and the
priest after prayer divides the windpipe and arteries
with a sacrificial knife.   The animal is next skinned,
and divided into two portions : one of which goes to
the people, and is cooked and eaten on the spot ; the
other part is divided between the punghulu and
priests.

Marriage amongst the wild tribes is a very simple
affair—in fact, it is a case of exchange and barter ;
for the enamoured youth has to make his arrangements with his intended's father, and give him what
is considered an equivalent for the lady's worth ; that
is to say a small quantity of tobacco, some cotton
stuff, such as a sarong, and a knife.   That is all ; and
the lady becomes the donor's wife.   But the affair is
far more ceremonious amongst the civilised Malays,
who surround the event with a considerable amount
of formula.

The engagement is generally settled by the lady
friends of the parties.   Then the friends of the bridegroom have to wait upon the bride's father and make
presents.   The bride's marriage-portion is talked over ;
the marriage expenses are paid ; and the portion, a
sum in accordance with the position of the parties, is
arranged.   Just previous to this the bride-elect has to
go through the ceremony of having her teeth filed : a
most unpleasant operation, which is performed by a
woman while the patient reclines.   It is no simple
ceremony, for the teeth are cut down perhaps a

fourth, and the effect is to render the gums swollen and painful for days. But there is this satisfaction for the maiden: she is now allowed to commence chewing the sirih leaf, and her teeth soon become blackened, and to a European eye repulsive, though it is considered a beauty with her own people. This blackening of the teeth is aided by the use of a liquid which is obtained from the shell of the cocoa-nut, prepared by fire in a peculiar way.

The hair also comes in for a certain amount of preparation, being cut off short on the forehead, somewhat after the fashion that has of late been popular in England. Henna is applied to dye the palms, and also to the nails of the hands and feet; and then matters are supposed to be sufficiently progressed for the approaching marriage ceremony. But it must be premised that probably the gentleman has never yet seen the lady; and very likely he will have to take her veiled, in the Eastern fashion, without a sight first of her face. This is often the case; and at the marriage feast, if the lady, on being unveiled, prove to be very plain, the bridegroom is bantered and laughed at unmercifully.

There are, however, certain concessions made to the lover when engaged. As with the native of Hindostan, who is allowed to taste rice that has been placed to the lips of his intended, so with the Malay. He is permitted to chew a piece of betel that has been tasted by his inamorata; and the young gallant feasts

on the delight of knowing that the lips of his lady
have touched the betel he masticates. If, after the
ceremony has been performed in accordance with the
rites of the Mahomedan religion, the wife is considered to be of sufficient age—that is to say, fourteen
or fifteen—the husband is allowed to take her home.
But as very frequently these betrothals and weddings
take place when the contracting parties are very
young, a young wife will sometimes be for years at
her father's house before she goes to one of her own.
In fact, it is no uncommon thing, says one observer of
the Malays, to see little girls running about one year
in the extremely light clothing of childhood, and to
see them married women and mothers the next. For
life is rapid in these hot climes, and growth in proportion ; while, on the other hand, the woman is
an aged wrinkled crone by the time she is forty ;
though, as has been stated, cases of extreme old age
are not unknown.

According to the means of those wedded, the ceremony is accompanied by more or less showy proceedings.
Both parties are liberally decorated with jewellery,
flowers, and gay attire ; the wedding paraphernalia
being to a great extent a kind of family heirloom,
like the plate of an English house, and having to do
duty again and again. The bride is, when dressed,
set up at the end of the house in state, and holds a '
kind of drawing-room, being visited by all her friends
and relatives, in company with vast numbers of guests

attracted by the occasion. After the wedding the young people are placed together in a seat of honour above the rest of the guests, when, amidst the feasting, the use of the sirih-box and betel-chewing are made prominent. Flowers are largely used; music is introduced; and the whole ceremony is made as much a feast and time of rejoicing as amongst the civilised nations of the West.

At these wedding feasts goats or buffaloes are killed for the feasting of as many as like to come and partake; for a large wedding is considered very honourable to the father of the bride. To the expenses of the wedding feast, however, large contributions are made by relatives, and even neighbours, who send rice and fruit. One end of the house is set apart on these occasions for the young women, who are screened from the other guests by curtains; and this part of the building is made gay with cotton cloth, chintz, and choice mats. As for the young men, they engage in various sports and pastimes, among which ball and cock-fighting take their places; while their elders sit and sagely discuss the doings of the neighbourhood, and probably canvass the various exactions of their chiefs.

One great peculiarity of the people is that they like these special events amongst themselves to be largely attended, especially if it be a matter of contract; for they argue that written deeds may be forged, destroyed, or altered, "but the memory of

what is transacted in the presence of a thousand
witnesses must remain sacred."

In the marriage agreement of the Malay the
stipulation is made that all effects and savings are to
be equally the property of both, and in case of divorce
all is to be equally divided; but if the man is the
party who insists upon the divorce, he gives half the
effects to the woman, and forfeits the sum paid as
addat—the marriage-portion or purchase. If, on the
other hand, it is the woman who claims to be divorced,
she makes forfeit, and can only take her personal
effects, and the husband may require from the relatives
the sum paid as addat, but this is rarely demanded.

The ceremonies at death are of a far more simple
character. The deceased is washed and shrouded in
cotton cloth, and partly clothed in the garments of
life, and then placed upon a bier formed of a couple
of planks, which, with the regular ceremonies of the
Mahomedan faith, is borne to the place of sepulture.
The graves are dug in accordance with a certain
custom which has obtained amongst them; and, so
far from being dependent on circumstances, are invariably of the same depth—that is to say, the digger
continues his work until his ear is on a level with the
surface. But it is not a simple fosse, as with us; for
a kind of niche or cavity is dug in the side, of the
necessary length, and about two feet high. This side
chamber, so to speak, is intended for the reception of
the corpse, which, on being lowered down, is there

placed—of course, coffinless—and is then shut in by means of the two boards that formed the bier. The body is thus enclosed in a rude earthen tomb, and the earth is thrown in—gently, at first, till on a level with the top of the boards, and afterwards filled up in the ordinary manner. Offerings to the dead, in the shape of spices and flowers, are made afterwards at intervals, and stones or wooden posts are put up at the head and foot of the graves; while, in accordance with old usage, the Malays plant at times the *chumpaka* and *sulasih.*

To return for a moment to their marriage customs : the Malays are on the whole a moral people; and though by the Mahomedan religion a man is allowed to marry four wives if he can support them, it is rare for a Malay to adopt this custom, which, with concubinage, is the practice of the more riotous chiefs. The ordinary native is a simple courteous being, who joins with an intense love of liberty a great affection for his simple home and its belongings; and is ever ready to greet his fellow in the peculiar manner adopted in the country, where the newcomer or visitor approaches his host, or the man he wishes to salute, with hands joined as if in supplication, while the other touches them lightly with his own on either side, and afterwards raises his hands to his lips or forehead. The custom of nose-rubbing has been attributed to the Malays in their greetings, but it has never been seen by the writer.

CHAPTER XXII.

HARDLY any weapon has attained to so evil a notoriety as the kris of the Malay. It has been accredited
with being deadly, fatally poisonous, and used upon
the most trivial occasions by its owner. In fact, there
have been writers who have made the Malay out to be
worse than the swaggering followers of the Japanese
chieftains, whose great delight is said to be to try the
temper of their keen blades upon anything or any
person they meet; and have accused them of plunging
a new kris into the body of the first comer to see its
effect, while the lookers-on curiously examined the
wound. Now, that the kris is a deadly weapon must be
at once admitted, and that its use is far too frequent
cannot be denied ; but when it is taken into consideration that in Perak every Malay wears a kris as part of
his dress, and that he is by nature quick to resent an
insult, it will not be thought surprising that wounds
are frequently given and deaths result. In fact, such
occurrences were only too frequent in our own land

when it was the custom for every gentleman to carry a sword; and it is not so very long since, according to our code of honour, it was considered necessary for an insult to be washed out in blood. Fairly speaking, with the kris always ready to their hand, the wonder is that it is not more frequently used amongst the Malays than proves to be the case. In our Settlements, however, the people are not permitted to wear either the kris or any other weapon under the penalty of a fine. There are exceptions, though, to this police regulation in the special permission given to followers of the Maharajah of Johore and some other important chiefs.

The great sin with which the kris is accredited by Europeans is that it is poisonous; but though there may be cases where a kris has had its blade smeared with some virulent concoction, these are decidedly the exceptions, for the rule is that the blade is not poisoned; and when on various occasions, while examining the weapon, the writer has alluded to the care necessary with so deadly an instrument, the Malay has ridiculed the idea of its being envenomed. In fact, it seems reasonable that this is not the case; for if prepared with a vegetable poison, as it would probably be, the effect would only be transitory, from the action of the atmosphere destroying the deadly nature of the preparation, which would have to be constantly renewed; while a Malay himself will say, Why should it be poisoned when it will make so

fatal a wound without? There is great force in this
last argument, for from its wavy flame-shaped blade,
the kris, with its double edge, divides the flesh in a
cut in a terrible manner, the wound being enormous
as produced by so small a weapon; and when it is
used with the knowledge gained by experience, as
in executions, a thrust seems to be almost instantaneously fatal.

To so wide a notoriety has this blade then
attained, that it will be only fair to give it the
precedence before firearms in describing the weapons
of the Malay. As intimated, it is worn by all—from
the *golo*, a kris made of very inferior iron, carried by
the poorest Malay, to the elaborate weapon ornamented with gold, ivory, and precious stones; one
of which, as seen in the sarong of a chief in Lombok,
was, from its diamond setting, valued at seven hundred pounds. A chief will frequently wear two or
even more of these weapons.

The spelling and pronunciation of this name have
often been a difficulty with Europeans: the Portuguese, according to De la Loubere, calling it
"christ," from the Malayan "crid," of which the
best in his day came from Acheen. Crawfurd, the
distinguished writer on Malay questions, thinks it
is an abbreviation of the word *karis*, a dagger; and
that it took its rise in the scarcity and dearness of
iron, which, unless imported, must have been rarer
and dearer than gold itself. "It is not to be sup-

posed," he says, "without a cause so adequate, that the Indian Islanders, any more than semi-barbarians acquainted with the use of iron, could have neglected the useful and formidable sword for the trifling and ineffectual dagger; and that the Indian Islanders have continued the use of their favourite weapon after the cause has in great measure ceased to operate needs not explanation to those who are aware of the obstinate adherence of barbarians to ancient habit and custom, particularly in matters where national pride and vanity are engaged."

The blade of the Malay kris varies in width from one inch to one and a half, and in length from fourteen to eighteen inches. It is of various forms, according to the taste or station of the wearer, and is formed straight, slightly curved at the apex, and waving throughout from hilt to point; sometimes with two or three curves, often with ten or a dozen. It is invariably two-edged, and very keen; and many of the finer blades are veined and damascened in a very beautiful manner, having a dull dead silvery appearance—for burnished steel finds no favour with these people. In the more ancient kinds it is no unusual thing to find the blade veined with gold or silver, which adds greatly to the beauty of the weapon. In fact, the maker of krises is looked upon by the Malays as a person of importance, just as the armourer was in ancient days with us; and his blades are considered, as he fashions them of various designs,

R

great works of art. This veining or watering a kris is called by the Malays *pamur*, and its mode of execution is admirably given by Mr. Newbold, who, in his "Straits of Malacca," dwells at some length on the method of damasking krises, a process which it has not been the writer's good fortune to witness. The recipe is doubtless obtained from the Malays themselves, and runs as follows :

Place on the blade a mixture of boiled rice, sulphur, and salt, beat together, first taking the precaution of covering the edges of the weapon with a thin coat of virgin wax. After this has remained on seven days the damask will have risen to the surface. Take the composition off, and immerse the blade in the water of a young cocoa-nut, or the juice of a pine-apple, for seven days longer, and brush it well with the juice of a sour lemon. After the rust has been cleared away, rub it with arsenic (*warangan*) dissolved in lime-juice, wash it well with spring-water, dry, and anoint with cocoa-nut oil.

The iron of which the blades is composed is a mixture obtained from Celebes and Java, which is blended with steel, and beaten up so that, as in our best gun-barrels, the welded metal shows a distinct grain, upon which the various artists pride themselves greatly—an immense amount of care and industry being bestowed upon this work, as there is also upon the handles, which, from their peculiar curve, seem to a European very unsuitable for grasping in the hand. But when it is taken into consideration that they are held dagger-wise, it will be seen that a good grip can be taken, and the weapon used with deadly effect.

These handles are made of either gold, ivory, ebony, or the kamooning wood, and occasionally of buffalo-horn; and in either case they are carved and polished with great taste, but generally with scrupulous attention to the customs of their ancestors.

Of late, a great deal of the manufacture of these weapons has been done by the Chinese, who are not only good smiths, but clever artificers in adorning and perfecting their work, especially the sheaths. These latter are composed of three distinct parts: the *sampiran*, which is the ornamental part of the hilt; the main sheath or envelope of the blade, which, like the garment, is called *sarong*; and the *buntul*, or ferrule, at the end. The sheath is mostly of wood, with ornaments of ivory, hard-wood, or gold, to form the ferrule; but in the case of valuable weapons it is formed wholly of gold; while gold, brass, or an alloy of the two metals, is used to form the ornament to the handle.

The kris is the instrument of execution, and one belonging to the Sultan of Salangore, which is used upon these occasions, is made with a straight narrow blade, and with a sheath of pure gold. The Malays are exceedingly punctilious in the shape, size, and general formation of their kris, and look upon its due perfection with superstitious awe; for to certain weapons they attach as much importance as to the Excalibur of ancient chivalry. Different forms of damask produce different effects. With one kind

the owner of such a kris cannot be overcome ; others
are generally auspicious ; another gives luck to its
wearer when trading or voyaging ; and, generally, the
value of the weapon does not depend on its costly orna-
mentation, but upon the accuracy of proportion in its
blade ; while a kris that has frequently shed blood
is greatly increased in superstitious value. There is a
reverse to this, however ; for where one of these
weapons does not answer to certain proportions in
its measurement with a piece of string, which is
doubled or folded in three according to a very puerile
formula, it is denounced as unlucky for the wearer—
not for him who receives its stab. The superstitions
are, however, many in connection with this blade.
If it has been an heirloom, or presented by some
superior, it is proportionately esteemed ; and no
greater reverence or higher qualities could have
been attached to any of the celebrated blades of
romance than is paid to this, the peculiar weapon of
the Malay.

The best krises are made by the Bugis, or at the
ancient seat of the Malay power in Sumatra, already
referred to as Menang Kabau ; but their manufacture
is common in many of the native states, though the
quality of the metal and the temper of the blade is
not considered to be so good.

The kris is held in far higher esteem than the
lance, and these various points of estimation, as
enumerated, are mentioned by several of the olden

visitors to the countries inhabited by the Malays; in fact, these peculiarities are very prominent, and are readily observed, having been handed down from generation to generation, and impressed upon the young as part of their education.   Considered an almost indispensable article of his dress, the Malay always wears his kris on the left side, where it is held up by the twisting of the sarong, with which during an interview it is considered respectful to conceal the weapon; and its handle is turned with its point close to the body if the wearer is friendly. If, however, there is ill blood existing, and the wearer be angry, the kris is exposed, and the point of the handle turned the reverse way.   To refer once more to the question of poisoning the blade, no instance of this has come to the knowledge of the writer, either in Perak or the other states of the peninsula.

The sword is also held in much veneration.   It is, to all intents and purposes, an ornament, being seldom worn or used in war, but taking its place amongst the various objects forming the regalia of a native state; and on state occasions it is always carried by a faithful and special attendant upon the sultan, rajah, or chief, who is styled the *Buntara*, or sword-bearer. His care of the sword is excessive, and when he rests it anywhere it is only upon his right shoulder, with the hilt uppermost, and not there till he has first placed for it to rest upon a handkerchief or cloth kept for the purpose.   Respect for the weapon demands that this shall invariably be done; and in the illustration representing Sultan Abdullah and his chiefs, these points will be seen rigorously attended to by the various buntaras who carry the swords or weapons of state. These frequently have the hilts jewelled very richly, and the scabbards covered with the royal yellow in silk or velvet; and the custom of sending the sword with its bearer as an ambassador in advance of the chief is not uncommon. In fact, if the buntara carries the Rajah's sword to a house where, as is elsewhere referred to, there is a maiden the chief desires, it is sufficient, and the superior's command is obeyed. This custom of sending the sword in advance has been more than once adopted by European officials in the peninsula, who have been well acquainted with the habits of the people, and who probably considered that this acceptance of their forms would be agreeable; but whether appreciated by the Malays is quite another matter. The sword seems to be associated by these people more with their idea of antiquity, and its use is tinged with religion. It is a weapon of form, like our own swords of state and those placed behind the judges; and the Malay's veneration for it is probably derived from the respect which they found the Arabs to possess for the sword as handed down to them by Mahomet. In fact, a Mahomedan conqueror of the Greeks is called by them one of the Swords of God.

There is a sword of state in the regalia of Perak; and this, with other articles composing it, including no fewer than twenty of the choicest elephants of the country—elephants being a part of the regalia—was carried off by Sultan Ismail during the "little war," in his flight from Blanja and Kinta, when startled by the Malays under Rajah Mahmood forming the advance-guard of our troops.

The Malays related to us an incident concerning this sword which is worthy of repetition, as it shows the great respect paid by the people to this weapon. During his flight Ismail was at a place in the jungle called Campong Kampayan, and in his distress he sent for his chief punghulu, or native chief, who, probably seeing the hopeless state of the country after the murder of Mr. Birch, and concluding that his master's chance was irretrievably gone, refused to come. Upon learning this, Ismail drew this sword from the scabbard, and planting it in the ground, thus addressed it: " If you are, as I believe, the invulnerable pillar of the state, I shall yet return to my country." Then reverently replacing the sword in its scabbard, he hastily mounted his elephant, and fled with his wives to Chumoh.

According to Newbold, the Malays consider the sword to have prior claims to antiquity to the spear, and it is said to be found sculptured on ancient temples and tombs in Java; while one celebrated weapon of legendary lore is said to have. been employed to kill an enormous serpent, which ravaged Menang Kabau in the twelfth century. Amongst the

other swords found amongst the Malays there is the
klawang, a long heavy blade, with a peculiarly-shaped
buffalo-horn handle, the blade increasing in width to
nearly the point, somewhat after the representations
of the old scimitar of the artist, but in this case the
blade is straight; and there is also the *naga*, or
dragon-headed sword, a somewhat similar weapon to
the last, only that its buffalo-horn hilt is carved into
the Malayan idea of a dragon, the same as the prows
of their dragon-boats. It is richly ornamented with
silver, and borne by the attendants as previously
described. The weapon worn by Sultan Abdullah in
the engraving, it should be mentioned, is probably
of European manufacture, and goes with his uniform,
both being extra Malay in every point.

A knife is invariably carried at the waist by the
lower-class Malay, or he may have instead the little
common kris known as a *golo*; but the peasant's
regular cutting instrument, one which serves the
purpose of both knife and weapon, is the *parang*,
which he wears slung at his left side like a short
sword; and the dexterous way in which this is used
in cutting a way through the jungle is often the
admiration of the European. It is so well weighted
and balanced at the point, that a very slight effort is
needed to cut through the brushwood of the forest.
They have also a sword with a thin blade, which
being of a finely-tempered steel, is capable of taking
a remarkably good edge. The Malays are very dex-

terous in its use, and perform one feat with it of which they are as proud as the horseman is of his tent-pegging on the plains of India. The Malay places a plantain-stem loosely on the ground, and then, without suffering it to fall, divides it again and again, slicing directly through the stem by means of a series of right and left cuts, delivered with admirable rapidity and effect.

The earliest weapons of the Malays were, after clubs, in spite of their own opinions, most probably spears, of which the forest would yield an inexhaustible supply in the shape of bamboos; which were hardened at the ends with fire, and then brought to a point, and used in connection with a wooden shield or buckler. At the present time the spear is still a favourite weapon; and in his attacks upon his enemies the Malay places great faith in its deadly qualities. It is called a *limbing*, and is not only used with great effect as a lance, but when driven to desperation the Malay hurls it like a javelin with almost unerring aim. The shaft is from five to seven feet in length, and is usually made of a hard red wood; but, unlike that of the ancient Malays, its head is of fine steel, dagger-shaped, and sharpened to an edge equal to that of a razor. The men of Perak are particularly expert in the use of this weapon, as many of us, in view of those we lost during the little war at the piratical village of Kotah Lamah, had only too accurate and painful evidence; for the thrower was

often unseen, while the spear came like an arrow in
its velocity, and inflicted a wound nearly as deadly as
a bayonet-thrust.

Another spear or lance used by these people is
known as the *tombak bandrang*, and this is more a
spear of state. Like the spear carried by the Bugis,
it is largely ornamented with hair, dyed red or black ;
and this flows down from the upper part of the
handle. These have their special bearers, and are
carried before the chiefs on state occasions. The
sling, it seems, was also known, but very little used,
as was also the case with the bow ; but both these
weapons seem to have been considered of light value
even before the introduction of firearms. Probably this
was due to the expert use made of the *sumpitan*, or
blow-pipe, which in some cases was made to act as
the shaft of a spear as well.

These blow-pipes are especially in use amongst the
Sakais, who also carry the parang and a long-shafted
spear. A small quiver of bamboo contains the arrows,
and these are decidedly of two kinds—the poisoned
and non-poisonous. Some of these slender darts are
sent with such swiftness from the long blow-pipe,
which is frequently nine or ten feet in length, that
for a considerable distance they are invisible, and the
aim is wonderful in its precision. The sumpitan is
of course a narrow tube ; while the arrow is about as
thick as a crowquill, eight inches long, and pointed,
the other end being covered with down or pith to

make it fit the tube. The point, if venomed, is coated
with the poisoning preparation for about an inch;
and where it ends the wood is cut, so that the point
may easily break off in a wound.

The Sakais use different kinds of poison for these
arrows, and prepare them with a great deal of the
mummery of superstition; so that the concoction
somewhat resembles the work of witchcraft. *Ipoh*,
or upas; *tuba*, the plant used for poisoning fish,
and which is apparently the *cocculus indicus* of our
druggists' shops; and red arsenic, or *warangan*, are
amongst the primary articles used in their preparations, mingled with others which probably only act
the part of vehicle. A decoction is, however, made
in various forms over a charcoal fire, simmered down
to a syrup, and afterwards poured into bamboos for
preservation. These various poisons are of a dark
colour, and emit a strong narcotic odour, probably
from the opium added. Their power, however, seems
to be evanescent, as they deteriorate by keeping.

In experiments made before Lieutenant Newbold,
a squirrel, after being shot, died in twelve minutes;
young dogs in about forty; a fowl in two hours,
though one lingered over seven. One of their preparations, however, is asserted by the Benua to be so
strong, that three arrows tipped with it will kill a
man in less than an hour, and a tiger in three.

The Malays must have been acquainted with
artillery from very early times, for De Barros, in

speaking of the taking of Malacca by the Portuguese
in 1510, says that the guns were of great size, "but
that they found no more than 3000 out of 8000, said
to be by Ruy de Arajo" (a prisoner of Segueera's fleet),
in this city. Among them was one "very beautiful
piece, which the King of Calicut had lately sent a
Hindu prince, called by the Portuguese, Zamosin."
And later still, the same writer, in giving an account
of an expedition sent by the Malays of Java against
Malacca, after its possession by the Portuguese, says
that the force was provided with artillery made in Java.

As to lighter pieces, matchlocks have also been
known to the Malays since at least the middle of the
fourteenth century, and the name they give them is
snapang, probably from the Dutch snap-pan, and
from these they fire tin bullets, in which it is said
they frequently insert pieces of common earthenware
or china. This has not been observed by the writer;
but in some that were fired against the expedition
during the late rising, it was no uncommon thing to
find a grain of rice. Old-fashioned blunderbusses,
too, seem to have been in favour, several of which
were seen in Kotah Lamah, which was a regular haunt
of fighting men.

The matchlocks made at Menang Kabau—which
for many generations has been famous for its arms—
are the most in favour, but they are clumsy pieces,
with stocks literally for holding the barrel, as they do
not fit the shoulder; while the gun itself is laid, on

account of its weight, in a rest, and the aim taken by
lowering the piece is very indifferent. They have
finely-worked locks of brass, which are made for holding the match of coir-rope ; but these pieces are naturally set aside when European guns can be obtained,
and muskets and rifles are now not uncommon. Like
the handle of the naga, the natives are very fond of
having their blunderbusses with mouths worked up
into the form of the dragon's head ; and this is done
with some skill. As to the barrels, the native smiths,
with very indifferent tools, twist a bar of tough iron
round a rod, weld it together, and after inserting the
barrel in the earth for steadiness, bore it smoothly
out, and produce twisted barrels of very handsome
workmanship, though they fail in the finer mechanism
of the locks.

The heavy guns employed in stockades are generally long pieces of brass called *lelahs* ; they are large
guns, but have a very small bore, and only carry a
two or three pound iron shot. These are the guns that
are used in the large praus in piratical expeditions, and
their ordinary range is four or five hundred yards,
though with elevation the distance can be much increased. In these more peaceful times, when piracy
is nearly extinct, they are kept for more harmless purposes, one Rajah at the native state of Tringanu—a
celebrated place for the manufacture of ordnance—
having four mounted on swivels upon the beach, where
they are used for firing salutes.

Occasionally, however, heavier guns are purchased
at Penang and Singapore, where they can easily be
procured, and in this way some of the rajahs are possessed of six-pounder iron guns and carronades. These
iron guns they call *miriams*, derived probably, says
Crawfurd, from the name of "Mary," as being known
to them first from the Arabs, who had obtained them
from the Christians — a derivation that might be
looked upon as of not much value, only for the
peculiar instances that are met with again and again.
The swivel is the favourite means of mounting their
guns, especially the smaller lelahs, which are found
with bores as small as an inch in diameter ; and from
these slugs are fired, as in the case of the matchlocks,
made of tin.   As may readily be supposed, these
bullets, from the lightness of the metal, have only a
short range.

For the manufacture of their gunpowder the
natives of Perak have a fair supply of nitre, or salt-
petre, in the state ; the preparation of charcoal is very
common ; and the sulphur has been probably obtained
from the Bugis traders, who brought it from Java and
the Celebes, or such volcanic islands in the neighbourhood as produced it in abundance.   A good deal of
nitre is easily procurable from the caverns in the limestone, where the excreta of bats lies to a considerable
depth, and gives forth this salt on preparation.   As a
rule, the native gunpowder—the art of manufacturing
which was probably learned from the Chinese—is poor

in strength and coarse in grain ; but, to meet this difficulty, they prepare a finer sort, which is retained for the purpose of priming their guns. Cartridges are not unknown, but cane is substituted for paper, and these seem to resemble the old bandoleers of our musketeers of two or three hundred years ago.

Taken altogether, the Malay has proved very slow at adopting the implements of war of more civilised nations, and though he possesses firearms in their various forms, the favourite weapons are still the limbing, or lance, and the kris, as shown by the native proceedings in the late war.

One of the principal features of their warfare is the stockade, in the construction of which defence the Malays are very expert. In fact, they are at their best when fighting under cover—a fact of which they are well aware, and hence the care that is taken in the woodland fortifications. As an enemy they are very little to be dreaded in the open, seldom if ever venturing to make a regular attack, except on single men or defenceless parties on the line of communication, as they showed during the war, when the postal runners were frequently speared while going with despatches from post to post. In making their stockades—which the reader is aware consist of strong fences of bamboo or other material, to keep out an enemy—they display great dexterity, both in the selection of a suitable locality to place the fortification, and the choice and manipulation of the materials at their command.

In Perak, excepting at Passir Sala, there were no stockades of any importance during the little war, probably because there was no real intention on the side of the chiefs elsewhere to forcibly resist the British authority, as there was in fact no *ankatan*, or rising : or it may have been that the measures taken by the authorities, consequent upon the murder of Mr. Birch at this place, were too rapid to enable a slow-moving people to erect defences and prepare for war.   Hence it was that all the principal villages which might have been provided with this means of defence remained open to attack.

In other parts of the peninsula, however, stockades of a very formidable nature existed, such as could not be taken by a European force without the aid of the vertical fire of artillery.   Among these were the defences erected by the Malays in the Terrachee valley in Songhy Ujong.   These were well manned, and would probably have held out against us, had they not been taken by surprise and gallantly turned by Major Channer, V.C., and the force under Colonel Clay.

The favourite positions for erecting these fortifications are often such as would be chosen by a trained European engineer, since natural strength is selected, and the protection afforded by defiles, hills, or a river or impassable swamp.   In some cases the walls are made of mud, in others of stout pieces of hard-wood laid side by side, while a favourite plan is to drive two rows of stakes deeply into the soil, point their ends, and fill up the space between with mud and stones, thus forming a strong wall. Outside this fence or wall, a ditch is dug of an average depth of five feet, and a similar width, the earth being thrown outwards, when it is not required inside the stockade to make platforms for the guns, or for filling up the spaces between the rows of stakes.

One stockade at Sempang, Malacca, was of a different form; in fact, it almost merited the title of a military blockhouse. It was built on a point of land with the branch of a river flowing on either side, and was capable of containing thirty or forty men. The sides were of stout planking, loopholed for musketry, with trap-doors to let down like the portholes of a ship, in which guns were placed to command the river. The roof was the feeblest part, being merely attap; but it was built on posts in a deep trench, the earth of which was thrown up at the sides, and sloped so as to form a glacis right up to the loopholes and embrasures of the guns. The entrance was by means of a ladder, which was afterwards drawn up within, effectually preventing further ingress, while the raised floor was perforated here and there, so as to enable the defenders to keep their enemy at a distance to the very last. The interior was shown in a drawing sent to the *Graphic* and published in November, 1875.

s

In the rear of this building were two more *kooboos*, or stockades, so placed as to give a command of fire right and left of the main defence. So cleverly was the whole designed, that all pointed to the fact that the Malay who constructed the place had obtained some of his ideas from Western nations, probably from what he had seen done by the British soldiery during the Naning War of 1832; or he may have profited by the works of the Dutch and Portuguese engineers, whose practice it was to build forts whenever a factory or trading emporium was established. These were erected all over the peninsula, and the remains of many of them exist to the present time.

The Malay is very ingenious in hampering the advance of an enemy, or hindering him when in pursuit. One favourite instrument for this purpose is the *ranjow*, which is of various sizes, and composed of bamboo hardened in the fire and sharply pointed. These ranjows, or stakes, are stuck about in the long grass, with their points towards the coming enemy, and in their native wars cause terrible injuries to the bare feet and legs of the people; and even with European troops they are obstacles not to be despised in a march through the jungle. In warfare a Malay will carry a bundle of these upon his back, ready to plant here and there, whilst larger kinds are not unfrequently placed about their stockades, which are often provided with an ambush in the shape of extensive growths of maize or sugar-cane.

Trees are often cut down, either to fall across a track, or with their tops towards the coming foe, and these form a serious obstacle to the advance of troops where the jungle is like an impenetrable wall on either side. This was done on the elephant-track to Kinta, near a place called Chankat Dungla, along which General Colborne and his forces successfully threaded their way with their guns in the face of obstacles of every kind. For the people of Perak, in spite of the frequent sounding of the gong for the signal to attack during the late war, proved themselves, probably from native jealousies, incapable of being organised, and led to perform a feat of any magnitude; the injury to our forces being for the most part in surprises or attacks upon the weak and unprepared.

CHAPTER XXIII.

ALLUSION has been made more than once to the love
of bathing displayed by the Malays, but their power
as swimmers has not been mentioned. In this pursuit
they are very able, and as divers exhibit qualities of
endurance that are surprising. One instance of their
power in this direction is well worthy of note. It was
in the case of a ship that had touched upon a coral-
reef and made a rent in the sheathing, when a Malay,
being furnished with a sheet of copper suitable in size,
and perforated with holes round the edge, dived down
with the piece, a hammer, and a nail, staying under
water long enough to fit the copper in its place over
the leak, and drive in one nail before coming to the
surface, and then going down to drive in nail after
nail till the plate was fixed, his movements being
perfectly visible through the clear water.

Tanks are favourite bathing-places ; and over
these, amongst the higher classes, it is a common
practice to erect a room for dressing and perfuming

themselves; and excursions in boats to bathing-places form the Malay idea of a picnic, for they will make their journey, and then spend the day in bathing, dressing, and the preparation of delicious dishes for feasting, while the return home from the trip amongst the lilies and lotus-plants is made pleasant with music and singing. Altogether, there is something very dreamy and delicious in these excursions, indulged in, as they are, in a soft climate, amidst the beautiful vegetation of the eastern land; and it is to be regretted that all the Malayan peasants are not so innocent and idyllic.

They are particularly fond of singing, and often engage in musical contests, displaying a good ear and readily catching up European airs. In fact, the Maharajah of Johore has trained a band of young Malays to play on the regular brass and stringed instruments of our own country, and their rendering of operatic airs is anything but despicable, their performances being, indeed, quite equal to those of the bands of Siam, which have obtained some notoriety.

Amongst the native instruments the violin is the favourite, but there is also a kind of guitar. The percussion instrument that stands first with the Malays is the gong, which is their *beau ideal* of martial music, and is sounded as a signal of assembly or alarm, and for commencing a fight in war-prau or stockade. They have also a kind of wooden gong or bell, formed of the trunk of a tree, a portion of which is hollowed out and suspended from a framework. When this is struck with a mallet, the hollow boom is carried to great distances, and the idea has been taken up and used for signalling at our police stations in the Settlements. In fact, the Malays have a very good idea of the sonorous properties of wood, as evinced in the wooden instrument, with its sad, but not unpleasing wail, suspended in their trees, and also in a kind of harmonicon, formed of graduated pieces of hard-wood or bamboo, ranged in a coffin-shaped box, and struck with a small hammer, having a pliable handle. The mosque drum has been mentioned, but they have also one which they call *tambour*, a very familiar and evidently borrowed name, just as the term *biola* for the one-stringed violin must be of western origin.

Dancing is indulged in occasionally at festivals, where the young people meet, but strict watch is kept the while by the elder dames, for a Mahomedan does not approve of our western customs in this respect. They have, however, professional dancing-girls, whose costume is made attractive with artificial flowers and a crown of tinsel and gilding ; these are, however, rare in Perak.

The people of Perak and the peninsula, though not players at cricket and lawn tennis, which will doubtless come with the spread of civilisation, have something in the shape of athletic sports, for the young men will indulge in wrestling bouts with some display of vigour. They are very expert, too, in

tossing the *raga,* or wicker-ball, which is thrown in
the air to one of the party, and the object then is to
keep it up, this being done with hands, feet, shoulders,
or knees, every part of the body being brought into
play to keep the elastic ball from falling to the ground.
Their dexterity at times over this is wonderful, and
the game forms a healthy, invigorating amusement,
that might well come into fashion in England, in spite
of its resemblance to our own football, upon which
it may by some be considered as a refinement.

Sometimes at their festivals a kind of imitation
war-dance is indulged in, which has the drawback,
however, of the opposing parties waxing warm with
excitement, and exchanging the artificial for the
genuine, getting up quite a real fight, and having to
be withdrawn. The Malays of Province Wellesley,
who accompanied Mr. W. Maxwell, our Deputy-commissioner to Perak, gave us at his request some very
amusing exhibitions of this kind. This was during
the expedition to put down the rising ; and these Province Wellesley Malays, who have been for some time
under British rule, were most loyal in their behaviour,
and certainly deserved some recognition of the action
they took—a recognition that it would not have been
bad policy to give them in some significant way. For
they stood bravely by their officers when under fire in
a most cheerful and steady manner ; and it must have
been very galling to their own countrymen and co-
religionists in Perak to witness this, while it was a

remarkably trying test of their own faithfulness to their Christian masters.

Among their quieter games the Malays are not unaware of the amusement afforded by riddles and enigmas, some of which, as propounded by the more educated classes, are clever and hard to solve. Chess too is known, and played by them on what they call *papun chatoor*—literally, a plank with chequers. Their pieces are very similar to the European, and they give them the names of—

Rajah.	King.
Muntri, or Vizier.	Queen.
Gajah (Elephant).	Bishop.
Koodah (Hare).	Knight.
Ter (Chariot).	Castle.
Beedah (Foot-soldier).	Pawn.

The game they call *gajah—main gajah,* "the game of elephant." Check is *sah* ; and *mat,* check-mate.

This word *main* signifies to play or gamble, and is in the latter case used in conjunction with the word *judi.* This was originally *main judi,* to gamble with small shells, or judis, hence the term. Gambling is one of the Malay's greatest failings, for a man will not only stake his all, but even his person, and, if married, his wife and children, becoming, as already intimated, the slaves of the more fortunate players. Dice and cards have been introduced by the Chinese, and over these considerable sums (for them) are lost : but it is with their more national games that perhaps the heaviest stakes are hazarded. For under the term national may be included the quail and cock fighting, and the bull and tiger fight.

Cock-fighting especially is much practised by the inhabitants of Perak and other parts of the peninsula, though wisely interdicted in our own settlements. Like many other Malay customs, it seems to have been first introduced from the island of Sumatra, probably from Menang Kabau, and has gradually spread itself all over the Archipelago, making its chief home in Manilla, where it is now recognised by the Government—though it is said not to have been known there till the arrival of the Malays to colonise or trade.

So great is the love of this sport, that not only have poems eulogising it been written, but codes describing the laws and best breeds of fighting-cocks. No less than ten good kinds are mentioned under specific names ; and their breeding and training is made more of an art amongst the people than, according to the writer's own knowledge, it was some years since amongst the princes of Central India. The Malays frequently use the artificial spur of steel, called by them *golok* or *taji*. This is from an inch and a half to two inches in length, about one-eighth of an inch in breadth, sharpened on both sides, keenly pointed, and straight or curved according to the taste of the owner —one being generally used, but two if to match a weak bird against one that is stronger. This spur is tied on the leg, either above, below, or on the natural spur itself. Upon important occasions large bets are made on the result of the contest in the *golongan*, or cockpit; and the losers, as is usual in most gaming transactions, are often driven to great desperation, and bitter feuds are consequently engendered.

Quails are often fought in the same way; for these and several other varieties of birds can easily be trained to display their pugnacity in a battle with a stranger-bird; while even crickets are matched one against the other, and fight with vigour.

The cock-fights are cruel in the extreme; for the spurs are sharpened on a fine whetstone, and the gashes inflicted upon the unfortunate birds frequently result in death; for the combatants are as daring as our own game-fowl. But they are not dubbed and trimmed, as used to be the custom in our own more barbarous days, but fight in full feather.

The grand national sport is the tiger and buffalo fight; but this is not very frequently indulged in, on account of the great trouble and expense necessitated in preparing a fitting enclosure, and also perhaps from the difficulty of obtaining suitable animals to pit one against the other in the contest.

Upon the occasion of the Duke of Edinburgh's visit to the Straits Settlements, one of these displays was prepared by a native prince; and on the day arranged the two beasts were placed in a strong enclosure made of stakes of the nibong-palm, thoroughly secured and strengthened with iron, so that there was not the slightest risk to the lookers-on. In the centre was a large curtain, which divided the buffalo from the tiger; and for a time the spectators had an opportunity of examining the peculiarities of each animal. The buffalo was a splendid creature of its kind, fresh from roaming about in its native pastures, but it was heavy and dull-looking in the extreme. The tiger too was a magnificent animal, with its glossy coat and lithe graceful movements; but it had the disadvantage of having been confined to its cage since its capture.

Upon a signal being given the two animals, which had been calmly observant of the crowd, were suddenly brought face to face by the quick withdrawal of the curtain, and then the change in each was remarkable. The dull and heavy buffalo suddenly assumed an aspect of intense ferocity. The horns, usually pointed back, were thrown forward; the thick strong neck seemed to swell out till it was twice its natural size; the body was curved into an arch; the tail erect: and quite motionless, but watchful in the extreme, the animal awaited the tiger's attack. The tiger on its part seemed nothing loath to engage in the contest. Its eyes dilated; the hair about its neck stood erect; its face seemed to flatten out and grow broader; and with its lithe tail twisting and writhing gently, it crawled for a short distance close to the ground, and then gathered itself up for its tremendous spring.

Meanwhile the buffalo remained, with its pointed horns and eyes fixed upon its adversary, awaiting the charge, which was not long in coming; for the tiger made one tremendous bound with apparently irresistible force, trying to catch the buffalo by the back of the neck; but in this case it was unsuccessful, and only made a flesh-wound with its powerful claws, before it was thrown off with apparent ease.

Foiled in its attack, it now began to sidle off like a great cat, when, before it could get ready for another spring, it was set upon by the buffalo in turn, the furious beast rushing at it, and with a roar of rage burying one of its sharp horns in the striped flank, and then following it up with a series of thrusts and tossings till its feline enemy was gored to death.

This was one of the now rare exhibitions of the kind; for the buffalo and tiger fight, and other barbarous practices, are rapidly dying out before the advance of .Western civilisation, and the introduction of more humanising games.

CHAPTER XXIV.

THE generally-received idea of a Malay is that he is
a pirate, who goes about in a prau, armed with a kris,
and robs and murders every unfortunate being he
encounters : but probably the reader who has gone so
far through these pages has come to the conclusion
that the native of the peninsula and the neighbouring
isles is a man a little higher in the scale. "Some
writers," says Marsden, "have compared the human
species inhabiting a country to the animals indigenous to the same place : hence the Malay is said to
resemble both the tiger and the buffalo of his land.
In his domestic state he is like the latter—indolent,
stubborn, and voluptuous; while in his adventurous
life and in his ire he is like the tiger—bloodthirsty,
cruel, and rapacious."

This comparison is greatly overdrawn, but there is
a grain of truth in it, for coupled as the Malay has
been by early association with the Arab, and having
embraced his religion, it is in no wise surprising that

we should find the "robber of the desert" converted
in some instances into the "inveterate pirate," with,
at the same time, that utter indifference to the future
which fatalism alone engenders. It must not, however, be supposed that as a rule the Malay is a pirate
of the old school, for the piracies are, for the most part,
chieftain-like raids. There is no petty thieving, but
bold attacks upon vessels by men who seem to have
considered that they had a right to mulct the travellers
on the great highway of the sea at their will. With
such ideas then, and having always been a great
maritime nation, whose wanderings have extended
from the east coast of Africa to the Pacific, it is not
surprising that to a great extent the Malays have been
freebooters. Good sailors they have always been, and
to the present day they are the best eastern seamen a
captain can obtain ; and the fame of the Lascars is
known to every trader on the sea, some captains going
so far as to say that they would infinitely prefer
Lascars to English seamen—for the former are always
sober, quiet, and to be depended upon.

A bad character has, however, attached to them in
the past, and to a great extent this has been deserved,
for the piracies of the chiefs have been many and
frequent. In the neighbourhood of the Straits they
have, through the vigilance of the cruisers, become
very rare ; but a few years back the smaller trading
vessels, such as those of the Bugis, had to run a
dangerous gauntlet, especially anywhere in the neigh-

bourhood of Borneo. Lingin, an island near the Straits of Banca, was a regular stronghold of piracy, and its inhabitants forayed principally on the Malay and Bugis praus, seizing the goods, and selling captain and crew for slaves. European vessels were pretty generally respected, especially those bearing the English flag; probably, says the narrator of the danger of these seas, from the fact that five praus attacked an English sloop-of-war one hazy morning in mistake for an Arab vessel. "In less than five minutes four of the five were sunk, each having received one broadside only, while the fifth got under the land by the help of her oars. These praus had six guns each and one hundred and seventy men."

We read, too, that in bygone times the Chinese vessels that traded with Ceylon and India were not only built in a superior manner to Indian and Arabian ships, but were very much larger, in consequence of having to defend themselves from the remorseless pirates who appear from time immemorial to have infested the Straits of Malacca. These ships were manned with from two to five hundred, and even a thousand men, were well-armed, and provided with naphtha to burn their assailants' vessels.

The boats built by the Malays are called *sampans*, whilst those intended for sea-going purposes, no matter what their size, are termed *praus*. They are in fact canoes, with plank built upon plank, to the height of bulwark considered necessary, while the sternpost

is carried up to a great height, from which the planks
curve down to the side. The material used for making
the bottoms of their boats water-tight is called by the
Malays *gala-gala,* and is a composition of the resin
dammar and lime ; the seams being caulked with either
the soft bark of a tree which grows in marshy places,
or the scraped peel of a kind of cane—in both cases
dammar is afterwards used as we apply pitch. Bar-
thema speaks of the praus of his day as being large
vessels, capable of carrying on a trade between Malacca
and Masulipatam, the port in India which, according
to D'Anville, Ptolemy refers to as being near to the
place whence vessels traded to Malacca.

The lines of the vessels are peculiar to the Malay,
and by those who are competent to judge they are
pronounced excellent ; though Mr. Wallace had strong
doubts of the stability of those in which some of his
trips to the eastern islands were made, the open ports
constructed at the sides for steering purposes being
dangerous from their liability to ship water in a high
sea : but the same writer speaks very highly of the
boat-building qualities of some of the people he encountered.

The sampans are capable of being propelled through
the water at a high rate of speed by means of the
Malay *dayong,* or oar ; and in a long journey, when
the powers of endurance would have to be called into
play, Europeans would have some difficulty in dis-
tancing the natives. When sails are used they are

272

of matting or cloth; and in steering, the paddle is frequently used in preference to the rudder, and managed with great cleverness and dexterity. Mention was made of their anchors being used in connection with a heavy weight of stone; and an old writer speaks of this in saying: "For their galleys they have only wooden anchors, for they know not how to melt the iron of their iron mines; and to the end that their anchors may sink to the bottom, they fasten stones unto them. They have neither pins nor needles, nor nails, nor chisels, nor saws."

This holds good to the present day concerning the anchors, which, in the common vessels, are frequently lost in the interstices of the coral reefs; but the captain of the boat has this advantage: he halts at the next suitable island, and fits himself with fresh anchors from the crooked wood of the jungle.

Specimens of the sampans of the Perak river are seen moored to the side in the illustration representing the general appearance of a Malay village on the river-bank; and in the accompanying engraving a representation is given of a sampan made specially, and under his own inspection, for the late Resident, and in which the late Governor, Sir William Jervois, visited the country prior to the disturbances. Such a boat is called by the people a *sampan naga*, or dragon sampan, from the representation on its figure-head of a fabulous serpent. It was when ascending the river in this boat that Mr. Birch was so brutally

T

set upon and murdered at Passir Sala ; and the boat was afterwards sent up the river to ex-Sultan Ismail by the murderers, but at once returned, and is now, to the best of the writer's belief, still in use at the Residency.

Such a barge is provided with a kind of matting-tent in the stern, giving room for sleeping, and for the arrangement of guns and spears on the sides. A kind of platform exists in the extreme stern for the steersman, and in front is an awning of mats, with seats for the rowers or paddlers, and poles laid along ready for punting through the shallows. The Malay boatmen employed by the Government wear a white tunic ; and a flat white cap resembling those of the Prussians.

The rafts, so cleverly constructed by binding bamboos together with rattans, have been mentioned in connection with crossing the rapids, and in the far interior the Malays even reside upon them ; but they always prefer to build their houses on the shore, and on posts well raised from the ground.

To turn to the praus that have been used by the Malays for their piracies : these average about ten tons burden, though some are made of fifty, sixty, or even one hundred tons, and are propelled through the water with paddles at a very great rate. The stockade style of fighting is introduced, for they erect wooden screens which will keep off musket-balls, and from behind these the crew fire their swivel-mounted lelahs till the vessel they attack shows signs of giving in, or boarding is attempted in answer to the signal given by the gong. Then the limbings, or spears, krises and klewangs, come into play, with hatchets and blunderbusses, and the onslaught is of a very daring nature. Malay praus generally attack in parties or fleets of several together, making their advance upon a ship disabled by the want of wind, while from their great power in paddling, the pirates are able to approach in any direction so as to take their prey at a disadvantage, and, if beaten off, can escape with ease; while, in cases where they are pursued, their local knowledge of the inlets and channels of the mangrove-fringed coast-line, with its many rivers, enables them to escape, and leave their pursuers baffled and impotent to avenge the injury.

At home then on the sea, of which they are great lovers, as shown even by their language, which contains many terms connected with an ocean life, and of a restless, roving nature, evident proof of which abounds in the numberless points and headlands throughout the islands and as far as Madagascar bearing names of Malayan extraction; loving, too, the excitement of adventure, the Malays became the terror of the Archipelago; for when prey was afloat they put out from the many creeks and inlets of the coast in praus thoroughly fitted in build and armament for speed and resistance. Of late however this spirit has been diverted into more peaceful channels, and such as will prove profitable to themselves and less injurious to their neighbours and the visitors to their shores. Still, every now and then there is not wanting proof that in native states, where the rein of government is held with slackened hand, piracy on the high seas is often indulged in and even encouraged by the chiefs.

It would be hard to say whether the east or west coast of the peninsula has had the worse character for piracy, but certainly a very unenviable notoriety has attached in the past to Salangore and Perak. To go farther afield, some of the inhabitants of the Nicobar islands, lying just to the northward of Sumatra, have exhibited a disposition of a remarkably savage kind ; and in this respect differ widely from the Samangs, or negro Malays, to whom they have a strong affinity. So serious have been their acts of piracy in quite recent times in seizing vessels, and also in attacking and murdering the crews of those putting in at the islands for water, that the British government was compelled to take special notice of their acts. The consequence was that an expedition was fitted out in 1867, consisting of Her Majesty's ships *Wasp* and *Satellite*. The expedition was accompanied by a brother of H.H. the Maharajah of Johore, and T. Dunman, Esq., as Commissioner. The latter was then the Inspector-general of Police at Singapore, and was not only possessed of a thorough knowledge of the language, but also of a singular aptitude in understanding the Malay character.

The vessels, after punishing the principal villages,

brought down three or four of the piratical leaders, who had severally dubbed themselves under English names and titles, such as " Sir George Brown," &c. These men were of the average height, had the thick lips and curly hair of the Samang race, combined with the high cheek-bones and expanded nose of the Malay. Photographs of these people, with a full de. scription, were sent by the writer to his friend the late Mr. Crawfurd, who read a paper on the subject before the Ethnographical Society. The late Captain Edye, of H.M.S. *Satellite,* also brought down a little captive girl, who had evidently been taken by these people from one of the vessels they had destroyed. She was a Eurasian, and only about ten years of age, having in all probability been taken when quite an infant, for the language she spoke was very mixed, and she had no recollection of her capture.

When received on board the vessel, she imme- diately became the pet of the sailors, and was treated with all the kindness for which the British bluejacket has made himself a worthy name, and was soon clothed in a dress made from navy serge, with a girl's hat of the latest fashion, cleverly improvised out of a man-o'-warsman's "straw," and ornamented with a cock's feather for plume.

On her arrival at Singapore, she was first placed in the girls' school attached to the late Mr. Keasberry's mission—one of the most valued institutions in the settlement—and upon its being closed she was trans-

ferred by the Government to the Chinese girls' school,
where she was tenderly nursed and educated, and
baptised under the name of little "Mercy." The
poor child, however, did not long survive, but was
one of the victims about two years later to cholera.

And here it would be unjust not to notice the vast
amount of good that has been done by the Society
for Female Education in the East. The task of this
Society is one that must bear fruit in connection with
our endeavours to civilise the native states; for its
efforts are directed towards the education of the Malay
and Chinese girls; each of whom must in time form a
centre from which will radiate the beneficent knowledge she has acquired, for the permanent advantage
of those around.

Among the more notorious acts of piracy in these
parts that have taken place recently may be mentioned the seizure of a junk, and the murder of the
Chinese crew and passengers. This vessel sailed in
1871 from Penang, bound for Laroot, the tin district
of Perak, only about thirty-six hours distant, but did
not arrive; and on enquiries being made, it was
found that an ingenious plot had been laid, by which
about fifteen pirates had gone aboard as passengers;
and that at an appointed time these people had risen,
murdering the crew and genuine passengers, number-
ing in all about thirty-four souls—men, women, and
children—and carried off the valuable junk and her
freight, a portion of which was a large sum in dollars.

The colonial steamer *Pluto* was immediately sent out with orders to search for the missing junk, which was found lying off Salangore, with the money gone, and the greater part of the cargo in the shops of the town. The junk was secured, with nine of the pirates ; but a rajah and his followers taking their part, krises were drawn, and firing took place upon the *Pluto*, which immediately left for Penang, where she arrived with the prisoners and her prize.

Such a resistance to the British authority, and so cruel an act of piracy on a vessel trading in our port, could not be allowed to go unpunished ; so the acting Governor despatched an expedition to secure the remainder of the pirates and recover the stolen property.

The expedition arrived off the Salangore river, entered it, and armed boats proceeded to search the vessels at anchor and some huts. Soon after, in a dispute about the Rajah going on board the *Pluto*, hostilities were commenced by the natives, who fled to the jungle; and in the firing that ensued seven men of the British were wounded, including the lieutenant in command of the landing-party, who received a cut on the hand from a kris. More could not be done then, as the men, crowded in boats, were exposed to the fire of an enemy hidden in the jungle ; so the forces were drawn off.

The next morning Commander Robinson steamed up the river in H.M.S. *Rinaldo*—a very risky proceeding, as there was a dangerous bar at the mouth. In addition, he had no surgeon on board; and he knew it would be twelve hours before the tide would allow them to pass out again. But this was a notorious piratical haunt; and after the treacherous attack of the previous day, it was necessary to punish the people for their insult to our flag, and to teach them that they were not secure in their positions. In a short time a hot and well-directed fire was opened on the steamer from the forts, and in five minutes there were three men wounded, and the *Rinaldo* had suffered severely; but by steaming on, the defences were turned, and before their guns could be got round, they were dismounted, or the forts knocked to pieces. Musketry-fire was then opened on the ship, but without much effect, and soon after she grounded in soft mud, presenting a fair mark to the enemy: but fortunately his guns were all silenced and kept down by the steamer's fire.

After awhile, the tide rising, the vessel steamed out of the river, returning with the *Pluto* soon after, bringing a detachment of the 19th Madras Light Infantry; and after a little firing the Malays fled, when the town was completely burnt down, the forts destroyed, and the guns spiked or broken up—Commander Robinson, who was in charge, saying that the town would have been spared had there been anyone with whom to make terms, and had the rest of the pirates been given up. In addition, five piratical praus were burned in this nest of pirates; three being armed with two twenty-four pounders and one small gun each, with an abundance of small-arms, spears, muskets, and pistols. They were of the largest class of praus, and measured from eighty to one hundred tons each.

The result of this expedition was that the Sultan of Salangore outlawed the Rajahs who had taken part in the affair; and all the pirates that could be found were sent to Malacca, one having died in the interim. His Highness then gave up a thousand dollars' worth of tin belonging to one of the offending chiefs, and presented Her Majesty with a very handsome pair of elephant tusks.

CHAPTER XXV.

EVEN so late as the year 1873, the piracies from the
native states, especially that of Salangore, were of so
formidable a nature as to again necessitate steps being
taken by our Government for their suppression. It was
in this year that a daring act of piracy took place in
the south of this particular state, namely in the Jugra
river. It was so serious in its nature that it will be
remembered in the peninsula for many years to come.
So swift, however, was the punishment enforced, and
so salutary the lesson taught, that it is gratifying to
know that a complete check was placed upon any
further attempts for the time being. Various other
acts of piracy had occurred just prior to this, notably
in the Laroot river, as will be described, the Laroot
pirates being routed, and their vessels and stockades
destroyed by H.M.S. *Midge* and *Thalia*, while other
stockades were finally razed in Perak, and a more
reputable state of affairs assured.

In the case of the Jugra piracy, which, as will be

told in the words of the sole survivor who escaped, as
given in a minute of the court, the perpetrators were
afterwards recognised and were cleverly taken by the
authorities of Malacca; and it was at first intended
to try, and punish them in one of our own courts;
but Sir Andrew Clarke, receiving an offer from the
Viceroy of Salangore, and probably believing in the
effect it would produce, decided that the criminals
should be tried by the native court, at the very place
where the act of piracy was committed. In this case
the writer was employed as joint Commissioner with
Mr. Davidson.

At the trial the charge against the eight pirates
was that they had plundered a boat at or near the
mouth of the river Jugra, and murdered eight men,
being the passengers and crew. The court was composed of the Viceroy of Salangore, with three Native
Commissioners appointed by the Sultan, while the two
English Commissioners watched the proceedings. The
sitting of the court took place at a stockade.

The survivor then gave his evidence, which, in
addition to its peculiarity as a sample of a statement
in a native Malay court, is interesting for the insight
it gives into the habits and customs of the boatmen
on the rivers and coast:

I live at Tranquerra, in Malacca, and am a seafaring man; I left
Langat on the 25th of the month of Poasah, in a naddy (boat) belong-
ing to Malacca; there were three Chinese passengers, whose names
I do not know, and six Malays belonging to the boat, named Hadjee

Doraman, who was the nacodah (skipper), Ah Kim, Tamb Itam, Meman, Mambi, and myself. The naddy was loaded with rattans; there were also boxes. There were 2000 dollars on board, belonging to Ah Kim, of Langat, and the nacodah. I assisted to bring the dollars on board the boat, and the nacodah told me there were 2000 dollars. We left Bandar Langat about six o'clock A.M. ; we arrived here (the stockade at the mouth) about one o'clock, and showed our pass to Arsat, who was in charge of the stockade. We went outside the river about a mile and anchored, because the wind was against us. We anchored about three o'clock; the nacodah told us to rest, and we would sail at night. About three o'clock, the juragan called the crew to boil rice. We cooked rice, and about five o'clock I saw two boats coming out of this river. I asked the juragan what boats they were, and he said two friendly boats from the stockade. They pulled up near us, and Doraman asked where they were going, and the reply was, they were going to fish. Musa replied from the boats. One of the boats came alongside, and Musa and three or four others came on board. The other boat came alongside on the other side. [There were about twenty men on the two boats.] They talked to Doraman. About six o'clock Doraman told us to bring the rice. When he was about to begin eating, shots were fired from both boats. Doraman fell to the shots. Musa then called out to "amok." Three of our people jumped into the water and were stabbed, and all the others in my boat were also stabbed and killed. I jumped into the water, hung on to the rudder, and after dark floated away to the shore: when I floated away the three boats were still together in the same place. I floated to the piles of this jetty and got hold of one. There was a Bugis boat lying about three fathoms off. I held on to the pile about an hour, and the pirates came in their own boats, bringing Doraman's boat with them. One man came out from the stockade on to the jetty and asked "Sudah habis?" (Is it all over?). From the boats a man replied "Sudah habis" (It is all over). "We are taking the property to Tunku Allang." They all went up the river with their boats and my boat. The two boats returned in about an hour without mine. They all came up on this jetty. People from the stockade asked if it was finished, and they said it was all finished. After all was quiet here, I went to the Bugis boat and asked them to assist me, and they took me into their boat. The Bugis asked me whose boat it was, and I told them Doraman's. The Bugis advised me not to say anything about the affair here or I would be killed. When I was speaking to the Bugis the people from the stockade came and asked them for me. The Bugis refused to give me up, but said they would show me next morning. All the prisoners were in the boats that attacked us. It was daylight, and I could see them quite well. No. 1 shot the juragan. No. 2 came into the boat and shot and stabbed people. No. 3 remained in his own boat and had a spear. No. 4 came into our boat and stabbed Tamb Itam. No. 5 was in his own boat, he had a spear and stabbed people in the water. No. 6 came into our boat and stabbed Meman and others. No. 7 remained in his own boat and had a spear and assisted to stab my friends in the water. No. 8 was in one of the boats, and I did not see him do anything.

The next day the Bugis took me on the jetty, and showed me to the headman of the stockade, named Marsat. All the prisoners were present with Marsat at the time. Nos. 1 and 4 asked the Bugis to give me up, but the Bugis refused. I saw on the jetty the boxes of many of my friends, also bags belonging to the boat scattered about, and met also two muskets belonging to my boat, and one spear and a sword. The Bugis then took me up to Langat to the Yam Tuan, who was asleep, and then they took me up to the Datu Bandar. He asked me if I knew the men who had done it. I said I did. He then asked me where they belonged to, and I said to the stockade. He then said to me : If you are asked, say you do not know who did it ; if you say you know them you will be killed. After this the Bugis took me back to the Yam Tuan, and I told him all that had occurred. He then asked me if I knew the people who had done it, and I said no, as I was afraid of being killed. When I was speaking to the Yam Tuan No. 1 and No. 4 came in and said: We want this man (pointing to me); Tunku Allang wants to take him to the Qualla. Yam Tuan told me to go with them. I said I was afraid. Yam Tuan said if I was afraid they had better let me go to Mahomed Syed's shop. Mahomed Syed was present, and I was given up to him. Mahomed Syed sent a letter by Belal Ismain to my uncle Mamoot at Malacca. My uncle arrived at Langat from Malacca on the 27th of the month of Poasah, and the same day I left Langat with my uncle. When I was leaving I saw our boat at Qualla Sungie Durien, in this river; no one was on board. Qualla Sungie Durien is Tunku Allang's place.

About twenty days after my arrival at Malacca I was on the bridge at Malacca, and saw two boats coming up the river, and saw some of the prisoners in the boats. I reported to Mr. Hayward, and I went with Duffadar Mahomed, and pointed out Nos. 1, 2, and 3, and Mahomed arrested them in their boats. Two days after that I saw another boat coming into Malacca, and reported it to Mr. Hayward; he ordered Mr. Warne to arrest, and I went and pointed out Nos. 4, 5, 7, and 8, and they were arrested. No. 6 was arrested at Ujong Kubu, in Malacca.

In the boat where Nos. 1, 2, and 3 were arrested we found a musket, a sword, and a spear, which belonged to Doraman, and were in his boat when she was plundered.

In the boat where Nos. 4, 5, 7, and 8 were arrested were found an anchor and a sarong. The anchor belonged to Allang, but was on board the naddy when she was plundered. The sarong belonged to Meman.

[The gun, sword, and sarong are produced, and identified by the witness.]

Two days ago I went up the Langat river in one of the man-of-war's boats, and saw Doraman's boat inside the Sungie Durien. It was tied to the mangroves as if hidden. There was a house on shore near the place; it belongs to Tunku Allang. The naddy was then brought down the river, and is here now. This is the naddy. After coming down with the naddy, I came on shore here, and found a water-cask in this stockade belonging to the naddy, and which was on board when it was plundered.

The case lasted three days, a great deal of corroborative evidence being given, sufficient to prove the facts without doubt; and finally the eight prisoners were all found guilty of piracy and murder of the eight British subjects, and seven were condemned to be executed on the following day; sentence upon one being suspended on account of his youth.

The execution by the kris is carried out in a very solemn manner, by men specially appointed to perform the duty. As a rule, execution is immediate upon sentence, but in this case it was deferred as above. Mention of the execution kris has already been made, as being perfectly straight and narrow in the blade; the one mentioned being kept in a sheath of gold.

Early on the morning of the appointed day an armed guard of seamen and marines was landed from Her Majesty's ships, and marched out to a rising ground behind the stockade where the trial had taken place. Some followers of the Viceroy were also in attendance with the executioner, the kris for the purpose having been sent down during the night by the Sultan : this weapon always being in the custody of the ruler of the country, who alone has the power of life and death.

The prisoners offered not the slightest opposition, their fatalist religion making them behave with a calm stoicism, as they placed themselves kneeling with their heads turned from the executioner. This latter official places then a small pad of cotton on the left shoulder to prevent the effusion of blood; passing the point of the kris through this he waits for a given signal, upon receiving which, one thrust in a slanting direction sends the blade into the criminal's heart, and death follows almost instantaneously, when the kris is drawn back nearly bloodless through the pad.

As soon as death had ensued, and each body was stretched out, the executioner made two or three brisk steps over and around it, the object of this custom being to drive away the evil spirits who might be hovering round, seeking to prevent the soul from ascending to the paradise of Allah. Generally the criminals executed are buried on the spot, a grave being previously prepared ; but in this case the bodies were at once removed by the relatives, to be interred on a point of land higher up the river ; while the Viceroy had a notice-board put up that in future this spot should be called "The Place of Execution."

After this it devolved upon the Commissioners to consider the amount of compensation that should be demanded of the Sultan of Salangore, whose people had committed this act of piracy, and taken the lives of eight British subjects, natives of Malacca ; and after due consideration, a note was despatched to him, announcing the decision as being a demand for five thousand dollars, or its equivalent in slabs of tin, and requiring also that this compensation should be at once placed on board one of her Majesty's ships lying off the Sultan's residence at Langat.

Very little time was wasted, for the lesson read of British power and determination to put down piracy was severe enough to insure immediate compliance. In effect, the piratical boat was handed over and taken off in tow to Malacca by H.M.S. *Rinaldo*, and the Commissioners received a note from the

Sultan, informing them that two hundred and eighty-
six slabs of tin (about seven tons) had been placed on
board H.M.S. *Midge*; and the next day, in company
with the Viceroy, the Commissioners visited other
places in search of piratical haunts, and during their
investigations warnings were issued which had due
effect.

But to show how indifferent the Malay, in his half-
civilised state, is to the commission of piracy at sea,
which he seems to look upon as his own proper poach-
ing-ground, a circumstance may be mentioned which
occurred at Langat just prior to the trial and execution that have been recorded. Our Admiral had an
interview with the Sultan, who was surrounded by his
chiefs and people, and in as much state as he was
capable of showing. The Admiral, in referring to the
barbarity of the Jugra piracy, advised and urged upon
the Sultan to caution his people against being guilty
of such acts in future, pointing out how it was impossible that they could be left unpunished, as in the
interests of the Settlements, as well as the native
states, our Government was determined upon putting
down the custom.

The Sultan listened very attentively, and then
turning quickly round to his people, he exclaimed:
Dungar lah, jangan kitah main main lagi!—" Hear
now, my people! Don't let us have any more of this
little game!"

U

CHAPTER XXVI.

Titles of chiefs—Taxation and tolls—The Sultan's slaves—Sultanas
—Court observances—The royal family—Ancient descent—
Vanity and superstition—A Malay document.

PRIOR to the occupation of the country by the British
forces, the government of Perak embraced a Sultan
elected from the princes of the royal blood of the
reigning house; the Rajah Muda, or heir apparent;
with four officers of the first rank, eight of the second,
and sixteen of the third.

The proper signification, by the way, of this title,
"Rajah," is a person over whose actions no one has
any control. He is one, too, who is exempt from
having to obey certain laws in the Malay code, and
hence his power is of a very extended nature, and can
be largely exercised for the good or evil of the people.
So great is the power, in fact, of the native chiefs,
that one of the ex-Sultans, in correspondence with the
Governor of the Straits Settlements expressed his
sorrow for certain crimes committed by the chiefs,
and owned that his control over them was next to
nothing, for they did what they pleased.

The chiefs of the first rank were—

I.—The RAJAH BANDAHARA, who was the Sultan's chief executive officer, minister, lawgiver, and ruler over the peasantry. His powers were very great, his sway extending over the extreme limits of the kingdom.

II.—The ORANG KAYA BUSAR, the keeper of the Sultan's privy purse.

III.—The TUMONGONG, or chief magistrate, preventer of oppression, and punisher of transgressors. This officer's place of honour in procession was at the head of the Sultan's elephant.

IV.—The MUNTRI, or chief adviser of the Sultan.

In the second rank—

I.—The MAHARAJAH LELAH, who was the commander of the land and sea forces.

II.—The LAKSAMANA, who was high admiral, his prau always taking the lead of the fleet. The Sultan's zenana was also under his charge when ashore; while in procession the Laksamana's post was by the Sultan's palanquin, or he bore his sword after him when riding in state upon an elephant.

III.—The SHAHBANDAR, or harbour and custom-house master.

IV.—The SEDIKA RAJAH.

V.—The PANGLIMA KINTA, who had charge of the regalia and the district on the left bank of the river.

VI.—The PANGLIMA BUKIT GANTANG, the high district officer of the right bank of the river.

VII.—The DATU SAGOR, the head of the river boats and navigation; and

VIII.—The IMAM PADUKA TUAN, or chief priest.

In the third rank were—

The SREE MAHARAJAH LELAH; and
The DATU MATA-MATA.

The others held offices of but little moment.

The subject of slavery was treated of pretty fully in a previous chapter, but the relations between the Sultan and his bond-servants was left to be dealt with under the question of Government. Here, no doubt, is the source of the whole evil, for the example set in high places has been eagerly followed by the chiefs, while their dependants in turn have gladly taken, in bygone ages, to a system that was aggrandising to a degree. The government under the late Sultan being arbitrary and despotic, and having but little control over the many chiefs, these latter have been as tyrannical and freebooting as the barons of the Rhine, or those of our own land in the days of Magna Charta John; but without making the slightest effort to benefit anyone but themselves. Their sole thought seems to have been to enrich themselves as rapidly as possible at the expense of the poor toilers in the field; and consequently every chief picked out a snug and convenient spot upon some reach of the river, and built himself a bamboo castle, with an attap roof, where he could sit in wait for every boat-load of produce coming up and down the stream, and by means of his followers levy black-mail, or help himself to the booty of the industrious bees, who, though they carried dangerous stings in the shape of krises, dared not use them against their more powerful, hornet-like oppressors. Tin, salt, fish, rice, fruit, anything would do for the chief so long as the quality was good and the quantity large; in fact, the unfortunate ryot seemed born to be oppressed, and oppressed he was, till his time for working had ceased to be. If he could be charged with some trivial offence he was fined; and when this levying of black-mail failed to provide sufficient for the wants of the chief, lawful indulgences were converted into offences, and the wretched people were compelled to pay for such absurd things as wearing a sarong a few inches too long or too short. In fact, nothing was considered too trivial by the ruling wolves who wished to prove that their subservient lambs had sullied the water flowing at their noble feet. Under such a government, as was most natural, every form of abuse and oppression was practised; and the only resource for the people was to connect themselves with the most arbitrary and powerful of the chieftains, so as to be robbed by one and one only, instead of having to submit to an indiscriminate oppression from the chiefs at large—who, fortunately for the poorer classes, were extremely jealous one of another.

The consequence of this state of things was that, naturally objecting to labour, the Malays grew thoroughly averse to every kind of work, caring little for doing more than providing for their simplest wants. It was no advantage to a man to cultivate a goodly piece of land, and raise crops that were not for his own eating; to grow fruits that were absorbed by Sultan or chief and their numerous followings; or to become the possessor of buffaloes that might be seized any day to draw the properties of his lord. All this has had much to do with the careless state into which the Malay has fallen, and it requires a good and safe government, with the protection of wise and just laws, properly carried out, to make the people take to the industrious life that means prosperity to his country.

This industry could not be expected where one chief levied a royalty of five dollars a *coyan* on rice, another sixteen dollars—tariffs being apparently regulated at the pleasure of the chief. These taxes were nominally levied for the benefit of the Sultan, who was supposed to obtain eleven dollars on every bhar* of tin, but he never received more than six. Then private owners of mines, though often imaginary beings, were sufficiently substantial in some form or another to levy their tax of ten dollars a bhar, making a total impost of twenty-one dollars—a sum which, as the late Mr. Birch said, no tin could pay. Tin and rice were only examples of the treatment of other articles of produce. In his own place, says the same gentleman, every chief took something. "At the Qualla Kinta" (or mouth of the Kinta) "the Bandahara sublets to the Rajah Makota a farm of extra customs-duties on every import and export, thus making the miners and inhabitants on that river pay at least double the amount paid by all other people in the country." . . .

---

* Coyan, about two tons ; Bhar, about three and a half hundredweight.

" At Sengang, where Rajah Yusuf lived, he used to stop every boat up or down, and levy one-tenth of everything, but he has lately given this up." Higher up the river, where the Sedika Rajah resided, they levied again a tenth on all imports and exports.

But in addition to all these oppressive levies of taxes, the inhabitants suffered from a system of forced labour, each male having to render to his chief a fourth of his year of labour, and to turn out to assist him in time of tumult or war.

Many of these oppressions have, through the efforts of the Residents, been ameliorated, but there is still this terrible custom of debt-slavery; and the chiefs, having the means and great power in the state, are always able to make the wretched people appear, in some form or another, in their debt. As this debt can rarely be liquidated, the unfortunate ryot is, as before shown, bound over with his family to serve the chief, sinking calmly into his wretched state of servitude and suffering with all the customary patience of the eastern believer in Kismet—fate. If the debt be liquidated, it is generally only for the family to change hands, and become the slaves of a new proprietor: it is to be hoped—though this is very doubtful—for the bettering of their condition.

The Sultan's slaves who are about his palace were acquired in an exceedingly simple manner—in a way, in fact, that thoroughly exemplifies the old-fashioned dealing of the eastern potentate, who, however, in this case, is but a petty sultan or rajah, living in no gorgeous Aladdin-like palace, but in such a home as Mr. Birch describes as that of Sultan Abdullah at Batarabit, where "the house compound is a most unwholesome swamp of green stagnant water, and the paths and streets sloughs of slippery mud." It was not surprising that this Sultan preferred to live on the river in boats.

When one of these rulers took a fancy to a slave, his custom was to send a messenger with his sword or kris to the house where the poor girl lived, and however much the parents might grieve at the loss of their child, the despot's command, as represented by the sword, was a law that no inferior thought of resisting. It was another case of kismet—the command of royalty—and the maiden was hurried off to the zenana, where she might in time attain to the high dignity of using a pestle and mortar to pound betel mixture for her lord to chew, if, like Abdullah, he were not a confirmed smoker of opium, and a reveller in the drugged drams that turn so many of these eastern rajahs into weak, mentally incapable rulers of the fair country that is at their feet.

The life of these sultanas is not an enviable one ; for though there is no bowstring in force for refractory or unfaithful ones, and no Bosphorus with saline tide, yet there are plenty of rivers, and, as has been shown, a very rugged and cruel drowning for the slave who dares to rise in spirit against her lord. But these are

EX-SULTAN ABDULLAH AND CHIEFS OF PERAK.

necessarily only the exceptional cases; for, as a rule, the slave-girl's lot is to be kindly treated, while in old age the Sultan or chief is bound in very shame to provide for her sustenance and clothing.

The observances in a Malay court are, as may be supposed, very strict, and the points of etiquette carefully studied and observed. Thus it was stated that the Tumongong and Laksamana have certain places by the Sultan's elephant. The Muntri has also to take his place at the head of his litter, and in the illustration given of Sultan Abdullah and his court, the various chiefs and officers are seen in their correct positions, according to rank and station, as they were placed for the taking of the photograph. The sword-bearers carry these weapons of state, and they are held, quite according to etiquette, upon the right shoulder. In this case the Sultan is seated on a chair, and as is always observed, no other chief can take such a seat unless it is of a lower level than that of his lord, and consequently they all sit or crouch upon their hams. Quite a difficulty occurred on board one of our vessels, when a Sultan and his officers paid a visit, the Muntri refusing to take a chair on account of one being already occupied by his chief. Indeed, Mr. Wallace gives an amusing instance of this Malay stickling for pride of place, in an anecdote that he relates of the chief of one of the islands he visited. This gentleman had a great love of European customs, and had gone so far as to order a carriage from England for his own use. Unfortunately, however, the vehicle had to be condemned on account of a great failing in its construction ; for, had it been made use of, the coachman or driver would have occupied a higher seat than his master, and in the code of Malayan etiquette such things could not be. In fact, sitting on the ground or standing is the attitude of respect.

Even in such a small matter as colour, the Malay is excessively particular as to his dress, the tint of his umbrella, and the envelopes he uses to send his Arabic written letters. The royal colour, as intimated, is yellow, and the envelopes used by the Sultan are always of this colour, and composed of silk.

When a Malay meets a European a polite salutation is accorded to him, and it mostly consists of the words *Tabik, Tuan*—"I salute you, sir; " but among themselves it is "Peace be with you!" the reply being, "And to you also." The etiquette as to the kris-handle will be remembered, as necessitating its being kept covered, and these points, along with all those relating to the due respect to be rendered to the various chiefs, the shape and style, colour and arrangement of garments, are rigorously kept up in the states at a distance from the European settlements. One of the most striking things, though, with respect to court observances, is the amount of superstitious veneration that exists for the person of the sovereign. To shed royal blood would evoke for the Malay, according to his ideas, a train of punishment which, in his superstitious awe, he could not contemplate without a shudder ; and in consequence the person of the monarch is perfectly safe, while the halo of his sanctity spreads around and illumines all his relatives present and, what is more, is reflected straight away down " the corridors of time " to come ; for every one who claims descent from royalty enjoys also this immunity from danger at the hands of a people who might be ready to resent an injury by the use of the kris.

The royal family of Perak, like most of those in the native states of the peninsula, traces its origin with the greatest care from the royal family of Menang Kabau, or Kabowe, as it is variously spelled. The chief city of this state is called by some writers Paggar-oodong, or Battang Selo, probably the Paggar-ooyoong of Marsden, the writer on Sumatra ; and the chief founder was Maha Raja de Raja, supposed to be a great-grandson of Mahomet. The late dynasty in Perak in more modern times is referred back to Sultan Mahomed Bansoo, who had issue by a former rajah's daughter—Rajah Eenoo, who married a daughter of Sultan Mahomed Muda, who had issue Rajah Cholam, who came to the throne of Perak as Sultan Mahomed Sapi. Rajah Cholam married a daughter of Rajah Kassim.

Sultan Mahomed Bansoo had also issue by four concubines, one being named Rajah Mundo Beeso, the second, Rajah Manda ; the third, Mahomed Kusso ; and the fourth, Mahomed Saboot.

We read in Moor's "Notices" that there were two
chiefs at Menang Kabau under a certain Rajah Allam,
who, though brought up in all the learning of the
age, gave himself up to vicious pursuits. Hence he
was seldom called upon to exercise his authority, which
was vested in the two chiefs. These were a Rajah
Addat, or rajah judging over cases of laws and
custom; and a Rajah Ebaddat, or judge of cases of
sacred appeal. They originally formed members of
the Paggar-ooyoong house, and though from length
of time relationship cannot be traced, yet the depen-
dence is claimed and admitted on all sides; and as the
Rajah Allam can only marry in one of these families,
and those of the *Eang ampat selo*, a proper understanding and subordination still exist.

The chiefs under the Rajah Allam were *Eang duo
selo*, and these resided at Soompoo Coodoos, now called
Lintow, of which Bangsa and Boohoo are the principal
cities.

Next in rank to these are the *Eang ampat selo*,
whose origin is altogether fabulous. Their names or
titles are Bandahara of Soongye Taru, Mangcoodoom
of Si Maneca, Endomo of Sooroowassa, and Caleca of
Padang Gunteeang. Of these four the Bandahara is
the principal chief, and is never called upon for personal service when the Rajah Allam moves, while the
remaining three, distinguished by the denomination of
Eang tega selo, accompany and attend upon the
Rajah Allam in all his processions and travels, each of

these possessing a large extent of territory, and a numerous body of dependants.

The grand assembly of the nation was formed of the six *Selo*, and all matters of judgment or policy were settled by them. The *Duo selo* had casting votes according to whether the case was secular or ecclesiastical; but final reference or appeal could be made to the Rajah Allam.

Tradition carries the Perak royal family safely back so far; but not content with that, they are, from their vanity and great love of antiquity of families, fond of trying to trace their descent to Mahomet, when, instead of being interesting, their account only tends to amuse, and reminds the listener of the account given by Dalton of the Sultan of Coti in the Island of Borneo. This great potentate was the chief of a large district in the south-east of that island, and his genealogical tree was written in these words, in the Koran of the Kragi of Tongarron, his chief city, by Nabbee Ahmet, who came down from heaven on purpose to perform this duty for the Sultan, who was one of the most barbarous head-hunters of that notorious land.

Soon after the great prophet Mahomet ascended into heaven from *Mecca*, his second and favourite brother, whose name was likewise Mahomet, dreamed that the prophet appeared to him in the shape of a comet, inviting him forth to preach the true doctrine. He accordingly arose, and embarked on board a ship with some chosen followers. They had no occasion for compass or sails, as the comet kept before the vessel, and the wind favoured them.

After being on the ocean one year, during which period no land
was seen, a country was descried in the west, over which the comet
remained stationary.   This was Coti.   Mahomet landed at a place
now called *Cinculeram*, when he fell asleep, and his brother again
appeared before him, standing upon the mountain *Baley Papang*.
With a loud voice he ordered a kingdom to be founded, and a
capital built, which should be considered second only to Mecca.
The prophet disappeared after leaving the Koran, written by a
celestial hand.   On awaking, Mahomet found himself in another
part of the country, where he built the capital, calling it *Tongarron*, after the name of the ship which brought them safe.   Here
it was the Koran was first opened by Mahummud Sali Hooden,
the first Sultan, who, after reigning forty-seven years, was taken
up to heaven in a flash of lightning, since which period the family
has given a succession of Sultans to Coti.

These facts the Sultan and his priest say are known throughout
the world, and acknowledged by all rajahs in India, who formerly
paid tribute.   He has no superior or equal except the Sultan of
Turkey.

This peculiar form of vanity runs strongly through
the whole family of Malay sultans, whose titles and
epithets are in some cases as extraordinary as they
are absurd.   Those of Menang Kabau excel in this
direction, as the following copy of a warrant from
that place will abundantly show.   The extract is from
Marsden, and in the original it commences with three
chops in the Arabic character.   A chop, it may be
necessary to inform some readers, is a seal in these
eastern lands, though very frequently it is adopted to
signify the trade-mark of some large commercial firm
in China.   The chop of a Malay sultan is generally
about a couple of inches across, is formed of silver,
engraved with Arabic characters, and is affixed at

the beginning of a document, the impression being made, not with sealing-wax, but with Indian ink, pretty liberally applied.

Here is the document, which was sent to a high priest :

(Three circular seals with these inscriptions in Arabic characters.)

(Eldest Brother)	(Second Brother)
Sultan of Rome	Sultan of China
Key Dummool Allum	Nour Allum
Maharaja Alliff.	Maharaja Dempeng.

(Youngest Brother)
Sultan of Menang Cabow *
Aour Allum
Maharaja de Raja.

The Sultan of Menang Cabow, whose residence is at Paggar ooyoong (after pardon asked for presuming to mention his name), who is king of kings, son of Rajah Izounderzulcar-nainny, and was possessed of Muncooto, who was brought from heaven by the prophet Adam ; master of the third of the wood maccummat, one of whose properties is to enable matter to fly; of the lance ornamented with the beard of Jangee, of the palace of the city of Rome, whose entertainments and diversions are exhibited in the month of Dul-hadjee, and where all Alims, Pukkeeahs (faquirs), and Moulahnocarrees, praise and supplicate God ; of the gold of twelve grains named coodarat coodarattee, resembling a man ; who receives his taxes in gold by the lessong (quasi bushel) measure ; whose betel-stand is of gold set with diamonds; who is possessed of the sword named Chooree-se-mendong-geree, which has an hundred and ninety gaps, made in the conflict with the arch-devil Se-cattee-moono, whom it slew ; who is master of fresh water in the ocean to the extent of a day's sailing ; possessed of a lance formed of a

---

* Supposed to be derived from two Malay words: *Menang*, to win, and *Kábau*, a buffalo; from a fabulous story of a fight between tigers and buffaloes, in which the latter obtained the victory.

twig of edjoo; of a calewang wrapped in an unmade chinday; of a crease formed of the soul of steel, which by a noise expresses an unwillingness at being sheathed, and shows itself pleased when drawn; of a date coeval with the Creation; possessed of a gun brought from heaven named Soubahanahououatanalla; of a horse of the race of sorimborahnee, superior to all others; sultan of the burning mountain, and of the mountains Goontang-goontang, which divide Palembang and Jambee; who may slay at pleasure, without being guilty of a crime; who is possessed of the elephant named Settee-dewa; who is vicegerent of heaven; sultan of the golden river; lord of the air and clouds; master of a balli, whose pillars are of the shrub jelattang; of gandangs (drums) made of hollowed branches of the minute shrubs pooloot and seelo-seoree; of the gong that resounds to the skies; of the buffalo named Se Binnooang Sattee, whose horns are ten feet asunder; of the unconquered cock Sengoonannee; of the coco-nut tree, whose amazing height, and being infested with serpents and other noxious reptiles, render it impossible to be climbed; of the flower named Seeree menjeree of ambrosial scent; who when he goes to sleep wakes not till the gandang nobat sounds; one of whose eyes is as the sun, and the other as the moon——To his subjects declares this his will, &c. &c.

In another communication to Mr. Marsden by Mr. Dalrymple, the same exaggerated language is taken up to show the antiquity of the royal family of Me-nang Kabau : God gave to Gaggar Allum, who had his residence in the clouds, " a bird called ' Hocinet,' that had the gift of speech. This he sent down on earth to look out for a spot where he might establish an inhe-ritance, and the first place he alighted upon was the fertile island of Lancapore, situated between Palimban and Jambee ; and from thence sprang the famous kingdom of Manancabou, which will be renowned and mighty until the Judgment Day."

When all that is worthless and fabulous in these documents is sifted out, there are, however, several grains of common-sense left behind; inasmuch as one can at least gather from the writings, their style, their allusions, and their use of so many Sanscrit, Persian, and Arabic terms, that the Malays must in early times have had most extensive dealings with the peoples by whom these several languages were spoken.

CHAPTER XXVII.

THE Malay language would present a very interesting study to the philologist; for, so far from being a barbarous dialect, it is a soft rich tongue, that has been worthily called the "Italian of the East." This is of course from its tuneful and flowing nature. The "French of the East" would be a more appropriate term, however; for as with that language a traveller may make his way right through the Continent, so with a good knowledge of the Malayan tongue a voyager can make himself understood through the whole of that enormous chain of islands stretching by the equator: beginning with Sumatra, and running right past New Guinea, with the innumerable places north and south.

This language, as is commonly, and probably very reasonably, supposed, took its rise in the seat of the Malayan nation itself; for doubtless tradition is quite right in setting this down as Menang Kabau. This district is opposite to Malacca on the peninsula, and divided from it by the straits of that name. It was at Malacca that the Malays of Menang Kabau first effected a landing, and doubtless gave to it the name which has been corrupted or altered into the one it now bears. The consequence of their migration was that the Orang Benua, as the aborigines of any country are called by the Malays, were driven into the fastnesses of the great jungles and back towards the mountains.

From the fact of the Malayan language being found in the island of Madagascar to the west, and also far away in the many islands of the Pacific, where there is scarcely a spot without its Malay words, some writers have concluded that these people are Polynesian in origin. Others again have thought that the Malays once peopled India, and were afterwards driven out into the countries and islands lying to the east of Hindostan. This, however, seems to be quite a fanciful conclusion, for the languages spoken in India show no trace of Malay words; therefore, in looking at the structure and composition of the language, it is far more reasonable to assume that it naturally had its origin amongst the people who spoke it in the central plains of Sumatra—that is, in or near Menang Kabau, where the Malays have remained less intermixed than in any other part of the peninsula or islands.

When first known to the European, the Malay tongue was considerably leavened with Arabic, Persian, and Sanscrit words, evidently due to a long-continued intercourse with the nations speaking those languages, and, as shown in the last chapter, existing very largely in documents and literary works. For instance, the Malays had from the Arabs, along with their religion, such words as related to the faith and laws of Islam ; and these were regularly imported into the language. So great an impress did this make upon the people, that they gave up the native character, in which their language was expressed in writing, and adopted the Arabic, in which they read the Koran. The Sanscrit and Persian words were probably added to the language by degrees, as the Malays traded with these people : the adoption of certain terms being a natural result.

Being a people who may be said never to have entered on the high road to progressive improvement, their language was never rich, nor did they possess anything worthy the name of literature for which they were not indebted to the Arabs, Persians, Indians, and Javanese, with the exception of a few works of traditional poetry, and a set of historical tales, called the " Sejara Malayu "—these being fictions of a highly-exaggerated character.

The nation may be considered as having been at its zenith in the sixteenth century, when Acheen was in its most prosperous state of wealth ; but even then there seems to have been no one sufficiently advanced above the general body of the people to leave any historical trace of their progress, or any record to show that cultivation of the habit of thought had had existence.

More lately, intercourse with western civilisation and with the Chinese has made its mark upon the Malay tongue by enriching it with many additions; and a more complete dictionary than that which we already possess, both from British and other sources, is greatly to be desired.

It is from the absence of combinations of consonants, and the prevalence of vowels and liquids that the language derives its soft and harmonious effect. Even the gutturals of the words introduced from the Arabic become toned down and pleasing when used by the Malays; and the effect of the harsh Arabic word, when uttered by Malay lips, is very remarkable for the alteration that has been made in its asperities. The purest Malay is said to be spoken at Malacca and Johore, Perak standing next in the scale; and those who have heard it spoken by the chiefs of these places will have had no difficulty in arriving at this conclusion, the dialect of Perak differing but little from that used in Johore.

Rhymes and poetry are in good favour amongst the people; and it is no uncommon thing to find amongst them those who are able to act the part of improvisatore, and extemporise stanzas of no mean order. When the writer has been on excursions far away in the interior, with only Malays for his companions, he has often been struck by the aptness of these people in putting the events of the journey or some adventure into verse, and singing it to one of their plaintive airs, keeping up the ditty in a whining melancholy way, till they fall off to sleep. This love of poetry may have been derived from the Arabs, who greatly esteemed such a style of conveying the thoughts, just as they were lovers of stories, and held in honour the man who was a good narrator. The Malays followed them in this latter, the extempore speaker or composer of verse being highly esteemed.

An example or two of the style of a Malay poem will not be out of place, as exemplifying the peculiar line of thought taken by these people in their verse ; for, as will be seen, the lines take the form of a proverb or aphorism.

> Apa goona passang paleeta
> Kalo teedah dangan soomboonia ?
> Apa goona bermani mata
> Kalo teedah dangan soongoonia ?

> What signifies attempting to light a lamp
> If the wick be wanting ?
> What signifies making love with the eyes
> If nothing in earnest be intended ?

This love of proverbs and ingenious or clever sentences is prominent amongst these people, and as was intimated in the chapter on that subject, is included in their amusements. Many of these sayings have been handed down amongst them as traditions in the language, and could an intelligent Malay be induced to undertake the duty, a collection would be of great interest. On such a thing being mentioned to them, however, they seem to be particularly averse to the proceeding, and we can readily understand how it is that so few records of the past exist, when even an account of the visit of a native ruler to England, which was promised at the time, has not yet seen the light.

Here is another extract from the same author, to exemplify the proverbs of the Malays :

Hearing of a person's death they say—

> Nen matee, matee, nen eedoop be-kraja.
> Kalo sampi-la, janejenia, apa boleh booat ?

> Those who are dead are dead ; those who survive must work.
> If his allotted time was expired, what resource is there ?

The "apa boleh booat" is a very frequent expression of the Malay to signify that the matter was inevitable, and is adopted in all cases of accident, death, or misfortune. It is, in fact, the saying of the fatalist. It was to be ! That is enough for the Malay, who shrugs his shoulders and meets death or misfortune with the same calm resigned aspect.

A dictionary of the language was compiled by Mr. Marsden, from whose pen a grammar also emanated. For this latter, however, there is but little need, on account of the extremely simple construction of the tongue ; though it would be the delight of schoolboys, and would, in their estimation, compare most favourably with the solemn Latin or sonorous Greek, since the verbs have no conjugation, and the nouns no

cases.   Hence, by means of a simple vocabulary, or
a dictionary, combined with conversation with the
natives, a European may render himself a Malay
scholar, and acquire the language sooner than any
that is spoken under the sun.

It would be surprising if a people who have held
so much intercourse with Arabia and Persia did not
possess their amatory poems or songs ; therefore it is
in no way astonishing to find verses breathing tenderness, and veined in some instances with true poetic
feeling. Amongst the pieces that have been preserved,
the following is from Newbold, and however much
the reader may object to the author for his bad taste
in alluding to the crow eating the young rice, when
his native forests teemed with more graceful and
pleasing images, nothing can be more poetical than
the idea in the two last lines :

> Tinggih tinggih poko lamburi
> Sayang puchok-nia meniapu awan
> Habis teloh puwas ku chari
> Bagei punei menchari kawan.

> Bulan trang, bintang ber chay-ya
> Burong Gagah ber-makan padi
> Jeka Tuan tiada per chay-ya,
> Bela dada, melihat hati.

TRANSLATION.

> Lofty, lofty grows the lamburi tree,
> Its branches sweep the clouds;
> It is over, my search is vain ;
> I am like the wild-dove bereft of its mate.

The moon gives her light, the stars glitter,
The crow is eating the young rice ;
If my mistress believeth not my faith,
Lay open my bosom and view my heart.

In these days, too, of drawing-room ballads that
are as empty, vapid, and inane—of course, allowing for
exceptions—as it is possible for them to be, what can
be sweeter than this song from a people whose home
is in the far-off jungles of their Eastern land? It is
taken from Captain Forest's Voyage, as given in the
" Asiatic Journal" of 1825.

Cold is the wind, the rain falls fast,
I linger though the hour is past.
Why come you not? Whence this delay?
Have I offended—say?

My heart is sad, and sinking too ;
Oh break it not! it loves but you.
Come then, and end this long delay.
Why keep you thus away?

The wind is cold, fast falls the rain,
Yet weeping, chiding, I remain.
You come not still, you still delay.
Oh! wherefore can you stay?

Amongst the favourite prose literary productions of
the Malays are their romances, which they derive from
India and Java. From Arabia and Persia naturally
come the various treatises on the Koran, and the
narrative fictions dealing with history and the demi-
gods and heroes of the traditionary past. The

"Hikayet Hamzah" is one that deals with the exploits of the uncle of Mahomet. The "Sejara Malayu" is another favourite piece, which tells of the gallant defence of Malacca by the Malays, when attacked by the Portuguese under Albuquerque, and is intended to rouse them to emulation. The first of these pieces strongly resembles the eastern tales that we have had from the Arabic, only that it is written in a strain of almost greater hyperbole. Chivalry and doughty deeds pervade it throughout, and it is considered one of their greatest compositions.

The "Hikayet Hong Tuah" is said to be of pure Malayan origin, and deals with the romantic adventures of a young noble, or Hong, of Malacca. He was a kind of King Arthur of his time; and, like other romances, it is listened to with great delight by the Malays. The custom is for these stories to be related by the elders or priests of the villages to admiring circles. The "Hong Tuah" has been praised by some writers, condemned by others; but is considered by Newbold to deserve the enthusiastic praise as little as the sweeping censure, being only a fair specimen of its class. There are several more of these *Hikayets,* or compositions—some of which approach the stories of the "Arabian Nights" in their highly-coloured descriptions; and among these is the "Hikayet of Isma Yatim," a story of Hindoo origin. This is a capital specimen of pure Malay language, and remarkable for its introduction of Malay customs.

The language is not wanting, either, in quaint peculiarities, many of which are figurative, while others are terse and to the point; while in many things they reverse our expressions in a manner that sounds to one unaccustomed to the people highly incongruous. Thus, in speaking of cattle or fish, a Malay will say "so many tail"—not head. A spring will be called an eye of water, and a policeman all eyes. The ankle is the eye of the foot; the sun the eye of day. Then as to time, they reckon by nights past instead of days; though this they often judge of by the opening and closing of a flower.

The word *soosa*, trouble, has been mentioned as very commonly used—in fact, it represents the view taken by the people of anything tending towards their advance. They speak of a friend as a place where you can store your cares and joys; of a neighbour, as one privileged to come up the ladder of a hut. In praise of a beautiful woman, a common expression is, not that she has a beautiful face, good figure, or small hands or feet, but that she has heels rounded like the eggs of a bird. The following sounds peculiar, but it is on consideration very apropos—viz. to speak of the metropolis as the mother of a country, for it really is. Regarding the situation of the Malay peninsula on the globe, they divide all countries as being to windward and leeward. Arabia, Persia, and the like are the former; their own peninsula, Sumatra, and Siam, the latter.

It would be out of place here to give many Malayan words and their meanings, but they are very quaint and original in numerous cases. For instance, the word *bunga*, meaning a flower, which is applied in many ways. They will thus speak of interest as the flower of money—the blossom it bears; of ground-rent as the flower of the ground, and so on. It is, however, in their proverbial expressions that the quaintness of the people is most marked. Thus, a cowardly despicable person is called, in allusion to their popular sport—cock-fighting—a duck with spurs. One who is intoxicated is said to mount the green horse. Their proverb with regard to investing, answers to dropping a bucket in the water of a well, and only pulling up the string. When the rain and sunshine come together, they say that some one is coming to a violent end.

There are numbers of similar expressions. They say those who in dry times empty the jar because thunder is heard in the air will probably die of thirst. "Clear water cannot be drawn from a muddy fountain." "A tiger cannot help showing his stripes." "How can a dog's whelp become a civet cat?"

Of treacherous people they have sayings such as—Sits like a cat, but leaps like a tiger; and a capital one of the garrulous person: "The tortoise produces thousands of eggs without anyone knowing it; the hen produces a single egg, and tells all the world."

Letter-writing is looked upon as a fine art, and the

pen used is formed out of the black spike of the gamooty palm. Paper envelopes are used by the inferior people, who wafer them with lac. It is only in the cases of chiefs or sultans that the yellow silk envelope or bag is used, in which the missive is sewn.

A highly-educated person's letter is according to the most rigid form. The introductory portion of the letter, the seals, folding, paper, envelopes, all are matters to be duly studied, and in many cases really are carefully attended to by the person who writes. In fact, according to Newbold, a Malay letter ought to consist of six distinct parts, namely : A short Arabic sentence ; the chop or seal; the exordium ; the substance of the letter; the concluding portion ; and the superscription—for each of which they have special terms. Mingled with the business-like or friendly letter are the *terassuls*, which are the flowery introductions or interpolations so popular amongst certain people—the "May your shadow never be less " type of compliment ; though frequently a letter will be accompanied by a pious prayer that Allah may cause the missive to arrive in safety at its destination.

Among the difficulties of the Malay language is that of getting good interpreters—that is to say men who will give a clear, succinct translation of a Malay speech into English, or *vice versâ*, without flowery additions, or rendering the one or the other at the expense of their clearness and perspicuity. Some very amusing passages take place in consequence of the native interpreter's want of knowledge of the weight and value of a word, and the exact sense in which it is applied. For instance, in one of the courts, when a case was in process of investigation before an English official, a witness, who was a poor shrimper and shell-fisherman, was brought up for examination, when the judge asked :

"What is he ? "

INTERPRETER (*in Malay*). What are you ?

WITNESS (*also in Malay*). Shrimp-catcher.

INTERPRETER (*importantly, in English*). He is an apprehender of shrimps, my lord.

It is hardly fair, though, to take the natives to account for these mistakes in our language, when it is said that amongst the European residents who have spent their days in the Straits, and the descendants of the old settlers who make their appearance on grand days in dress-suits as antiquated as the days of George and William IV., blunders of the most humorous nature are perpetrated from forgetfulness or sheer ignorance of our tongue. Of these, one gentleman is credited with having pleaded, in excuse for not making a longer stay in one of the settlements, that he was only "a bird of paradise," when it is to be presumed " passage " was intended.

CHAPTER XXVIII.

So far but little has been said respecting the ancient
history of the Malay people of Perak; but they have
a history which shows that, in place of being a poor
spiritless body of tribes, they have been, from the
earliest times, a race whose enterprise has been wide-
spreading to a degree.

Crawfurd, in his dictionary of the Indian islands,
says in regard to the Malayan state of Perak, that
when or how it was founded is unknown—"a mystery, like the founding of all the other states of the
peninsula."

Doubtless it is involved in obscurity, and very
little has come down to us by which we can trace its
early history before it became known to Europeans;
but still, some approximation may be made as to
its first colonisation by an inquiry into the rise and
progress of the Malayan race, which is now dominant
there, and in the various native states adjacent.

Now, this race, which is at the present day so widely scattered over the Eastern archipelago that they may be found in the great majority of the islands, while in the others there is frequently a trace of Malay occupation, is believed by some writers to have first had its origin on the Malabar coast of the continent of India ; others, again, who class the Malay as a branch of the great Mongolian or Tartar race, consider that they gradually progressed southward, peopling first the peninsula, and then extending gradually through the many islands of the eastern group.   Others, and among these not a few who have visited Sumatra, Java, and other islands of the archipelago, and, better still for observation, resided for a long time amongst the people themselves, favour the theory adopted by the higher-class Malays—that their parent state was Menang Kabau.

In the sequel we shall see that the views of the last portion of theorists· appear to be most consonant with the past history of the race, who, occupying this portion of the earth's surface from extremely early ages, migrated across the Indian ocean, conveying the productions peculiar to their country, while ever looking to Sumatra as their original home, and to the district of Menang Kabau on that island as the seat of their ancient power.   Crawfurd, who is perhaps our best authority, says that this district is eminently favourable for the development of an early civilisation.

In these early migrations, possible enough to a

maritime people whose vessels were imposing, and who had by experience learned the ease with which a voyage across the Indian ocean could be made, and its return secured by taking advantage of the monsoons, which robbed that voyage of the dread felt by the early navigators that they might never be able to return, the Malays became closely associated with the Arabs, whose connection is so strongly marked in religion and custom to this day; and, consequently, it will be quite in keeping with the character of this work to endeavour to trace out the early intimacy of this latter nation with the countries of the east. In this we are much aided by an examination of the products which the Arabs appear to have been the first to import westward.

About sixteen hundred years before the Christian era we find in Holy Writ that cinnamon was one of the ingredients used in preparing the anointing oil. Now, this cinnamon, or rather kinnamon, is the peculiar growth of India, Ceylon, and the Eastern archipelago; and Herodotus, writing about twelve hundred years later, says Kitto, "describes Arabia as the last inhabited country towards the south, and as the only region of the earth which produces frankincense, myrrh, cinnamon, cassia, and ledanium; and, as to cinnamon, he says: 'Which we, as instructed by the Phœnicians, call kinnamon.' Herodotus, moreover, states that the Arabians were unacquainted with the particular spot in which it was produced, but that

Y

some asserted it grew in the region where Bacchus was educated. From all this we can only infer that it was the product of a distant country—probably India—and that it was obtained by the route of the Red sea."

There appear to have been two kinds of this spice known to the ancients—and even to the present day—as cassia and cinnamon; the former being a coarser product, and known in the Hebrew as *kiddah*; and the latter as *kinnamon*, probably derived, according to Kitto, from the *cacyn-nama*—*dulce-lignum* of the Cingalese—or the Malayan *kayoo-manis*. It is true that cinnamon is now known to the Malays as *koolit-manis*, or sweet skin; but this designation is more probably of later date, as in contrast to *kayoo-manis*, or sweet-wood; and these people still have the *kayoo-pait*, or bitter-wood. The name given to cassia by the Hebrews as *kiddah* is not so easy to determine; for though it may have grown in the country of Keddah, or Quedah, and been obtained originally from thence, it would rather appear that the state of Keddah takes its name from one given by the Malays to an elephant-trap.

Kitto adds, there can be no reasonable doubt, as cinnamon and cassia were known to the Greeks, that they must have been known to the Hebrews also, as the commerce with India can be proved to have been much more ancient than is generally supposed. It is moreover sufficiently clear that the ancient Arabians obtained this spice from the three sources of India,

Ceylon, and the Malay islands; and as we proceed, we shall see that this was not the only product early imported by the Arabians from the far East.

In an able disquisition on a work called the "Periplus of the Erythrean Sea," written probably about the year 129 B.C., Dr. Vincent informs us that perhaps the most ancient record that we possess of a trade between Arabia and the countries of the east is obtained in "Ezekiel;" and this trade, then, must have been carried on before the siege of Tyre, or about 588 B.C. The articles then imported by the Arabians from India and these countries seem to have been gold and spices. But in those days Tyre had the commerce almost entirely in her own hands; excepting during the reign of Solomon, who, though he exacted a tax from the kings and governors of Arabia upon their imports, and shared in the profits of their trade, had not, says Dr. Vincent, any fleets in the Mediterranean, nor commerce on that sea. This circumstance, he adds, gave Tyre a monopoly of the whole communication with the Western world.

The extensive trade which the Arabians had with the East gave them great power and influence, not only upon the Red sea and the north-east coast of Africa, but as far south, upon the eastern coast of that continent, as Cape Corrientes. This trade was at its height long before any visits paid to the Red sea by Greek or Roman; and the chief ports at which their imported produce was received seem to have been

Mosyllon and Point Aromata. So particular was the trade in gums and spices that their productions were, in the markets of Alexandria, always designated by the term " Mosyllitick ; " and probably our term aromatic, as applied to such articles, is derived from the name of the ancient port of Aromata.

In the occupation, however, of the island of Madagascar, and probably of certain ports—though this is not so clear—the Arabs were forestalled by the Malays ; and for this information we are indebted to the researches of Dr. Pickering, among others. This gentleman says, in his " Races of Man," that the Malayan race is actually present upon the island of Madagascar, and dominant there ; and as to the time of their arrival, it is sufficiently evident that Malay influence has preceded the visits of the Arabs.

Some writers have, however, questioned this assertion of the prior occupation of Madagascar by the Malays ; and excellent authorities have, while acknowledging the fact, demurred to the inference sought to be drawn from it of a migration thither of the people of this nation. Let us take, then, the evidence. First, we have upon the island a class of man bearing such clear traces of being a hybrid between the Malay and the Negro, that Dr. Pickering unhesitatingly classifies these people under the title of Malayised Negroes, evidently the same race as the Samangs of the Nicobar islands and the interior of the peninsula. Then, again, if the Madagasci language be taken, we shall find that it contains many words from the Malayan tongue, the Malay numerals being wholly imported into it. For names of places on the island, there are on the east coast—where the Malays would naturally first land — such terms as *Manambatoo, Manam Hari*, &c. ; *batoo* being the Malay for a stone, and *hari* for a day; while the word *manam* is evidently a corruption of the Malay term *anam*, six.

In the etymology of the island itself, says Dr. Vincent, we should rather make our researches in the Malay than in any other language. The Arabs called it the Island of the Moon ; but it was first known to them as Madaster, or Magaster, and it was this name that was the first brought into Europe by Marco Polo, who doubtless had it from the Arabs. *Ma* or *maha*, and *daster* are both Malayan words; but the former would more likely have its origin in the Sanscrit, and the latter in the Persian language. These words might, however, be readily imported into the Malayan tongue from an almost simultaneous intercourse with India and Persia ; which is subsequently confirmed by the visits of the Malays to India and the Persian gulf, for purposes of trade, in conjunction with the Arabs. The Persians themselves were not a maritime people, neither were the inhabitants of India, as compared with the Malays ; while the Arabs themselves would scarcely have borrowed a name from another tongue.

Another thing in favour of the supposition that

Madagascar was peopled by the Malays, and known to have been by the Arabs, is that we find an early Arabian chart in the twelfth century giving the island in question, not as lying on the east coast of Africa, but contiguous to the Straits of Malacca; doubtless from the fact that reports had reached the Arabs of there being Malays upon it, rather than from the supposed error of Ptolemy, in carrying the coast of Africa round to the east. From these points enough evidence may surely be drawn to prove that the Malays held intercourse with, and peopled the island, long prior to any visit paid to it by the Arabs.

In further testimony, however, of the early migration of the Malayan race westward, we have undeniable proof of their adventurous journeys by sea; for, unlike many other eastern nations, they had no religious or other obstacle to prevent their crossing the ocean; the voyages to and fro being made, as suggested, remarkably easy by the regularity of the monsoons. If, then, we recognise this conclusion—one which seems almost forced upon us—it stands to reason that with the Malay came the merchandise of his own land; which in due course fell into the hands of the Arabs, and was by them carried into Arabia, Judea, and parts of Egypt.

We have it recorded distinctly by Pliny, in the first century, that a regular communication was known to be open between Arabia, India, and parts beyond; and that the Arabs, who were established at Ceylon

— then known as Taprobane, and the people as
Singalese, from *singha*, a lion, from a fable of a
king of Ceylon born of a lion—were spreading their
superstitions amongst the natives on the coast, and
were receiving the trade of China (the country of silk)
from the Ceeres, or Chinese, who had reached this
island; and that the father of the Rajah who came on
an embassy to Claudius had been in that island.
Which statement on the old historian's part, shows
that prior to his day an intercourse had existed
between China and Ceylon by way of the sea; and
the route for this trade must have been, as it is at the
present day, by the Straits of Malacca, between the
peninsula and Sumatra, then inhabited by the Malays.

In the second century Ptolemy tells us of a port
on the Coromandel coast of India which was a rendezvous for this trade, and that fleets were fitted out to
sail from thence to the Golden Chersonese — the
modern Malay peninsula. This port was called by
the old geographer Nigama, and is said to correspond
to the position of the modern Negapatam—a place
which bears evident traces of having been an important mart for trade at a very early period. And
the visits there of the Chinese seem amply confirmed
by the remains which they have left, especially one
particular pagoda, which, says Colonel Yule, in his
" Marco Polo," is constructed in a style of architecture
not unlike the Chinese. The trade from this port,
with occasional fluctuations, has continued down to

the present time ; and vessels are still fitted out there for the ancient Aurea Chersonese, not merely to convey the produce of India, but to embark large numbers of emigrants and coolies for our eastern settlements.

But Ptolemy elsewhere refers very definitely to the Aurea Chersonese, and seems clearly to indicate it as the country of the Malays. He mentions in connection with it especially two places, Malai-oo-kolon and Ta-mala. Some geographers have placed the former near the modern Cape Roumania—perhaps the most southern part of Asia—and the latter as far north as the Tenasserim coast of Burmah. If, however, we look a little into the etymology of the word, we shall be rather inclined to agree with Dr. Vincent in assuming that Malai-oo-kolon could be no other than the modern Malacca ; and being, moreover, placed in the neighbourhood of the pirates, who have given a character to the Malays in all ages, adds strongly to the same supposition. The view taken is strongly supported by the etymology of the words *ta mala*, which, without attempting to force a conclusion, can only be associated with *Tanah-malai*, which, literally translated from the Malayan tongue, is the "country of the Malays."

We have here, then, without trying to build up a wild theory, Ta-mala, or the country of the Malays, and Malai-oo-kolon, or Malacca, as probably then their chief city, to which they had doubtless migrated from their primitive home upon the island of Sumatra, then known as Java Minor, and, somewhat later, as Pulo Percha—Pulo being the general name for an island with the Malays; while at this period Singhapura—the modern Singapore—was known, according to different authorities, as Zaba and Sebana, and the state of Perak was probably Ptolemy's Argusa.

Dr. Vincent was quoted a short time back as referring to the Malays of quite ancient times as pirates. This character of the people may need some support; and it is given here, by reference to Yule's " Marco Polo," where we read that—

This character for piracy and adventure the Malays seem steadily to have borne until the year 1267 A.D., when they became so powerful by sea as to fit out a fleet for the invasion of Ceylon, and which they successfully carried out under a leader named Chandra Baun. Marco Polo, who visited Ceylon in the same century, thinks this leader to be the same as Sendeman.

It would be reasonable to assume, in fact, that the Malays, having become more powerful by virtue of this trade with the Arabs in the west, and, in all probability, with the Chinese also in the east, had migrated to Malacca as a convenient *entrepôt* on the high road between China, India, and Arabia. Colonel Yule, however, considers, from the evidence at his command, that Singhapura was rather the first great mart in these seas, and any demur to his statements must be made with great diffidence ; but as he refers

to a place called by Marco Polo *Malai-an*, and of
which, he adds, there is no clear evidence to show
what country or place was really meant, might not
the reference have been to Malacca? for Malai-an
would seem to indicate a place of collection for
Malays. We have certainly this very clear evidence
—that while Malacca on the main bears evident traces
of having, at some remote period, been very largely
peopled, there is not the slightest indication of this in
the island of Singapore; a point which is fully sustained by Crawfurd, who considers that there is
nothing there to support the old traveller De Barros
in speaking of the celebrated old city of Cinghapura,
"to which resort all the navigators of the western
seas of India, and of the eastern of Siam, China,
Champa, and Camboja, as well as the thousands of
islands to the eastward."

Lastly, from Marco Polo we have ample testimony
of the increase in number of the Arabs on the coast of
India, and the dissemination of their doctrines. He
mentions that the trade from China no longer met
that from the Red sea in Ceylon, but on the Malabar
coast, probably at Calicut, where the ships from Aden
obtained their lading from the east, and carried it up
the Red sea for Alexandria, from whence it was taken
into Europe by the Venetians.

Enough has now been said in regard to this trade
between Arabia and the east to show that it existed
from the very earliest times—that it was known in

Egypt and India ; and though we do not gather from the sacred writings that any nations corresponding to the Malays or Chinese took part in this trade, it is not unreasonable to believe that they did, from the frequent reference made to them in the subsequent testimony of the profane writers of the first and second centuries. Were further corroboration necessary, it could be added from the writings of the voyager Cosmas in the sixth century, and from the journals of the Arabian geographers published in the ninth.

CHAPTER XXIX.

A FEW words have now to be said to show that the
Asiatic Malays treated of in this work have, in their
first migration eastward from Sumatra and the district of Menang Kabau, first landed at Malacca.

It has been stated that these people at the present
time all refer to Menang Kabau as their original
home, and the seat of power of their race and nation;
and although there is no written history to confirm
this, we have it on the testimony of their chiefs, both
in Perak and the other states, that such is the case.
Moreover, to this day they treat with veneration and
respect any Rajah who can trace his descent from one
of the leading families of that state. In addition,
Mr. Crawfurd, though he gives up as hopeless all
endeavours to accurately trace the exact locality from
which the Malayan nation sprang, yet admits the fact
of this tradition in the following words :

All the central Malays of the peninsula claim their origin from Sumatra and from Menang Kabo, the most powerful state of that island; but they do not pretend to state the time or the cause of their migration. Some of the states of the interior even call themselves men of Menang Kabo, the chiefs receiving an investiture from that place; indeed, the migration from Menang Kabo to the peninsula, although in driblets, goes on down to the present time. The Malays of Borneo, in like manner with those of the peninsula, claim their descent from the same Menang Kabo.

In further support of this we have the authority of Mr. Braddell, the Attorney-General of the Straits Settlements, a gentleman whose long residence in the country, and intimate knowledge of the language and people, entitles his statement to be received with the greatest respect. He, however, places Singapore as the first seat of Malayan power on the peninsula, and not Malacca. He says, in reference to the singular fact of nine petty governments bordering on Malacca, that it is difficult to understand how these little states, the whole of which, when taken together, do not equal in size one of the recognised modern Malay dominions, should have been established and allowed to remain; and goes on to mention a tradition that soon after the foundation of the first Malay empire at Singapore, by members of the Menang Kabau, family in the twelfth century, a settlement was made in Malacca by a chief who, with his followers, had crossed from Sumatra. These people married the women of the aborigines, and formed a large colony, the people of which were called by the

old Dutch writers Menang Kabowes. Afterwards
they divided into and formed the nine states, or, as
they are called, Nagri Sambilang.

If the view be correct that the first migration
eastward made by the Malays was to Malacca, we
can then understand how the first colonists would,
in accordance with their national habits of government, land under their respective chiefs, spread
themselves in different localities, each chief independent of the others, but all subordinate to the
parent state of Menang Kabau; the fact of their
allegiance to so powerful a state preventing them
from being molested, and enabling them to maintain
their independence amidst the wars and changes
around them—a separate independence, which is a
source of great pride amongst them to the present
day.

We may now pass on to take in rapid review the
intercourse carried on since the days of Marco Polo by
Europeans with the Malays and people of the Eastern
archipelago.

John the Second of Portugal, in the year 1484,
fitted out three ships, and placing them under the
command of Bartholomew Diaz, sent them out with
instructions to try and skirt, and, if possible, circum-
navigate the continent of Africa; and about the same
time he despatched a tried soldier named Covilhan,
who had served in Africa, and was well acquainted
with the Arabic language, to make his way to India

by the route of Egypt and the Red sea. Covilhan learning from the Arabs of the great trade carried on at Calicut, made his way to that port, and also to Goa, which was then a great rendezvous for merchants from all parts.

A few years later, in 1497, Vasco di Gama made his famous voyage from Lisbon, and rounding the Cape of Good Hope sailed up the eastern shores of Africa. He had visited the coast of India, and made port at Calicut, giving to his nation the paramount power of the Indian seas from Malacca to the Cape of Good Hope, a power which was maintained for upwards of a century.

It is worthy of notice in this voyage of Vasco di Gama, that upon his arrival off Mozambique, he states that they were visited by the natives in boats which had sails made of palm. This roused the attention of those on board, who looked upon it as a remarkable circumstance, but their attention was taken in a more significant manner in a few days time, for two men of a superior rank came on board, dressed in garments of cotton, silk, and satin. This was the first infallible token the voyagers round these unknown seas had received of their approach to India, and hope glowed in every heart. The language of their visitors was, however, unknown to them, and the new arrivals could not comprehend either the negro dialect or the Arabic spoken by two of the voyagers, though one of them seemed to have a slight knowledge of the latter tongue.

They conversed, however, with the Portuguese by
signs, and seemed to indicate that in the north they
had seen ships as large as that upon whose deck they
stood.

The point most noticed by these early navigators
was that their visitors were a different race of people
to those of Mozambique, which was at that time under
the government of Quiloa, whose sovereign ruled from
Sofala to Melinda, and over most of the neighbouring
isles.

Now, it seems quite possible that these men of
superior rank, who differed from the people of Mozambique, were Malays.   From their intercourse with
the Chinese, they could easily have been dressed, as
described, in silks; and might either have been
settlers, or merely there as the result of one of their
commercial voyages across the Indian ocean.

Later on—in 1503 or 1504—Benthema gives a
description of his hazardous voyage, and of his
having proceeded from Borneo to Java, and from
thence on to Calicut, at which port he arrived in
1506, just seven years before the Portuguese reached
Malacca.   This writer says that the people of India
were then no seamen, but entrusted their navigation
to foreign sailors, " who were Mahomedans."   Here,
again, there seems little doubt but that these people
were Malays, who to this day are the Lascars of the
native vessels navigating the Eastern seas.   He also
relates, respecting Calicut, there were then about

fifteen thousand Arabs there, who also abounded in Ceylon and on the Coromandel coast.

About this time the port of Goa having become of considerable importance from its trade, and from its being the rendezvous for the Mahomedans who came from all parts of India and Ceylon to embark for Jeddah, to make their pilgrimage to Mecca, the Portuguese had determined to occupy it, and it was taken by Albuquerque in 1510, was recovered by the Mahomedans the same year, and finally retaken by the Portuguese in 1511.

In 1513 we arrive at very distinct and important statements respecting the Malay peninsula ; for King Emmanuel, of Portugal, thinking it to be his duty, writes to inform the Pope of his successes in India, and tells him how the Portuguese general, Albuquerque, had sailed to the Aurea Chersonese, called by the natives Malacca. He had found it an enormous city of twenty-five thousand houses, and abounding in spices, gold, pearls, and precious stones. This city he had attacked twice ; taken, slaughtered the *Moors*, sacked it, and finally burnt the place. The king, who fought upon an elephant, was wounded badly and fled. After this the general built a fortress at the mouth of the river flowing through the city, making the walls fifteen feet thick, and using for the purpose the stones taken from the ruined mosques. At that time there were many foreign merchants at Malacca, including those from Sumatra, Pegu, Java ? (Ja'aes), Gores, and the

z

extreme east of China. Great store was obtained from
the people by the conquerors; and upon hearing of
the fall of the city the king of Ansiam—meaning Siam,
called by the historian the most powerful monarch
of the east, from whom Malacca had been usurped by
the Moors—sent a golden cup, with a carbuncle and a
sword inlaid with gold, as a token of his friendly
feeling towards the conquerors.   In return, Albuquerque sent some of his ablest men with presents,
and instructions to explore the country for the benefit
of their faith.

Here then we have distinct proofs of the wealth,
power, and size of Malacca in the sixteenth century,
and allusion to its former position under the king of
Siam—a condition that has not been unfrequent with
Malay states; instances being quite lately given of the
paying of tribute to the Siamese, who exact the gold
and silver flowers mentioned as of such exquisite
filigree work in an earlier chapter.   The statement as
to the size of Malacca is quite possible, though the old
historian may have exaggerated; but at the present
day there is every trace of the city having once been
of great extent, while the eastern houses are of such
a slight character that a conflagration would sweep
an enormous number away.

In 1589, less than one year after the defeat of the
Spanish Armada, a body of English merchants sent a
memorial in to the queen, asking for permission to
send ships to trade with India and examine the

Portuguese settlements, with their occupations of
Malacca and certain islands of the archipelago. They
pointed out that there were a number of important
places that might be visited with advantage by English
ships. The queen, who was ever alive to the interests
of commerce, and ready to give the weight of her
authority, granted the petition, and three vessels sailed
in 1591, under the command of Captain George
Raymond. Hakluyt gives an account of this expedition, taken from the lips of Edward Barker, the
lieutenant of the voyage. Purchas gives another
account, derived from the purser, and other writers
have dealt with the subject; but all agree that the
vessels were overtaken by a storm and separated, that
the captain was never heard of again, and that after
many extraordinary adventures—extraordinary then,
but matters of course to-day—the voyage was accomplished by Master James Lancaster. The ad-
venturers were disappointed in their speculation, but
the knowledge obtained of the feasibility of the scheme
encouraged others to make the attempt. This it is
stated, by more than one authority, was the first
English voyage to the East Indies. Accounts, however, of two previous voyages are to be found in
Purchas and Hakluyt—one having been undertaken
in 1579 by Thomas Stephens, and another in 1583
by Ralph—wherein the then novel accounts of the
peoples they encountered, with their trade, manners,
and customs are carefully described.

The next voyage to the east of which there is any
account is that of Captain Benjamin Wood, in 1596—
a voyage that turned out to be most unfortunate.
Three ships were fitted out, mostly at the charge of
Sir Robert Dudley, and sailed from England the
bearers of Queen Elizabeth's letter to the emperor of
China; but this attempt to open up trade with the
east failed, for not one of the company ever returned
to give an account of the fate that befel the rest.   It
is a quaint specimen of the *naïveté* and simplicity of
the times that the letter borne by the little fleet recommended two merchants of London to the emperor,
and vouched for the probity of their dealings; at the
same time offering protection to any of the Chinese if
they liked to come and open a trade to any port in
Her Majesty's dominions.

By the year 1600, the Portuguese, into whose
hands had fallen the major part of the commerce in
the Straits of Malacca, now carried on a great trade
at Arracan in Pegu, Siam, Tenasserim, Quedah, and
other states in the peninsula.   Sumatra was at that
time divided into so many separate kingdoms, the
most important of which was Acheen—the state that
has of late given so much trouble to the Dutch.   The
king of this state besieged the Portuguese more than
once in their stronghold of Malacca, sending an
" expedition of more than five hundred sail, one hundred of which were of greater size than any then
constructed in Europe, and the warriors or mariners

which it bore amounted to sixty thousand, commanded in person by the king."

The king of Acheen is described by Captain Best,
who voyaged there in 1613, as being—

A proper gallant man of warre; of thirty-two years; of middle
size; full of spirit; strong by sea and land; his country populous;
his elephants many, whereof we saw 160 or 180 at a time. His
gallies and frigates carry in them very good brasse ordnance, demi-
cannon, culverine, sakar, minion, &c. His building is stately and
spacious, though not strong; his court at Acheen pleasant, having
a goodly branch of the main river about and through his palace,
which branch he cut and brought six or eight mile off in twenty
days, while we continued at Acheen.

He desired the captain, whom he had called
Orang-Kaya-Puteh, or white lord, to commend him
to the king of England, and to entreat him to send
him two white women for his wives, saying that if he
had a son he would make him king of the coast from
whence the English fetched their pepper, so that they
should go no more to Calicut, but to their own
English king, for their commodities.

The narrative goes on to say: " Wee all this while
dranke tobacco in a silver pipe given by his women,
which are in a close roome behind him "—giving an
accurate account of the custom observed in an ordinary Malay house to this day. Captain Best, however, does not speak very highly of the people he
encountered, saying that with their king they were
griping, base, and covetous; that the trade was bad;

and that any ship going to Acheen should be furnished
with some one who could speak Malay.

It should, however, in fairness to this monarch, be
said that, when visited at a somewhat earlier date by
Captain Lancaster, " at an audience to take leave, the
king said to him : 'Have you the Psalms of David
among you ?' The captain answered : 'Yea, and we
sing them daily.' Then said the king : 'I and the
rest of these nobles about me will sing a psalm to God
for your prosperity ;' and so they did very solemnly ;
and after it was ended the king said : 'I would have
you sing another psalm, although in your own language ;' so there being in the company some twelve
of us, we sang another psalm ; and after the psalm
ended, we took leave, the king desiring God to bless
us on our journey, and to guide us safely into our
own country."

We find, too, about this time, the first mention of
Johore, or, as it was called, Jhor, and Perak. The
Portuguese had another powerful enemy in the king
of the former country, who had formed a close alliance
with the king of Acheen by marrying his sister.
These kings united their forces in their attacks upon
Malacca, but were each time heroically repulsed by
what was, as compared to their own men, a mere
handful of Portuguese. These latter had, however, an
ally in the king of Perak, then a very powerful and
wealthy state, to which many ships resorted for trade.
On one occasion, in 1813, as related by Captain Best,

the Shahbandar of Acheen had gone on an expedition
to this country, but had been driven from Perak by
the Portuguese, and as this officer had set off without
the knowledge of the king of Acheen, the latter con-
fiscated the Shahbandar's state, making excuse that
he had gone to Perak, the home of his enemies.

Perak is again spoken of in the instructions given
by the East India Company to their factor, John
Jourdain, in 1614, where, in giving a list of the
places for trade in the east, it is mentioned in connection with several better-known places, such as
Bengala, Pegu, and the Coromandel coast, and with
Malacca and Patani, both states of the peninsula;
while later on, when it was conquered by the
Acheenese, Perak is stated to have been possessed of
" much wealth."

The Portuguese were, in the face of these powerful
native enemies, whom, by their crusades against
Mahomedanism, they had converted into the most
bitter opponents, unable to maintain their position
for any great length of time in these seas; besides
which they had to contend against the jealous hatred
of the Dutch, who, readily gaining the friendship and
aid of these native princes against the Portuguese,
besieged them in Malacca in the year 1606 and 1608 ;
but though repulsed with loss on both occasions, in
the year 1641, after a blockade of nine months'
duration, the town fell into the hands of the Dutch,
and this was followed by the downfall of Portuguese

influence in the archipelago, after an occupation of one
hundred and thirty years.

It was while the Dutch were in possession of
Malacca, and, saving for the piracies, comparative
peace reigned in the archipelago, that M. De la Loubere
was despatched by the French king as Envoy extraordinary to the king of Siam, and his account of his
voyage, which is a most ably written narrative, was
afterwards published in France, and translated into
English in 1693. So important a country as the
Malay peninsula, lying contingent to Siam, of course
did not elude his notice, and in describing it he
says :

> In fine, the mountains which lie on the common frontiers of Ava,
> Pegu, and Siam, gradually decreasing as they extend to the south,
> do form the peninsula of India *extra Gangem*, which, terminating
> at the city of Sincapura, separates the gulfs of Siam and Bengala,
> and which, with the island of Sumatra, form the famous Strait of
> Malacca, or Sincapura. Several rivers defile from every part of
> these mountains into the gulfs of Siam and Bengala, and render
> their coasts habitable. Opposite to Camboya, viz. in the peninsula
> *extra Gangem*, which lies on the west of the gulf of Siam, the
> gulf of Siam extends to Quedah and Patana—the territories of the
> Malayans, of which Malacca was formerly the metropolis.

In describing the boundaries of Siam, and
enumerating its provinces at that time, he includes
Jor (Johore), and Patani, going on to say that
"the governor of Jor renders obedience to the king
of Siam no longer, the Portuguese having given him
the title of king; and it may be he never intends to

obey, unless the kingdom of Siam should extend itself as relations declare, to the whole peninsula *extra Gangem.* Jor is the most southern city thereof, seated on a river which has its mouth at the cape of Sincapura, and which forms a most excellent port."

Furthermore, he says, in describing the peninsula state, Patani:

> The people of Patana live like those of Acheen in the island of Sumatra, under the domination of a woman, whom they always elect in the same family, and always old, to the end that she may have no occasion to marry, and in the house of whom the most trusty persons do rule. The Portuguese have likewise given her the title of queen, and for tribute she sends to the king of Siam every three years two small trees, the one of gold and the other of silver, and both loaded with flowers and fruits; but she owes not any assistance to this prince in his wars. Whether these gold and silver trees are a real homage, or only a respect to maintain the liberty of commerce, as the king of Siam sends presents every three years to the king of China, in consideration of trade only, I cannot allege: but as the king of China honours himself with these sort of presents, and takes them for a kind of homage, it may well be that the king of Siam does, not less value himself in the presents he receives from the queen-of Patana, although she be not perhaps his vassal.

This gold and silver flower is the *bunga amas*, given by some native states to the king of Siam to this day as an evidence of tributary allegiance.

In De la Loubere's book is a quaint but very correct map of the Malayan peninsula, prepared by M. Cassini, the Director of the Observatory of Paris in 1668, from which is gathered the fact that Perak then continued to be looked upon as second only to

Malacca on the western coast. The river Perak is not very correct in its representation, being made more to resemble a tidal creek. This is doubtless due to the information received that the rivers to the north joined the Perak, which, in the case of the Juramas and the Bruas is very nearly correct.

Perak has always maintained an independent position, and has exhibited great pride of authority. After the defeat of the Portuguese, however, it was overrun by the Acheenese; and its inhabitants were carried away by thousands to repeople that part of Sumatra after the many sanguinary wars in which the Malayan kings of the state had been engaged. Later on, as the power of the Acheen sovereigns was on the decline, Perak again began to assert a powerful independence, and was treated by the Dutch as a state of some considerable importance during the whole of their occupation of Malacca. Evil times however were in store for the country, and in the year 1818 it was attacked by a very large, force from the state of Quedah, to the north, with which it had always been on friendly terms. But the rajah of Quedah, being a tributary of the king of Siam, and Perak refusing to own all such allegiance, the rajah of Quedah was ordered to invade the country, and punish its Sultan for his contumacy. From this date it is stated that the chiefs of Perak have always resided on the left bank of the river.

The Siamese retained control over the country for

only four years, when the people of Perak formed an alliance with Rajah Ibrahim, the powerful and warlike chief of Salangore, by whose aid the Siamese authority was overthrown in 1822. A few years later a treaty on behalf of Perak was made by the English—now established in Malacca—with the king of Siam, which provided that the country should be governed by the Sultan according to his own will, and the British power bound itself to protect Perak from attack on the side of either Siam or Salangore ; but if the Perak Sultan chose to send his tribute—gold and silver flowers—to the King as of old, no interference was to take place on the part of the English to prevent him.

Since then Perak has been in a state of chronic anarchy and confusion, extending back for some time, caused principally by disunion among the chiefs. This culminated during the last few years in a disturbance foreign really to the state, though it was of such extent that the chiefs were necessarily mixed up with it. For years past large numbers of the Chinese had made their way into the country, pursuing various industries—becoming wood-cutters, charcoal and lime-burners, gold-miners, and traders ; but the bulk were employed at the tin mines of Laroot, where, after various displays of petty jealousy, open warfare was commenced between two rival factions of these people.

CHAPTER XXX.

LAROOT, which has been so frequently mentioned in
these pages as the district in the north of Perak, has
been for some time ruled over by an officer or chief
known as the Muntri of Laroot, or, as it should be
more correctly, the Muntri of Perak ; but his power
had of late become so great, and his connection with
the district in question so fully acknowledged, that he
was almost invariably spoken of as the chief of the
subsidiary place.

The late Muntri is the son of one Inchi Long
Jaafar, an enterprising man, who, prior to 1855, was
appointed by the then reigning sultan of Perak to
take charge of the Laroot district, which at that time
was limited to the river and the mines. He bore no
title, being a mere trader, whose dealings were with
the then small colony of Chinese miners who had
settled in the place ; but by his keen management he

soon became a person of some importance. His duties were appointed by the Sultan, and no doubt he had to receive the greater part of the revenues of Laroot; his appointment being endorsed by every successive Sultan. These revenues were the tithes of the rice cultivation of the district, and later on, the tax or royalty on the tin that was smelted, so that in time his privilege became very valuable, especially as for some reason the district had its borders largely augmented towards the south, and fresh Chinese were constantly arriving to increase the workings, and of course the produce of the tin.

The Sultans being careless, indolent men, and it is believed unwilling to take the management of an extensive district, now inhabited by large numbers of Chinese, who were of a very factious nature, Inchi Jaafar would have very little difficulty in keeping them in ignorance of the vast revenue he was gradually receiving; and kept them satisfied by means of large presents given to them from time to time as tribute; so that he rapidly grew in power, wealth, and position as ruler over this enormously rich district, and, it seems, kept the Chinese miners in a good state of subjugation till his death, when he was succeeded by his son.

The Chinese, being a clannish people, were divided in Laroot into two parties, namely a body of Macao men, of four districts, and one of Keh Chinese, of five districts, the two parties being known as the See Kwan and the

Go Kwan; and between these rival factions a serious
outbreak took place soon after the death of Jaafar.
This ruler had held a nominal command over the
people, siding with neither faction; but as they
rapidly increased in numbers, and the disturbances
arose, the present chief, Nga Ibrahim, lost control
over them, and his power was set at naught.

At first during this period, the chief was merely in
correspondence spoken of as Nga Ibrahim, but shortly
after the Sultan promoted him to the high rank of one
of his four chief officers, making him Muntri of Perak ;
and before long he was practically acknowledged to be
the independent ruler of the district between the rivers
Krean on the north, and Bruas on the south. His
political management was clever, for on the outbreak
of the great quarrel between the Chinese, when the
two parties were quite beyond his control, he joined
one of the rival factions, and aided it by throwing the
Malay influence into the scale, thus reducing the other
párty to submission.

This was in 1862, and was, not taking into consideration minor quarrels, the commencement of the
disturbances in Laroot. After the fight, one of the
leaders of the defeated party, who was a British subject, raised a complaint to our Representative concerning the destruction of his property at the mines ; and
the result of this was that his cause was espoused by
our Government, and a claim made by General
Cavenagh upon the Sultan for compensation to the

defeated party to the amount of seventeen thousand dollars. This was enforced by a blockade of the Laroot river by a British man-of-war. The Sultan replied that this money ought to be paid by the ruler of Laroot ; and by him the indemnity was found. It is considered that the title of Muntri was bestowed upon him for supplying this large sum—but at all events the honour was conferred; and subsequently Laroot became one government, and the Muntri enjoyed the revenues of the country, whose inhabitants so increased that at the end of 1871 the Chinese mining population was estimated at forty thousand, and the value of the tin annually exported was somewhere about a million of dollars.

With the increasing strength of the Chinese, that of the Muntri began to fail. They made demands of him which he yielded; for principally through the fact of having sided with one party, he could not maintain his prominent position as ruler over both ; and so it was that, though he was able to exact the regular royalty paid to him on tin, the Chinese refused to pay to him the revenues obtained through the gambling farm on which he had levied dues, and also that which had accrued to him from the sale of their favourite drug opium. Further signs of contempt for the Muntri's power too were being shown ; for one of the great sugar-planters who rented the farms of the Krean district refused to pay his rent, alleging that the amounts were due to the Sultan, and not to the

Muntri, whom he treated as a subordinate officer, and not as the ruler of the district.

Soon after—that is in the beginning of 1872—fresh quarrels arose between the rival Chinese factions, whose position had now altered so that the defeated party had grown the stronger ; and consequently the Muntri threw over his former allies, and sided with his old enemies, with the result that the conquerors of the preceding fight were beaten, and literally driven out of the country.

Rumours of these fights reached England ; but it is probably not known what sanguinary engagements they were, inasmuch as they were looked upon as the petty riots of some Chinese, in an out-of-the-way part of the world. But this is far from being a correct idea of their extent. The Chinese are a busy, industrious people, and, when in small numbers, are glad to obtain the protection of the Malay chiefs ; but as soon as they are in sufficient strength, they display a disposition to set that power at defiance, refusing to acknowledge their rule over the mines, and declining to pay the revenues ; but having no control over the rivers by which they carry off their metallic produce, they pay the royalties here to the Malay chiefs who live on the banks and hold the stream under their control. In their quarrels the Chinese run to great excesses, and the disturbances between rival tribes arise from small matters—a squabble between two boys, or some case of petty jealousy—when the whole party on either side will be drawn into the ensuing fight.

In the autumn of 1872 the Go Kwans who had been expelled, and had spent their time in warlike preparations, made an effort to regain their position. Arms and ammunition were sent up the Laroot river, and at last a desperate attack was made upon the faction in possession of the mines. The engagement seems to have been most sanguinary; three thousand Chinamen are said to have lost their lives. The way of retreat was strewn with dead bodies; and great numbers of fugitives, many of whom were wounded, made their way to Penang, while the conquerors installed themselves at the mines. The Muntri again espoused the cause of the victorious party, which was strongly aided by the Chinese merchants in various parts, who equipped junks, and furnished the sinews of war; but so little was this state of affairs appreciated by the more wealthy and thoughtful Chinamen, that one leading man is reported to have said : " When the British flag is seen over Perak or Laroot, every Chinaman will go down on his knees and bless God ! "

In this latter disturbance fighting men were recruited from China ; while on the side of the Muntri, and for the preservation of law and order, the Chief of Police in the district, Captain Speedy, with one hundred men, went to his aid ; but on the whole the effect produced was not very great, for in spite of the moral support of the Government and the

2 A

aid of Captain Speedy's trained men, the Muntri's
enemies could not be driven from the country ; while,
being short of provisions, they took to sending out
large row-boats to forage. But from this they gradually
took to genuine piracy; till, in 1873, they were attacking everything that came in their way, and committing
such atrocities that finally the Government was forced
to seriously interfere.

Prior to this, though, attempts had been made
to settle the difficulties; for in September, 1873,
H.M.S. *Thalia* and *Midge* proceeded to the scene of
these piracies, and sailing up the Laroot river, were
fired upon by the pirates, and, after various little
encounters, proceeded to attack the powerful stockade
which defended the stream, in company with well-
manned row-boats; the enemy firing from muskets, and
also sending rounds of grape from their larger guns.
The engagement was continued for some time, when
our forces were drawn off, the stockade not having
been destroyed, though great loss was inflicted upon
the enemy, ours being confined to two sub-lieutenants
dangerously wounded.

This gross insult to our flag demanded immediate
action; and a few days later H.M.S. *Midge*, in company with the boats of the *Thalia*, ascended the river,
where they were soon within reach of the pirates,
who received them with the fire of three large war-
junks and that of a strong stockade.   Our forces were
not long in replying, and soon after the boats dashed

in ; the junks were boarded, and the stockade carried, with very little loss to ourselves; while finally the junks and a second stockade were totally destroyed.

The Chinese were well armed, mounting, as they did, some five-and-twenty guns, though of small calibre, and having plenty of Snider rifles. They however were very severely punished, and the town of Laroot surrendered unconditionally, with nearly four thousand men ; and the report of the officers in command stated that everything was done for the relief of the enemy's wounded; while, as a specimen of the fighting powers of these Chinese pirates as opposed to our seamen and marines, our losses were only two men wounded, as in the previous action.

This was a severe lesson to the piratical party, but it proved impossible to capture their swift row-boats, which evaded pursuit in the various creeks with which the coast here is intersected ; and soon after the departure of the men-of-war the action of the Chinese became bolder and more serious than ever, while the fighting was renewed.

Such being the state of the country, steps were absolutely necessary on the part of the Government to prevent the contagion from spreading to our own Settlements, especially to Penang and Singapore, where the Chinese had many sympathisers, and from whence the rival tribes were frequently receiving supplies of men, arms, and ammunition ; the result being constant attacks upon defenceless trading-boats

passing up and down the Straits.   In fact, these Straits
—notorious for their Malay piracies—were now gaining an evil name for those perpetrated by the subjects
of the Celestial Empire.   To so great an extent were
these proceedings carried, that attacks were planned
and carried out upon our own isolated police stations,
and notably upon the light-keeper and his party at
the lighthouse at Cape Rachado.

This being the state of affairs on the accession of
Sir Andrew Clarke to the governorship in November,
1873, he proceeded to try and obtain a settlement of
the disturbances by dealing personally with the
matter, and procuring a general peace in the troubled
districts ; for it was believed that the Chinese factions,
whose fighting had degenerated from a little war into
open piracy, must have now suffered to such an
extent as to be willing to make terms for the general
and peaceable occupation of the mines, "if they
could be relieved from the complications arising out
of their alliances with the contending Malay parties ;"
for at this time influence on the part of ex-Sultan
Ismail was being brought to bear against the Muntri
of Laroot, who had grown too powerful and rich to
give satisfaction to the princes of the country, of
which his was, after all, but a division.

To further these arrangements the Governor
decided to go from Singapore to Perak, to discuss
the troubles with the Perak chiefs ; but first it
was necessary that all fighting should cease.

Mr. Pickering, one of our officers, who, from his intimate knowledge of the Chinese language and customs, had obtained great influence with the Chinese of the Settlements, was then sent to Penang, where he conferred with the head men, to find out whether they were willing to come to terms with each other, disarm, and let the arbitration of their disputes be arranged by Government. Mr. Pickering succeeded most fully. The head men agreed to leave their differences to be settled by the Governor, and to give up their arms. Whereupon Captain Dunlop and the writer were despatched to carry out the disarmament, and receive all arms and row-boats, and at the same time to obtain such information as was possible respecting the dispute then existing amongst the Perak chiefs, as to the right of succession to the country. After some difficulties this was done, and the chiefs of Perak, and the leading men of the Chinese, met the Governor at the Dindings, where, as regarded the preservation of peace in Perak itself, it was decided that the Rajah Muda Abdullah should become Sultan, and in spite of his vacillating behaviour with the Chinese, it was thought better in the interests of peace that the Muntri's appointment should be ratified as governor of Laroot, and these arrangements were made to the exclusion of Ismail, with the full assent of the Perak chiefs.

In dealing with the Chinese difficulty the rivers were searched in pursuit of row-boats and arms;

among the guns taken being a Krupp. A number of
women and children, who were kept in a state of
slavery, were searched for, so as to set them at liberty,
which was subsequently done; and the leading Chinese,
many of whom were men of property, bound themselves over to preserve peace towards each other and
towards the Malays, in a penalty of fifty thousand
dollars, and furthermore undertook to disarm and
destroy all their stockades. For the further settlement of all difficulties, three officers were appointed,
with the full consent of the Sultan, to settle all points
of disagreement with respect to the mines, and who
were to discover and set free the women and children ;
the Chinese agreeing to accept the decisions of these
officers as final.

Following upon this, the result of the discussion,
and the feeling of the Malay chiefs that they could not
of themselves deal with the Chinese immigrants, was
that the Sultan Abdullah requested the Governor to
appoint Residents in the country. This, with the full
consent of the native princes, was done ; a Resident
being appointed at the Sultan's court at Perak, and an
Assistant-resident at Laroot ; the expenses connected
with which appointments were to be borne out of
the revenue of the state. The two Residents were
Mr. J. W. W. Birch and Captain Speedy ; the former
taking up his abode at Banda Baru, and the latter
as Assistant-resident at Laroot. Their duties were to

advise the respective rulers in matters of revenue, and
those of a judicial character especially. Mr. Birch was
a man of great experience and knowledge of the people,
and had held high administrative and judicial offices
at Ceylon and Singapore ; and, had he lived, would
have greatly added to the development and prosperity
of Perak. Captain Speedy had been busily engaged,
with the hundred trained men under his command, in
assisting, as Chief of the Police, in putting down the
disturbances on the Laroot river—boarding junks,
making seizures, and the like, and acting generally
on the side of law and order on behalf of the Muntri
of the country. This officer's position now as a
partisan chief of armed men being no longer tenable
in Laroot, and the necessity for the disposal of his
body of fighting men having arisen, he was formally
appointed the Assistant-resident, and his men discharged and re-enlisted as the Resident's Guard. For
it was considered that this officer, being held in high
respect by both the Malays and the Chinese, would—
now that he was freed from all engagements with the
Muntri, and acting under government — become a
power, from his knowledge and his influence with the
above chief, in the pacification and management
this part of the country.

These arrangements having been made, all that
was now necessary was to send back the disarmed
men and boats to Laroot, towed by two steamers ; and

the miners, satisfied of the peace that was in future to reign, returned cheerfully to their avocations at the mines.

In this way, then, was a serious chain of outbreaks —begun by the Chinese, but with which the Malay chiefs had gradually embroiled themselves—on the disputed question of the right of succession and the position of the Muntri of Laroot, brought to an end ; while, had the new Sultan proved, in his fresh career, equal to the opinions formed respecting him by Sir Andrew Clarke, when only Rajah Muda, or next in succession, a career of prosperity would have begun for the country, in place of the troubles which subsequently had place.

CHAPTER XXXI.

THE engagement made with the chiefs, as described in the last chapter, was signed on January 20th, 1874, and was called the Pangkore Treaty, and among the arrangements embraced by it, the acting Sultan Ismail was allowed to retain the title of Sultan Muda only, and had a pension and a certain small territory assigned to him suitable to his position as ex-Sultan. The rest of the treaty was taken up with questions of boundary, the payment of the Residents, the appointment of native officers, and matters of revenue and the collection thereof.

The ex-Sultan Ismail was deposed, but he had only been intended, it seems, to be a temporary occupant of the throne on the death of the late Sultan ; for he was not of the blood-royal, and his only claim to the position was that he had married into the royal family, and when placed in the ruling seat he was kept there by intrigue. He had occupied important positions during

the past two reigns, and from his high office and
age seemed to be a suitable man for temporarily
occupying the throne ; while once there, as he interfered scarcely at all with the matters of government,
living a retired life far up the country on the Perak
river, it is probable that the principal chiefs wished to
keep matters as they were, and therefore resisted the
claims of the Rajah Muda Abdullah, to the disturbance
of the state.

These difficulties it was the Governor's aim to end,
and after his discussion with the chiefs wherein it
was elicited that the claims of Ismail were not good,
and that his position as sultan would, if continued,
lead to the continuance of the troubled state of the
country, proceedings went on for the confirmation
of the Rajah Muda Abdullah as sultan of Perak ; and
here it will be interesting to the reader to have the
portion of the discussion relating to this matter as
given by Mr. Braddell, the Attorney-General of the
Straits Settlements, in his report of the proceedings
at Perak and Laroot on the occasion of the Governor's
visit.

The Governor then asked all present: If the Rajah Muda accepts
the Sultanship, are there enough great men of the country present
to confirm him ? To which there appeared to be a general assent ;
but the Muntri fenced, and at last, on being pressed, he said I
think there are enough, if the Rajah Muda thinks he ought to be
made Sultan. ·

The Governor then addressed the whole assembly and intreated
them to state if there was any objection to the Rajah Muda as

Sultan, and did they know of any other person who should be installed? The Muntri said, whatever the Bandahara says, I am bound to obey.

The GOVERNOR. But tell me your own opinion.

The MUNTRI. The proper thing would be to inquire of all the inhabitants of the country.

The GOVERNOR. Have you ever heard of the people (ryots) being consulted in a Malay country as to who is to be king?

The MUNTRI. When Ismail was chosen the people were there, and, I suppose, took a part in the business. (This, however, was denied by the other chiefs.)

At this time the Laksamana arrived, and took his place.

The GOVERNOR. What would become of Ismail if the Rajah Muda is made Sultan?

The Muntri said he did not know; but the Laksamana said, in times gone by there had been ex-Sultans, called Sultan Muda, as the present Rajah Muda's grandfather was, and Ismail might have a revenue, and a small district to govern as Sultan Muda.

The GOVERNOR. What ceremonies should be performed for the installation of the Rajah Muda as Sultan?

The LAKSAMANA. He should be crowned at Banda, in the Perak river; and even if some of the great men were not present, it would suffice if the Bandahara and Rajah Muda were present.

On this the Governor asked all: Are you ready to have the questions as to Ismail and the Rajah Muda settled now?

The LAKSAMANA. How about those who are not here?

The GOVERNOR. This point has already been discussed. Are you yourself willing to give your adhesion to the Rajah Muda as Sultan?

The LAKSAMANA. Individually, yes.

The BANDAHARA. Yes.

RAJA OSMAN. Yes.

RAJA ABBAS. Yes.

The MUNTRI. If the people like it I have no place, I of course follow them.

The TUMONGONG. I follow the course of the Bandahara.

The DATOH GAPAR. Same as Tumongong.

The MAKOTAH.   I follow the Bandahara.

The DATOH ROUAH.   Yes.

The SHAHBANDAR.   I will follow the Raja Muda.

Hajee Hussain and Hajee Mohamed Syed and five others all agreed.

The GOVERNOR.   Does Ismail take any interest in the government of the country ?

The BANDAHARA.   He lives a retired life.

The Governor then said that what they had been discussing would form the subject of a treaty, and asked them to name deputies to attend for them.

All agreed.

The following were then chosen : Rajah Muda, Bandahara, Laksamana, Muntri, and Shahbandar ; and at the request of the Muntri, his friend the Tumongong was added.

The Muntri, on being asked to state anything he might have in his mind, said : "As to the succession I have nothing further to say."

On this, sireh and tea was served, and the conference broke up.

Great expectations were formed of the result of this Pangkore treaty ; but shortly after Mr. Birch had taken up his residence in Perak, troubles began ; for the Governor was soon obliged to write to the Sultan, complaining of his not taking the advice of the Resident, and calling him to account for breaking the solemn promises he had made.   In fact, it seems that, from the first, great dissatisfaction was felt by both the Sultan and chiefs who had signed, and they objected strongly to Mr. Birch's plans for collecting the revenue.   Later on, a full and comprehensive scheme for this purpose was laid before the Sultan— one that had the approval of the Governor—but it found no favour with the ruler and chiefs of Perak.

In fact, Mr. Birch soon found that he had a task of a most onerous nature in dealing with a man whom he describes as being eminently silly and foolish, and one who indulged largely in opium. He could hardly ever be kept to a subject for any time when on questions of great import to the state, but was, with childish vanity, constantly asking questions and drawing attention to his dress. In short, he was a weak sensual man, whose sole thoughts were devoted to his own gratification when not taken up by trifling matters of the time.

At the end of a year—namely in January, 1875—Mr. Birch was so out of favour with the Sultan that the latter wrote to ex-Sultan Ismail not to sign the Pangkore treaty, lest it should strengthen the Resident's authority in Perak. In fact, on other occasions, the Sultan showed a disposition to take part with his old opponent Ismail against the Resident; and as time wore on, ominous little signs began to tell of the coming of mischief. The Maharajah Lela, a powerful chief, began to erect a strong stockade round his house at Passir Sala. The Muntri of Laroot took precautions for the safety of his family by removing them from Durian Sabatang to Laroot; while in many other instances little clouds began to form, indicative of the coming storm.

At last, in April, Sir Andrew Clarke wrote another letter to the Sultan, reproving him for his resistance to the reforms proposed by Mr. Birch, and telling him

that he was breaking the Pangkore treaty. At the
same time he enclosed a proclamation under his own
hand, which warned all men against collecting the
revenue in any form excepting only such as were appointed by the Resident. Soon after this the Sultan
sent to the Governor at Singapore, making complaints
against Mr. Birch, so as to get him removed from the
Residency ; but Sir Andrew Clarke declined to interfere, as he was leaving the Straits. This letter not
succeeding, and being still more embittered against
the Resident, who was pressing him to sign certain
papers in connection with his scheme of taxation, it
seems that the Sultan called together his chiefs at
Durian Sabatang; and it is believed that at that time it
was decided to kill Mr. Birch, and, by a combination
of the people, to attack Banda Baru, and drive the
English completely out of Perak.

Later on—that is in September, 1875—Sir William
Jervois, having now succeeded Sir Andrew Clarke as
Governor, visited Perak, and, during his progress
through the country, made proposals both to the ex-
Sultan at Blanja, and to Sultan Abdullah at Banda
Baru, that the country should be handed over to the
management of British officers ; proposing certain
allowances for the chiefs if they agreed to the arrangement, as this seemed to him the only way of settling
the knot into which affairs had run : for the treaty was
openly violated, the government was wretched, slavery
ran riot, and Mr. Birch had embittered himself still

more by interfering in certain slavery matters. After consideration, the ex-Sultan Ismail refused these proposals, and declared that he was not bound by the Pangkore treaty, while Abdullah expressed his wish to abide by the treaty, but asked for time for consideration, and received fifteen days.

At last the proposals were accepted by the Sultan, and he received a promise in writing from Mr. Birch that he should be paid two thousand dollars per month. On the same day a letter was brought to Abdullah, by the colonial steamer, consenting that the government should be carried on in the Sultan's name ; another letter being at the same time conveyed to Mr. Birch for the Rajah Muda, or heir to the throne, Yusuf, offering to make him sultan if Abdullah had declined the Governor's proposals as to the government. Matters however still hung fire, the Sultan hesitating to sign the proclamations placed before him by Mr. Birch, and it was only under the pressure of a threat to send the Governor's letter to Yusuf that the Sultan affixed to the proclamations his chop, or seal.

One of these proclamations, in the name of the Sultan, announced to the people of the country that it had been found advisable to place the land for its better government in the hands of British officers, who were to try cases ; but in matters of life and death no capital sentence could be executed without the Sultan's consent. The other proclamation dealt with

the new arrangements to be made as to the gathering
of the revenue, and stopping the illegal squeezing
carried on by the chiefs. Following upon these, a
proclamation was issued by the Governor at Singapore, and was afterwards sent up to Mr. Birch. But
meanwhile troubles were thickening. Three slave
women had fled from the Sultan, and sought and
obtained protection at the Residency; the Sultan
was receiving visits from his chiefs, and is believed to
have given his signed consent to the murder of Mr.
Birch. Then the women were claimed, and consent
was given for them to go; but Mr. Birch declared
that, now he held full authority from the Sultan, he
should interfere if the women required his protection.

The plot too was thickening in another direction;
for communications were being opened up with ex-
Sultan Ismail, and it was in consideration what steps
should be taken to defeat the British authority. At
last matters came to a climax; for soon after, that
is at the end of October, copies of the Governor's and
the Sultan's proclamations were brought to the
Residency at Banda Baru, and were posted under
a salute of twenty-one guns; while just about the
same time, bullets were being made, powder obtained,
and men were gathered preparatory to a rising.

On the 1st November Mr. Birch ascended the river
Perak in his dragon boat, the same given in the illus-
tration. He was accompanied by Lieutenant Abbott,
R.N., and a small native guard, in a large and small

boat, as escort; and they made their way up to Passir
Sala, where, as soon as it was known that they had
arrived, announcements were sent round in all directions. Passir Sala was the residence of the Maharajah
Lela, a chief who had shown all through a most
determined opposition to the Governor's proposed new
method of administering the affairs of the country;
but so little was danger apprehended, that the two
officers dined and slept that night on board the
Resident's boat, in the belief of their absolute security.

The next morning—a memorable one in the history
of Perak—Lieutenant Abbott crossed the river for
awhile to shoot, and Mr. Birch shortly after sent Arshad,
his interpreter, into the village of Passir Sala, to post
the Governor's and Sultan's proclamations. This was
resented, however, by the Malays, who kept tearing
them down as fast as they were posted up; which
so enraged the interpreter that at last he struck one of
their number with a stick, an indignity which was at
once resented with the kris, and the poor fellow ran
bleeding to the river and jumped in. This was the
spark that set fire to the train; a cry of *amok*
immediately ensued, and the infuriated Malays, armed
with spears and krises, made a rush in a body down
to the river-bank, where Mr. Birch was ashore at the
bathing-house, his orderly being on guard with a
revolver. He let his leader, however, be taken completely by surprise, and at a great disadvantage, leaping
into the river, holding up his revolver, and swimming

2 B

for his life.   Mr. Birch was a lithe active man, of un-
daunted bravery, and had he been in the boat, where
he was well provided with firearms and spears, he
would have sold his life most dearly. As it was he was
savagely attacked, some of the Malays driving their
keen limbings through the rattan mat that formed a
screen, while others went to the end of the bath, and,
as the wounded Resident struggled up out of the
water, one man cut at him with a sword, when he
sank, and for the time being was seen no more.

Meanwhile Arshad, wounded as he was, made for
the dragon boat, and got hold of the gunwale, trying
to sustain himself; when two of the Malays jumped
into the boat, and cut at him with their swords till he
lost his hold, and floated down the stream to be
picked up by the coxswain of Mr. Birch; who had in
the *mêlée* swum off to one of the two boats which
accompanied the dragon, and who now tried to save
the interpreter, and dragged him in. A portion of the
escort of Sepoys were in this boat, and they now
commenced firing at the Malays, driving them off
for the time; but as this boat now dropped down
the stream they took courage and followed, firing at
the guard; and then taking a sampan, they crossed the
river and began firing again, scaring the escort so that
they took to the water. A few more shots were ex-
changed, and then the small boat was allowed to
proceed in peace; but before they had gone much
farther it was found that the interpreter, who by his

rash act had commenced the trouble, was dead, while
several of the Sepoys and boatmen were killed and
wounded, the larger boat having been sunk during the
disturbance.

The native guard had been ordered by Mr. Birch
not to use their firearms, for he had said if the Malays
made a disturbance he would leave. In fact, the
men were cleaning their rifles, and were so taken by
surprise by the large party of well-armed Malays that
resistance seems to have been the last thing dreamed
of; while the whole attack was so sudden and un-
expected that nothing seems to have been done to save
Mr. Birch; the English companion on whose aid he
could have counted, and without whose lead the
Sepoys seem to have been helpless, being far away.

As soon as the disturbance was over, Mr. Birch's
dragon boat was taken by one of the chiefs for a short
distance down the stream, and plundered; the principal
part of the Resident's things being afterwards found
in the house of the Maharajah Lela, who was considered to be the leading spirit in the attack, aided by
another chief, known as the Datu Sagor; and proof is
not wanting of the preparations that had been made
for the cowardly attack. No doubt the train was
already laid, and it wanted but the spark to be
applied. In fact, just before his death, Mr. Birch had
noticed a body of about forty Malays, all armed with
spears and krises, crowding towards his boat, and
warned them to keep away; but he evidently felt so

2 B 2

secure that he took no further heed to their proximity, although such a gathering was unusual. The excuse for the rising was furnished by the interpreter's act, one which he paid for dearly in the loss of his own life ; while he was the immediate cause of the death of a valuable public officer, whose body was some four-days afterwards taken away, towed behind a boat, by some Bugis men, and was afterwards found ashore in the jungle, about two hundred yards from the river, by Rajah Dein, a Bugis.

Lieutenant Abbott was in the meantime unaware of what had taken place, being absent for about three hours, shooting on the farther shore ; but, on his return to the river, he was met by the Datu Sagor, who had but a short time before taken part in the *émeute*, and now told the lieutenant that there had been a disturbance at Passir Sala, advising him to take refuge in the jungle, as his life was not safe for a minute where he then was.

This advice savoured strongly of treachery ; for, under the circumstances, concealment in the jungle would have been a very hopeless proceeding, and must have resulted in the fugitive being hunted out and shot down. It is evident that Lieutenant Abbott took this view of the position—alone there with his one companion—and rejecting this advice, and feeling that with his leader and escort gone, his best plan was to flee to the Residency, he watched his opportunity, and seized a small canoe, or dug-out, in which he and his follower embarked, and paddled off into mid-stream, so as to allow it to drop down with the current to Banda Baru.

If he had had any doubt before of the wisdom of trusting to himself, instead of the Datu Sagor, it was swept away directly; for fire was opened upon him from both banks, the gauntlet of which he ran till he was beyond the reach of the Malays, and arrived at the Residency in safety, where he at once made up his mind to put it in a state of defence. Fearing that an attack would soon follow, he called in all the Sepoys and police to the small island upon which the Residency was built. Mr. Swettenham, of the Straits Civil Service, who had a few days previously ascended the river, for some distance, on the same mission of posting the proclamations, heard on his way back of the events at Passir Sala, where he was told that the Malays were on the look-out to kill him. He, too, was advised by a friendly rajah; but the advice he received was not to land, but to retreat; and this he did, making the best of his way down the river under the cover of the night, an unusual mist fortunately prevailing at the time when he reached Passir Sala, and concealing his little craft till he was safely by; and he finally succeeded in joining Lieutenant Abbott at the Residency. Thereupon the determination was made to hold the place, and defend the flag to the last.

The island being only separated by a small creek from the bank of the river, and having but sixty men at his disposal, Lieutenant Abbott entrenched his position, told off his four seamen to the native detachments to work the field-pieces on the spot, and generally put the place in a good state for resisting the enemy. But previous to this being fully accomplished he had written to the Sultan, telling him of the murder of Mr. Birch, and asking him to collect men and come to his assistance. To this Abdullah responded by coming at once, accompanied by the Laksamana, the Shahbandar, and a large following. Mr. Swettenham, however, did not feel full confidence in the presence of these Malay chiefs and their followers in the little British camp, where they might easily convey information to the enemy; and, consequently, while accepting their services, requested them politely, but with firmness, to move lower down the river, ready to act when called upon, and this was acceded to at once.

CHAPTER XXXII.

The attack on Passir Sala—Repulse—Burial of Mr. Birch and Captain Innes—Proceedings of the Government—Reinforcements from China—Capture of Passir Sala—Mr. Birch's dragon boat —Troops from India—Proceedings of the northern column— Qualla Kungsa and Kota Lamah.

THE position of the young Englishmen at the Residency was a perilous one; but their prompt behaviour was not without its influence on the people, and they were not long left in suspense; for the news having been conveyed to Penang by Captain Welner, of the Straits Government steamer *Pluto*, the Lieutenant-governor lost not a moment in sending off a detachment of Her Majesty's 10th Foot, and some police, under the local head of the force, the Hon. H. Plunket. At the same time, Captain Innes, of the Royal Engineers, an officer of great judgment, was sent to act as commissioner, and Mr. Kynnersley, of the Straits Civil Service, as interpreter. The news of the coming of these reinforcements was conveyed in a letter from Captain Innes, and was gladly received at the Residency, as it contained the information that the little force would be at Banda Baru on the following

day. On the arrival of the troops no time was lost,
preparations being hurried on; and Mr. Swettenham's plan for attacking the enemy by sending a
small force up each bank of the river, supported by
two guns lashed in the boats, was generally approved,
while rockets were also to be taken in the boats for use
if required.

It was at this time that the body of Mr. Birch was
brought in, the Bugis who were its bearers giving
information of there being a strong stockade at Passir
Sala, and another four or five hundred yards inland.

The party marched to the attack on November 7th,
preceded by Malay scouts, and accompanied by a rocket
party with four blue-jackets, the troops being under
the command of Captain Booth and Lieutenant Elliot.
On approaching the stockade, the attacking party had
many difficulties to hinder them—the thickness of the
field of Indian corn and padi, and the trees, fences, and
height of the stockade, which, in spite of their efforts,
was but little injured by the rocket party. A heavy
fire was opened upon the little force as soon as they
came within range of the stockade, which was found
to be held in force; and in spite of the vigorous
reply of our troops, the men fell fast. But the
advance was still kept up until the infantry were close
up to the Malay stronghold, when Lieutenant Elliot
was wounded severely, and his party fell back behind a
tree. The firing was however still kept on, and
another of the 10th men went down; and on his

being carried to the tree where the lieutenant was taken, it was found that Captain Booth was also wounded, and the lieutenant and Captain Innes had both been taken to the rear, the latter shot through the heart.

Under these circumstances, three officers of the little force being *hors de combat*, it was considered wiser to retire until reinforcements could be procured ; and after carrying the wounded to the rear, a volley was fired into the stockade, and the little party, burdened with its injured men, steadily began to retreat. They had a distance of about a couple of miles to traverse to reach the boats, where all were embarked, and proceeded to the Residency, the Malays being satisfied with beating off the attack, and making no attempt at pursuit, or even at hindering the re-embarkation.

This was a severe repulse, the losses of the little force being no less than seventeen killed and wounded, two of the killed being Captain Innes and a man of the 10th, whose body afterwards floated down the river, shot through the head and chest. Fortunately, however, surgical assistance was at hand, and the wounded were well attended to.

Mr. Birch was buried beneath the palms close by the Residency—a faithful representation of the place being given in the accompanying engraving, produced from the series of photographs taken by the writer during one of his visits to Banda Baru.

This spot was chosen for Mr. Birch's interment, as

being one of the portions of the jungle which he had
cleared for about two or three hundred yards along
the bank for the site of the new Residency he meant
to build, where the barracks, armoury, and magazine
had been established, as shown in the cut, with a
police station a little lower down.   On the occasion of
the bringing in of the body, and its interment, the
people, who were greatly attached to their leader,
made bitter lamentation.   It was an impressive scene,
the more especially as it took place at a time of peril,
when no man felt that his life was safe.   The service
was read by Mr. Swettenham, and due military
honours were accorded to the fallen man, three volleys
being fired by the Sikhs over his grave just as the
sun was sinking.   Only a short time later the ground
had to be again disturbed to form a grave for Captain
Innes, who was buried with the same ceremonies
beside Mr. Birch, as the moon was rising on the night
of the day on which he fell.

A few days later the Governor visited Perak in
person, bringing with him in H.M.S. *Fly*, Captain
Bruce, a detachment of H.M. 80th Foot with some
artillery, and leaving his instructions with Major
Dunlop, R.A., who had come up as Commissioner, he
sent on also H.M.S. *Thistle*, Captain Stirling, which
was then at Klang, farther down the coast.   Prior,
however, to leaving Singapore, the Governor had instructed the Colonial Secretary, Mr. C. J. Irving, to
telegraph to Hong Kong for more troops, and to

summon H.M.S. *Modeste* from Labuan; and with praiseworthy despatch General Colborne arrived at Singapore by the 16th, with three hundred of H.M. 80th Foot.

But before the general had had time to leave Singapore, Major Dunlop and Captain Stirling had concerted measures for a combined attack upon Passir Sala by land and water. At the same time it may be mentioned in passing, that the Governor's idea for reducing the Malays to submission was for one force to proceed up the river by Passir Sala, while another crossed the country from the Laroot river to Qualla Kungsa, so as to proceed down the Perak river—these two points giving a practical control of the country.

Major Dunlop and Captain Stirling's plan was carried out on November 16th, and in this attack upon Passir Sala, Sultan Abdullah, who had been applied to for help against the rebellious chiefs, furnished sixteen boats for the transport of the men and artillery, but without "polers." This difficulty was however got over by the seamen, though it was an onerous duty for men unaccustomed to the work, and in a sharp stream. The plans were well carried out, Captain Stirling's naval force taking up its position in the river, and Major Dunlop's land forces theirs near Passir Panjang, bugle signals being arranged so as to keep up the co-operation when the two forces were separated. The fire was opened from the stockade upon the boats in the river, and vigorously kept up

on both sides ; while leaving the jungle, the land forces
advanced through the thick Indian corn till fire was
opened upon them. Then a gun (a 12-pound howitzer)
was brought up, and after four or five rounds of case-
shot had been discharged into the stockade its fire was
silenced, and the troops dashed in to find it deserted.
It was a strong place, with deep ditch, earth-work,
wattled fence, and pointed bamboos, while it was
armed with a large iron gun and a small pivot
"lelah."

These guns were spiked and thrown into the river,
and the force then moved on through a dense plantation
of bananas till fire was opened upon them from another
stockade, a short distance from the spot where Mr.
Birch was murdered. The Malays in the second
stockade were driven out by the blue-jackets, and the
attention of all was then directed to a formidable one
close into the village, which was firing on the boats.
No time was lost, for the eagerness of the men was
roused by the sight of Mr. Birch's boat and the bath-
house where he was murdered, and with a rush they
charged and took the stockade, the land and river
forces entering it at the same moment, to find that
the Malays had retreated. Here were found four
guns, one being the small brass piece taken from
Mr. Birch's boat ; two were lelahs, and the other an
iron 6-pounder, which had just burst, evidently having
been struck by one of the English shells.

By this last stroke, Mr. Birch's dragon boat and

his row-boat were recovered, and the village was in the possession of the English, who now turned their attention to the Maharajah's house, which was found to be strongly fortified, being surrounded by an earthwork eight feet high, with ditch containing water, and on the top of the earthwork a stockade formed of short sharpened bamboos. The place might have been held and given a good deal of trouble to capture, but it had evidently been left in a hurry, and on search being made, a number of the articles belonging to Mr. Birch, which had been plundered from his boat, were found.

The village was then burnt, and soon after Campong Gaja, a place a little lower down, the residence of the Datu Sagor, who, as we have seen, either took part in or countenanced the murder of Mr. Birch, by being present at the time. This place had also been fortified with a couple of stockades, but very little attempt was made to defend it. At the other stockades, however, a gallant defence was made, and the enemy must have suffered heavily. They however retreated in good order, carrying off their arms with their wounded and dead; the principal trophies obtained, beside the guns, being the war-gong, shot through by a bullet, and several drums, with powder and cartridges in some quantity. The loss on our side was not one man killed, while only two men, one of whom was a civilian following the forces, were wounded.

Consequent upon the condition of Perak, and the inflammable nature of the Malay character, the other states began to show strong symptoms of a rising, as if contingent upon the Perak outbreak, and further reinforcements being urgently needed, India was appealed to by telegram; and so rapid now are the movements of forces when summoned by wire that by the 27th of the same month the first portion of the reinforcement reached Penang. It was so admirably adapted for the service in hand, so complete in itself in every detail of its composition, and showed throughout how all had been contrived by a prevailing mastermind, that it may be well here to give an account in full of this miniature army designed for jungle fighting.

The head-quarters and 600 men of H.M. 3rd Regt. (Buffs), Col. Cox, C.B.; head-quarters and 400 men of 1st Ghoorkhas; 3–5th Royal Artillery, with four mountain guns (7-pounder M.L.R. steel, 150lb.); two 5½-inch mortars, with 500 rounds per piece, and 200 rockets; a field telegraph of 100 miles of wire, one superintendent, and ten signallers; a company of the Madras Sappers and Miners; a proportion of medical officers, doolies, and doolie-bearers for conveyance of sick; with sea provisions for six weeks and shore provisions for ten days, camp equipage, light tents, and "Lascars' pawls."

This force was capable of division into three parts, and was composed with this view in officers, men, equipment, guns, and ammunition. Each ship had a complete equipment for the number of troops aboard, so as to make them independent of the movement of the other vessels.

Brig.-Gen. Ross was in command, with staff as follows : Major Mark Heathcote, Assistant Quarter-master-General ; Major H. J. Hawkins, Major of Brigade ; Lieutenant Preston, Rifle Brigade, A.D.C. ; Capt. Badcock, Deputy-Assist. Commissary-General ; Major Twigge, R.E., Capt. Crawford, R.E., Lieut. North, R.E., Field Engineers.

H.M.S. *Philomel* also came from Bombay, and Admiral Ryder sent from China H.M.S. *Egeria* and *Ringdove*; H.M.S. *Modeste*, Capt. Buller, senior naval officer, which was on her way when the disturbances commenced, reached the Straits about the 20th November.

General Colborne (now Sir F. Colborne, K.C.B.) had now a considerable force under his command, one that must have made a great impression on the Malay chiefs, as an example of the power and promptitude of England when called upon to maintain the dignity of the Empire, and avenge so cruel an insult as the present to her flag. In conjunction with the Governor, then, it was arranged to hold the country until the murderers of the late Resident were given up—a reward having already been issued for the capture of the Maharajah Lela—and satisfaction duly rendered for the outrage.

The Indian column, which was appointed to occupy the upper portion of the country, had to march by way of Laroot, a distance of twenty-seven miles —the pass they had to traverse has been mentioned in the early part of this work—arrangements having been made and stations appointed for their encampment. In this work the Muntri lent every assistance in his power, by furnishing elephants and men for the improvement of the track, which is now occupied by the first good road which was made in Perak. Detachments were left at Bukit Gantang and Campong Boyah, with which places communications were kept up; these being spots that had been chosen as sites for encampments by Captain Satterthwaite, R.E., in concert with Captain Speedy, the writer being the Commissioner and Mr. W. Maxwell the Deputy-commissioner with this force.

. The southern column was under the command of General Colborne in person, with Majors Lloyd and Huskisson as Brigade-Majors; and Commissary Robinson, of the Control Department, a gentleman who, from previous visits to the country, was able to render most valuable assistance. The artillery force was commanded by Major (now Colonel) Nicolls. The medical officers in charge were Drs. Randall and Orton, the former of whom was wounded, and is since dead. Major Dunlop was the Commissioner with this force, and Mr. Swettenham Deputy-commissioner.

The naval portion was under the command of

Captain Buller, C.B., and the naval brigades formed from it were under Captain Buller and Captain Garforth — the former with General Colborne and the southern column, and the latter with Brigadier-General Ross in the north.

The northern column duly crossed the country from Laroot to Qualla Kungsa, which became the military station for the time being ; and it was while the troops were here that an absurd alarm took place. An attack from the Malays was at any moment deemed imminent, and careful supervision was exercised during the night over the various sentries ; therefore a sudden outcry from one of the camp followers, who had been lying asleep, was quite sufficient to produce a stampede amongst the undisciplined portion of the people, and it was some time before the cause of the cries could be made out. The matter was very simple : the alarmist had been lying asleep on his back beneath a cocoa-nut tree, and one of the huge husk-covered nuts, being over-ripe, had become dislodged in the night, and in falling had struck the poor fellow in the epigastric region, causing, no doubt, as much pain as fear.

The chief value of this northern column was in its presence in Upper Perak, where it kept the disaffected chiefs in check, and thoroughly prevented them from combining in any active measures against the Government, and also from joining those below stream in the disturbances. It had however its actual work, among

the principal events of which was its attack upon
Kotah Lamah—a place that had long been noted as a
resort for the worst characters, and freebooters of the
vilest description. In fact, Mr. Birch, during one of
his visits was threatened by the people with loaded
guns. On the arrival of the troops at Qualla Kungsa
these people were not openly hostile. The acts of the
head men of the place however at last called for interference ; and as it became necessary to make an
example of the village before the departure of the
troops, it was determined to disarm the people. For
this purpose a small force was sent up the river
beyond Qualla Kungsa, and the demand for arms to
be given up was acceded to on being made by Captain
Speedy ; but armed men were seen rushing off, in two
or three instances, to the jungle. The military force
made their way right through the campong and back
without being opposed ; and after this General Ross
and his party landed at the middle of the village, and
were searching the various houses to see that they
contained none but women and children, when, under
cover of a brisk fire, well maintained from the jungle,
they were assailed by a body of fifty or sixty spear-
armed Malays, who had been hidden amongst the trees.
These men suddenly rushed out, and nearly succeeded
in surrounding the little party, which had to retire
fighting as they went, the marines and sailors main-
taining a most gallant front till the river was reached.
Shortly before this several officers had gone in the

direction of the river, and Major Hawkins is supposed
to have been following them when he received a
frightful spear wound, the blade passing right through
his chest. A sailor named Sloper ran to his help,
and shot two Malays who were running up to continue the attack, when Major Hawkins is reported to
have exclaimed : "Save yourself, you can do me no
good now." The officers who had gone on towards
the river now returned, and tried to move him, but
they were compelled in turn to fall back towards the
river, Surgeon Townsend being the first to be assailed
by three Malays with spears. One he shot with his
revolver, but the man struck him down in falling, and
his two companions dashed in to spear him, when
they were bayoneted by a couple of the seamen. This
engagement was successful, however, from the fact that
a large quantity of arms were taken, including lelahs
and a 12-pounder iron gun, which was spiked and
thrown into the river.

Far from being disconcerted by their losses, the
people of Kotah Lamah began soon after erecting
stockades, and were guilty of so many lawless acts,
that the Governor finally decided that a severe chas-
tisement should be inflicted upon them, and for this
purpose he consulted with General Colborne. The consequence was that a further expedition was arranged
to be carried out against the Kotah Lamah people, the
great body of whom had now gone farther up the
river, to the two villages of Enggar and Prek; and this

expedition was somewhat hurried by an appeal for help which came from Rajah Muda Yusuf, whose people had been attacked by a body of the Kotah Lamah people, under Toh Sri Lela, their chief. This party was driven off by some of the Ghoorkhas, but unfortunately two of Rajah Yusuf's friendly Malays were killed and two wounded by mistake.

The next day our forces were sent up the river to Enggar, where the Malays opened fire from two or three lelahs, but after a short and sharp return fire they were effectually driven out of their village. A portion of the force was then directed to bivouac in the village for the night, and then move forward and attack Prek, to which place Toh Sri Lela and his followers had fled. Here, the next day, the enemy were again driven out, making a precipitate retreat, a result which, when achieved, was followed by the return of our troops to Qualla Kungsa, the power of the Kotah Lamah chief being completely broken.

CHAPTER XXXIII.

THE brunt of the work however in the Perak outbreak
fell upon the southern column, which had to be
brought up the river in boats against the rapid stream,
the means of progression being by "poling," which
was admirably performed by the blue-jackets—whose
behaviour throughout, whether in boating or skirmishing in the jungle, was always gallant and deserving of
praise.

It was on December 8th that the forces left Banda
Baru, but with so large a flotilla—forty-five boats
crowded with troops—the current strong, and the
heat of the sun very great, only about eight miles
were accomplished on that day; and the little army
encamped on an island just above Passir Sala. The
9th, 10th, and 11th were passed in the same slow toil
up the river; and on the 12th the force encamped
about a couple of miles below Blanja, the site of their

projected operations—for here the Sultan Ismail had
had his place of residence.

The next day the troops marched into Blanja by
eight o'clock in the morning, but to find no enemy;
for the news of the coming of the little force had preceded them, and the place was deserted. On every
side lay the traces of a hasty flight: boxes and
packages prepared for conveying away lay in all directions, but had evidently proved too cumbersome for
the ex-Sultan's retreat, and had therefore been abandoned. Had there been any doubt as to the line of
retreat, the information could have been readily obtained, for the way open was by the elephant-track,
running nearly at right angles to the river towards
the interior, where the capital of Perak—Kinta—lay,
on the river of that name—the river which, after a
course nearly parallel with the Perak, empties itself
into the latter near the Residency at Banda Baru.

This elephant-track presented plenty of obstacles
to the passage of a little army; for the peculiarity,
already described, of the elephant, in always placing
its feet in the same holes, no matter how deep they
are in mud and water, soon results in the formation of
a series of pits, which are almost impassable, except
by the huge animals themselves, who, feeling satisfied
of the safety of a place where an elephant has planted
his feet before, wallow through them in a slow pon-
derous way that is remarkable, when firmer ground
might easily be found. Under the circumstances of a

beaten track being in such a deplorable state, it might be supposed that the troops could make a fresh one to the right or left; but it must be thoroughly understood that, saving to wild animals, the jungle is impassable, presenting as it does a dense green wall of vegetation on either side, that cannot be penetrated, on account of the manner in which the trees and undergrowth are matted and woven together by creepers and the wiry rattans. In addition, there are thorns of the most pungent kind, one of which is known by the natives as tigers' claws, from its hooked and formidable nature, while to crown, or rather to form a base to, these difficulties, the soil is often one continuous marsh or swamp, covered with vivid green moss, which gives way beneath the traveller's feet.

This density of the jungle is the more insisted on here from the fact of its being explanatory of the difficulties of the troops, and to prepare the reader for the statements of the march being arrested by the Malays felling a tree or two, so that they lay across the track. To the ordinary reader, the obvious way of escape from such a difficulty seems to be to strike out into the jungle, as might be done in a forest-path in our own country; but this can only be accomplished by literally cutting, hacking, and clearing a way through the wilderness of vines and creepers.

Three hours after the arrival of the troops, Blanja was garrisoned, and the force, now quitting the river, took to the woods to cross to Kinta, where a

severe fight was anticipated, in consequence of the
reports that had come in respecting the collecting
together there of disaffected chiefs, now joined by the
ex-Sultan Ismail, who was stated to be sheltering the
Maharajah Lela, and to have the intention of protecting him.   To meet these difficulties the little land
force consisted of two hundred infantry and forty
artillerymen, with two 7-pounder rifled guns, and
forty seamen, with a couple of rocket tubes—the rocket
being a missile that creates great consternation
amongst the Malays. Consequent upon the difficulties
of the task, and the weight of the guns which had to
be dragged over and through a variety of serious
obstacles, only four miles were advanced in two hours
and a half, and at the end of this time the first
symptom of the presence of the enemy was found in
the shape of several trees felled across the track, interlaced with bushes, behind which the Malays were
making a stand, receiving the advance guard of the
force with a sharp fire of musketry, which resulted in
Dr. Randall being severely wounded.

A halt was immediately called, and while the
enemy was held in play with return fire, for the most
part at a completely invisible foe, one of the 7-pounder
guns was got to the front, well served, and a few
rounds sent crashing through the trees in the direction of the enemy, in company with a couple of
rockets. The Malays then retreated, and the obstacles
having been hacked and cleared away, the troops,

who had suffered no other casualty, proceeded, feeling
their way cautiously along a jungle path that might
have been easily defended by an able enemy. Nothing
further occurred for a couple of hours, when the
advance was again checked by trees felled across the
path and another innocuous fire of musketry; but a
rocket sent hissing through the trees a second time
dislodged the Malays, and the march continued for
another half mile, when a strong stockade arrested
further progress. This, however, the enemy did not
attempt to hold, but evacuated it before it was reached
by the troops, who found plenty of traces of hasty
flight in the shape of water-bottles and sleeping-mats
left beneath the huts which had been set up; the idea
having apparently been to turn this into what it could
easily have been made—a very formidable place for
defence.

The stockade having been destroyed, the advance
was continued till the troops came to a halt, having
succeeded in dragging their guns and camp necessaries
about eight miles through the jungle. This halt was
called after every effort had been made to overtake
Ismail, who was evidently only a short distance ahead,
making his escape to Kinta on elephants. But the
progress of our men was too slow, for they had to
carry the heavy 24-pound rockets and tubes through
a series of quagmires, and at last all hope of overtaking
the ex-Sultan was given up for that evening. The
next day was spent in getting up supplies, and on the

following day the little force marched to a place called
Pappan, some six or seven miles farther—the general
rate of progress through the dense jungle being only
about one mile an hour.

From here Mr. Swettenham, in company with a
friendly rajah and a body of Malay scouts, proceeded
onward, finding the road grow worse, consisting at last,
as he describes it, of nothing but logs, roots of trees,
and elephant holes full of water; but the bad ground
was passed at last, and he halted a short distance from
Kinta, to send forward scouts to discover the whereabouts of the enemy, and two more to give information
to General Colborne of his position.

The next morning the war-gongs were heard close
at hand, and an attack was evidently intended, when
the advance guard of the forces came up, but beyond
a little scattered firing nothing took place till the
arrival of the main body of the troops, when rockets
were discharged in the direction of Kinta and a campong close at hand. These were followed by shells as
soon as the gun was brought up. There was a little
firing then amongst the Malay scouts, who encountered
the scattered enemy; and the advance continuing, the
force at last stood on the banks of the Kinta river,
here about fifty yards in width, with the village upon
an island in mid-stream. As the skirmishers advanced
the enemy began firing upon them from their lelahs,
but these were soon silenced by the gun and rockets,
and the river being waded, an entry was made into the

little capital, which the soldiers found now to be quite deserted, Ismail and his followers having fled up the stream—report saying that the Maharajah Lela was with him, and that the whole party were well furnished with elephants, the departure taking place just before the entry of the troops.

The troops then encamped in the deserted village, and on making search they found nine brass guns by way of trophies. It was soon found, however, that Ismail had contrived to take with him the whole of the Perak regalia, his purpose being apparently to make his way due north, and to cross into Patani, on the borders of Quedah. The commanding officer had, however, though unsuccessful in capturing the ex-Sultan, the satisfaction of making this most toilsome march of three days through the jungle, and taking possession of the capital without the loss of a single man, excepting Dr. Randall, who was wounded soon after the start from Blanja.

The troops now thoroughly occupied the country, and beyond a few petty attacks upon boats and isolated police by the Malays, all of which were promptly punished, no attempt was made at resistance; while at the beginning of January reliable information was brought in of the whereabouts of Ismail and the Maharajah Lela, the people friendly to our Government having been stimulated by the large rewards offered for the capture of these chiefs. The report stated that Ismail was in the mountains

near the source of the Perak river, when an armed
force of police were sent to ask the co-operation of a
friendly native chief for the capture. The attack was
made, but Ismail and the greater part of his people
escaped once more, though with the loss of nine
followers and seventeen elephants. Four of the men
were killed—one being reported a chief, and another
Pandak Indut, who was believed to be the actual
murderer of Mr. Birch—while a short time later three
more of the assassins were secured.

Meanwhile the proceedings in Perak had not been
without their effect in another part of the peninsula;
matters having assumed a threatening appearance at
Sunghie Ujong, while the Malays in the neighbourhood of our settlement at Malacca were becoming so
disorderly that the Government had further to consider what steps should be taken for quelling the
movements of the lawless in these parts.

Sunghie Ujong is a state lying to the south of
Perak, from which it is separated by the state of
Salangore, while on the south it nearly approaches the
boundary of our settlement of Malacca.

H.M.S. *Thistle* was called into service, and a
portion of the Indian column of General Ross was
detached for service in the disturbed districts, the
various reports coming in being of a very alarming
tendency. Colonel Anson went as the Government
representative, with Mr. Neubronner as interpreter.
Before their arrival, however, hostilities had com-

menced; for the Malays who were disaffected had
been collecting in armed force at a place in Sunghie
Ujong, called Terrachee, and made a threatening
attack upon Mr. Daly, who is the Government Surveyor, and who was engaged in making certain topo-
graphical researches. They confined themselves, however, to threats; but on Captain Murray, who was in
charge of troops there, coming upon the scene, he was
fired at by the Malays. A short skirmish ensued,
which resulted in Captain Murray's men running short
of ammunition, and having to retire towards the Residency; when the Malays followed in a very threatening manner, stockading a pass in the Terrachee valley,
and also occupying a village called Paroe, a few miles
distant.

During the next few days the disaffected kept
increasing in numbers and erecting stockades, whereupon a reconnaissance was made by the troops
under Lieutenant Hinxman, who found the enemy
so strongly entrenched that he and his men were
forced to retire. Later on, however, the Malays were
attacked, and compelled to retreat from the village of
Paroe, the Lieutenant-governor of Malacca, the Hon.
C. B. Plunket, being present on the occasion, and
some native police, under Bird and Skinner, who ably
supported the small detachment of H.M. 10th Foot.
The Malays, says Captain Murray, numbered from
three to six hundred men, and were encouraged by
the greatest men in the country. But in spite of

their number and strong defences Lieutenant Hinxman's small force carried all before it, and at the point
of the bayonet drove the enemy in full rout from
their stockades.

From here the enemy made for the Terrachee
valley, where they took up a very strong position at a
place called Bukit Putoos. To give some idea of the
kind of country in which the troops had to operate, it
must be understood that though about Paroe the
land was tolerably open, though uncultivated, farther
on towards Terrachee the jungle became thick,
with a narrow ascending path, which gradually grew
steeper, till it reached the narrow defile or pass
of Bukit Putoos, which forms the way across the
mountain.   Here the path is only eighteen inches
wide at the bottom, the sides of the rock being nearly
perpendicular, and twenty feet high, so that it was
only possible for one man to go forward at a time, and
a bold enemy might have kept an army at bay.   In
addition there was the jungle on either side, with
sharp mountain streams to cross, rough boulders, the
path of the worst, and the enemy in front, who had
stockaded the place to the best of their ability ; while
at the various approaches trees were felled, and the
way made perilous with *ranjows*—the spikes of bamboo or palm these people force into the ground, with
their points towards the enemy.

Upon the relief forces coming into the country,
they marched for the Terrachee valley, and finally

were divided into two columns, the first under Lieutenant-Colonel Hill, who had with him Captain Stirling, R.N., Captain Murray, Assistant-resident, with about one hundred Ghoorkhas, a naval brigade from H.M.S. *Thistle*, ten artillerymen, a 7-pounder steel gun, and some rockets. This little army was directed to make a *détour*, marching for the villages of Pantay and Terrachee, while the other division, under Lieutenant-Colonel Clay, made direct for the pass.

This latter force consisted of a detachment of H.M. 10th Foot, with artillerymen, under Captain Rigg ; Lieutenant North, R.E., with intrenching tools ; a hundred and fifty Ghoorkhas ; an Arab contingent under Captain de Fontaine ; a gun, a mortar, and some rockets.

The day after the marching of Colonel Hill's force, Colonel Clay's was set in motion, so as to attack the pass in front as soon as time had been given for the former to make a *détour* and come upon the enemy in the rear.

On reaching the foot of the pass, a reconnoitring party, consisting of a small body of Ghoorkhas, was despatched under Captain Channer, and after some delay he sent word back that, on account of the density of the jungle, it was impossible to discover where the stockade was situated ; when orders were sent by the commanding officer for him to go as near as possible, and endeavour to find out whether an available place could be found for the guns and rockets if brought to the front.

Captain Channer, with whom was Lieutenant North, R.E., pushed on—his route having been along the bed of a torrent till the way was blocked by felled trees. A rearguard was left to cut through these obstructions; and nothing daunted by the rough nature of the country, Captain Channer threw out men right and left, himself leading the left body of twenty-five men. He had given up his guides, for they evidently knew nothing of the position of the enemy; and trusting to himself, he went on working cautiously through the jungle, till he saw the enemy's smoke and fires, and soon after came upon one of the stockades, and reconnoitered the Malay defences. This jungle fort was composed of logs surrounded by a palisade, and sharp spiked bamboos were everywhere about the ground.

This was an important moment; for if the Malays had caught sight of the attacking force the alarm would have been given at once; but by using precautions, and watching the enemy, Captain Channer was able to learn the easiest way into the stockade. Then, supported by two Ghoorkhas, he leaped over the palisade, where he could hear the Malays talking inside— no look-out being kept, as the enemy was cooking; and then dashing forward, followed by his two men, he boldly attacked the twenty or thirty who constituted the garrison, shot down one man with his revolver, while the two Ghoorkhas each shot down theirs. Five Malays in all were killed in the first instance, and the remainder of the little flanking party coming up, the enemy, believing themselves to be surrounded, took to flight, making for two other stockades at about eighty and one hundred and sixty yards distance, the latter extending right across the pass.

The first of these—in which a 4-pounder iron gun was found—from being a defence, was now turned into an attacking point ; and Captain Channer, getting his men well under cover, opened a sharp fire on both strongholds in his front, with the effect that, after half-an-hour's fighting, the enemy evacuated the lower stockade, and soon after the rapid firing drove them out of the one that crossed the pass. As the Malays always, when they have time, carry off their dead and wounded, it was impossible to ascertain exactly the full extent of their losses ; but, from the traces left, it was evident that they must have suffered severely. On our side we had only one killed and three wounded.

The duties of Colonel Hill's little column were not light, though they encountered less active opposition. Their presence had no doubt great influence in pacifying the district, which was crossed under great difficulties, the Muar river having to be forded nearly twenty times, while swamps, dense jungle, and the various obstacles of a country unprovided with roads

harassed their march.   Neither had the natives been
idle in trying to stay their advance.   Trees were
felled wherever they could hinder the march.; the
river Muar was staked with ranjows at the crossing-
places ; and in the Terrachee valley a stockade had to
be attacked, the Ghoorkhas taking it in the rear
after some skirmishing and a shot or two fired
from the guns.   Altogether it was a most arduous
march—one which would have been impossible but
for the information obtained from the Malay scouts by
Captain Murray.   As it was, the advance was made
under most untoward circumstances, heavy rains often
falling, and the troops having nightly to clear away
enough of the dense jungle for them to obtain a place
whereon they could bivouac.   Finally they reached
the rear of Bukit Putoos, and a party was sent out to
arrest the defenders, who were reported to be in full
retreat ; but they got clear away, escaping into the
jungle, where it was impossible to pursue.

These well-directed efforts completely broke the
spirit of the disaffected in these parts, and by the time
the two columns formed a conjunction, the rising may
be said to have been completely at an end.   But about
the same time there were troubles at Klang, in the
south of Salangore, where Mr. Davidson was the Resident; the turbulent characters in these parts, thinking this a favourable opportunity for plundering and
showing their opposition to Toonkoo-dia-udin, the
Viceroy of Salangore, who holds Klang under the

authority of the Sultan of that country; though a claim for it has always been set up by one Rajah Mahdie, who was, however, kept from all active measures in the disturbances by being lodged under police surveillance at Singapore. In fact, some time before the rising the British government had thought it necessary to issue a warning that if Rajah Mahdie made any hostile expedition against Klang they would not feel justified in interfering to save his life, and therefore any such piece of aggression would be entirely at his own risk.

A little sharp work took place over these risings, but Mr. Davidson, the Resident, considered himself quite equal to cope with them; and though the offer of the Arab contingent was made by the Government, he declined it, and beyond the occasional visit of a man-of-war, he received no aid whatever. The little force he raised for suppressing the marauding parties that were formed, consisted of his own faithful Malays and some Chinese miners. By the aid of these men he dispersed the lawless bands in a few vigorous attacks, with the result that he completely pacified his district, and maintained authority throughout.

In this manner were the risings in Perak and the neighbouring states effectually suppressed; but there yet remained the punishment of the instigators of the rebellions and the murderers of Mr. Birch. Condign measures, however, were adopted for this purpose, as will be stated in the following chapter.

2 D 2

CHAPTER XXXIV.

COINCIDENT with arrangements for the return of a portion of the troops, whose services were no longer needed, steps were being taken by the Government for securing the persons of the offenders who had fled from Perak; and to effect this, one of the first things done was to communicate with the Government of the king of Siam, in one of whose dependencies—namely Patani—they had taken refuge, and to request that they might be removed into Singora, and kept there until their future should be arranged. The result of this request, as brought before the Siamese power by her Majesty's Consul-General at Bankok, was that it was decided to send a gunboat to Patani, bearing a Siamese commissioner, who should take charge of any of the chiefs of Perak who should be found in Patani, or any of the Siamese provinces; and that they should be taken to Bankok; and such of them as were reasonably supposed to be implicated in the murder

of Mr. Birch were to be handed over to the British
government, while the remainder should be kept
under surveillance until it was decided what should
be their fate. The whole of this arrangement was
made by Mr. Knox, whose position was rather a delicate one, as not only had we no extradition treaty
with Siam, but the offence with which the chiefs were
charged was not committed on British ground.

The Rajah of Quedah, in whose state the fugitives
were believed to be at times harbouring, on being
communicated with, also expressed his willingness to
deliver up Ismail and his followers; and it was near
his territory that the unsuccessful attempt was made
to capture the ex-Sultan—the one which resulted in
the death of four of his people—among whom was the
Sedikah Rajah—while several were wounded, and the
seventeen elephants were captured.

For a whole month longer, however, Ismail and the
remnant of his followers remained at liberty near the
head of the Perak river; until, feeling that if they
were permitted to remain unmolested in their retreat,
they would form the nucleus of a fresh disturbance,
the Governor sent orders to Penang for another effort
to be made from that settlement to effect the ex-
Sultan's capture. The plan proposed was that, after
obtaining information as to the exact whereabouts of
the fugitives, three combined movements should be
made—by Malays under Rajah Muda Yusuf, by men
from Salama, and a force from Quedah.

In accordance with these orders, an expedition
started, under Mr. Hewick, the Assistant-superin-
tendent of Police of Province Wellesley ; and he soon
found, by the action taken by the Patani men, that
the orders of the king of Siam for the prevention of
the entrance of the fugitives into his province had
been stringent : but they acted in a double-edged
manner ; for the instructions being to the authorities
to prevent all Perak men from entering Patani territory, and as there was no road from Perak to Quedah
that did not pass through Patani, the whole expedition, with its Perak men, was brought to a standstill.
While matters were in this state news was brought in
that Ismail was wearied out and ready to give himself .
up, and was on the frontier waiting.

There were still some difficulties to get over, as
now there was a chance of hindrance being thrown in
the way of the capture ; for the Patani men showed a
disposition to meddle, and sent parties out to interfere.
By a little judicious management, however, Mr.
Hewick, had Ismail taken to a place called Cheeah,
and following him there, found him encamped in the
jungle with his people, to the extent of about one
hundred and seventy men, women, and children.   In
the interview which followed the ex-Sultan undertook to proceed quietly to Quedah, and from thence to
meet the Lieutenant-Governor at Penang.

When questioned as to his participation in the
murder of Mr. Birch, he denied all knowledge of it,

saying that it happened in Sultan Abdullah's territory, and therefore he left it to him to inquire into the matter; while his reason for not coming in when summoned to meet Her Majesty's Commissioner was that as he was starting, a rumour was brought in of the approach of an inimical rajah with a force, and not wishing to submit his wives and children to the chances and horrors of war, he had fled with them into the jungle, where he had continued roaming from place to place ever since. Mr. Hewick states that it was perfectly evident that Ismail had no power over his chiefs, who rendered to him no respect whatever; and in hut building, catching elephants, or other offices of a similar kind, he had to act for himself, like the rest.

By careful marches Ismail was then brought down till he met the Sultan of Quedah, whose well-armed force of about a thousand men had been so disposed in the rear of the ex-Sultan and his followers that escape was impossible, though great care was exercised not to let him know how he was surrounded. The march was afterwards continued to Qualla Muda, where the ex-Sultan, the regalia, and the chiefs and followers, to the number of eighteen, were embarked and taken to Penang, while the women and children and twenty-seven elephants were left in Quedah.

It seems that the sufferings of Ismail and his followers must have been very severe; for when he surrendered he was in a destitute condition, his people emaciated, many of them ill, while many more had been left behind in the jungle and had died off. But one of the most important of the chiefs was still at liberty in the person of the Maharajah Lela, who was stated to be somewhere in Upper Perak ; but neither he nor the Orang Kaya Besar was taken on that occasion, though the latter was willing to surrender— the Superintendent of Police being too anxious to secure the ex-Sultan and his large following.

From Penang, Ismail, with his two sons and the attendants, was sent down in H.M.S. *Ringdove* to Singapore, and from thence by the same vessel to Johore, where the Maharajah had consented to receive them ; and here they were detained on parole, with the arrangements necessary for the prevention of intrigue.

The capture of the Datu Sagor, the chief who stood by while Mr. Birch was murdered, was effected through the instrumentality of Mr. Swettenham, a few days before the surrender of Ismail. The Datu had for the most part kept in hiding in the neighbourhood of Banda Baru, and he was at last captured where he had taken refuge with Sultan Abdullah at Pulo Tiga. As for the Maharajah Lela, he was still at large ; and though an effort was made to effect his capture at Kendrong, he escaped across the river into Patani, where the authorities refused to give him up to Mr. Maxwell, the Deputy-commissioner, who was in quest of him with a following of forty Malays. Finally however he surrendered with his followers, in July, 1876, to the representatives of the Maharajah of Johore at Kota Lamah, and was conveyed to Johore Bahru, with the understanding that he was to have a fair trial; and after a week's stay he was removed to Singapore, and thence to Laroot—as the murder having taken place in Perak, it was necessary that the trial should be held in the same state.

Whatever may have been the expectations of the Malay chiefs, they had a severe lesson to learn in the proceedings taken against them by the Government. Ismail and his sons were prisoners; the Maharajah Lela, Datu Sagor, and Pandak Indut, who had been falsely reported slain, were also under arrest, as well as several of their followers. In addition, the three men who had been seized and tried for the murder at the native court of Sultan Abdullah, were sentenced to death by Rajah Dris, the judge appointed by the Sultan; but the Governor subsequently advised that the sentence on two of the men should be commuted to penal servitude for life.

In the trials which followed, the Maharajah Lela, Datu Sagor, and Pandak Indut were found guilty of the murder of Mr. Birch, and were hanged; while such important evidence came out in connection with the cruel outrage as determined the Government upon requesting the attendance of Sultan Abdullah, and also of the Laksamana and the Shahbandar at Singapore, serious charges being also made against the Muntri.

In the protracted and careful inquiry before the
Commissioners a number of facts transpired which
implicated these chiefs, and showed that they had
favoured the determination to kill the British Resident and drive his staff out of the country. In
fact, that they were all in the conspiracy, and had
held meetings to discuss the question. The Sultan
was charged with authorising the deed; with pur-
chasing and supplying arms and ammunition; with
assisting the plans; with issuing his warrant to the
Maharajah Lela for the murder; that after the murder
he aided and protected this chief, and, furthermore,
sent him arms and provisions to aid him in resisting
the British officers; and that he aided and protected
the Datu Sagor.

These charges were generally denied by the Sultan,
who asserted that the papers and instructions he was
said to have issued, with their chops, or seals, were
forgeries.

As an example of the superstitious nature of even
the best educated Malays, it may be mentioned that
in the evidence it was asserted that certain incanta-
tions were made at Abdullah's instigation, and that
these were continued for three successive night; on
the last of which the spirit invoked declared that
Mr. Birch would be dead at the end of three months;
while other witnesses asserted that the Sultan wanted
to kill Mr. Birch by sorcery, and to injure him by putting poisonous plants in the place where he bathed.

The charges against the Muntri and the other chiefs were of a similar character, the Muntri being accused of favouring the Resident's death, counselling the Sultan against the British, and instigating attacks upon them.

During the time occupied in the examinations connected with these inquiries by the Commissioners, Abdullah and his chiefs resided, under supervision, in Singapore; and as soon as the inquiries were concluded, and answers received from the Home Government to the Governor's despatches, the now ex-Sultan was, with his chiefs, arrested, their case was heard, and they were finally lodged in Singapore gaol to insure their safe custody while their future was taken into consideration; the sentence upon them being that they should be deported from the country. The Muntri received the same sentence, and orders were issued also for his arrest, which were fully carried out.

The circumstances of the case against Sultan Ismail and his following were considered sufficient also to justify their continued detention at Johore, where the Maharajah undertook to provide against their being intrigued with in connection with the future affairs of Perak; while for the maintenance of the various chiefs provision was arranged for out of the revenue of Perak.

In connection with these arrangements, a proclamation was issued by Sir William Jervois, in March of the present year (1877), abrogating that of Sir Andrew Clarke of 1874, and concluding in these words :

Now be it known to all Men, that Abdullah has ceased to be Sultan of Perak, and that the Government of the State of Perak is, for the present, conducted by the Rajah Yusuf, son of the late Sultan Abdullah Mahomed Shah, as the Chief Native authority in the State.

Rajah Yusuf, heretofore mentioned as the Rajah Muda, was thus made ruler of Perak, the government being carried on in his name, and with the aid and advice of a Resident—Mr. Hugh Low receiving the onerous appointment.   Yusuf gained the confidence of the British Government by the way in which he refused to join in the contemptible little plots of the chiefs against Mr. Birch, and also by the spirited way in which he came forward with his following of friendly Malays to aid in the capture of the various fugitives, and in the pacification of the country.   He is a man over the middle age, and is described as being of considerable ability, feared and hated by many of the chiefs, and as being of a fierce and cruel disposition ; but he was a proved man as to his loyalty ; and there being no desire on the part of Government to annex the state of Perak, his appointment was the wisest course that, under the circumstances, could be pursued.

The last steps for the full pacification of the state had been the appointment of a Resident's guard of two hundred men, and a police force of five hundred ;

and finally, in July this year, the transportation of ex-Sultan Abdullah, and his three chiefs with their families to the island of Mahé, one of the group of the Seychelles, in the Indian Ocean—an island lying only about ten degrees north of Madagascar, the seat of the early Malay migrations. The embarkation, according to the *Straits Times*, of July 21st, caused but little excitement, and a guard of six police was deemed sufficient for the charge of the four chiefs and their fifty followers, principally, however, women and children—the few male servants, like the chiefs, being quite unarmed. The report adds, that the chiefs did not appear dejected or cast down, but rather " pleased with the change from prison walls to the deck of the ship."

In this case, history seems to have repeated itself. In bygone ages the ancestors of these chiefs, from their own wandering and investigating nature crossed the ocean westward to the Mauritius and Madagascar, while now they have been transported to similar westward homes, though for the purposes and at the command of the dominant power.

The Perak regalia, which was captured with ex-Sultan Ismail, consisted, besides elephants, merely of a few golden krises, swords, bells, dragons, and various gold and silver articles of a personal character.

CHAPTER XXXV.

LIFE in Perak, though as yet tested to a very small extent by Europeans, is very bearable, and the contented mind would meet with a continuous feast of enjoyment, if only by paying heed to that which is spread on all sides, without taking pains to investigate the wonders of the land. During the three last months of the year the rains are so heavy as to make an umbrella the best of friends to him who ventures to travel, while it is almost as welcome during the heat of the day of the other nine months. The mornings and evenings are, however, deliciously cool and fresh.

It may be taken for granted that amongst the more enlightened Malays there is a disposition to welcome the English, and to avail themselves, ·for the benefit of their country, of our knowledge, laws, and capital. To the present day the visit of the Duke of Edinburgh to the peninsula is talked of with pleasure, and the incidents in connection therewith are well remembered by the Malays. In connection with this visit, it may be mentioned that the two cocoa-nut trees obtained from Dr. Little's cocoa-nut plantation, which were with due ceremony planted by His Royal Highness in the grounds of the Government House at Singapore, are thriving well, and promise to be fine fruit-bearers.

Safety to life and property is increasing daily; and any person who chooses to make himself acquainted with the Malay people, and by his consistent conduct shows his respect for their customs and religion, may find himself amongst stanch friends ; for any one who has read so far through these pages must by now be convinced that in character the Malay approaches far nearer to the gentleman than to the bloodthirsty savage he has been so often painted. True there is the kris always worn at the waist of his sarong, but so was the rapier worn by our gentry of a generation or two back ; and, however much we may have advanced during the past few years, no one will charge our fathers and grandfathers with being bloodthirsty because the small-sword formed a portion of their attire.

Granting this safety, then, from the natives, the next question that seems to arise is as to the noxious beasts of the country. The only one of these to be really dreaded is the tiger, and the accidents from it are far more rare than may be supposed, espe-

cially since measures have been taken to keep down
its increase.   Where mishaps have occurred, they
have been generally amongst the Chinese coolies engaged in the plantations, or in similar work, which
rendered them very much exposed to attack ; while in
the course of years, as the country is opened out,
these must grow less and less frequent. From serpents
there is scarcely anything to fear, the python, as far
as the writer knows, never attacking man, while the
poisonous kinds are always ready to flee from the
sound of his foot.   What he has to fear from the
animal world is really the attack of the tiniest of insect
plagues, which up the rivers of the country are indeed
a pest, and require all possible caution to keep them
at a distance.

The next great question is the health, and the
most insidious of its assailants, jungle fever ; but taken
altogether the country is salubrious, and with due
precaution there is very little more to fear than one
may encounter in one's own land ; in fact, many of
our native ailments are escaped.   There can be no
doubt that several of the diseases from which the
natives suffer are brought on by their own defiance of
the simplest sanitary laws ; while, from his superior
knowledge of such matters, the European may go
comparatively scathless.   At the same time, nature
has undoubtedly aided the inhabitant of the East and
of tropic lands, and protected him by the colour given
to his epidermis.   After violent exercise the white skin

cools very rapidly, and causes the chills, colds, rheumatic pains, and bowel complaints from which a European may suffer in the East; while, when in the same heated state, the black or brown skin cools slowly, and the inflammation is averted.

Care in the choice of an abode, in cutting down the jungle, in picking out a resting-place when camping out, are all conducive to the health. For when the trees are cut down the miasma that rises from the ground has nothing to absorb it; hence the advice not to clear away the jungle without leaving the brushwood. When camping out, the writer has seen in the morning the value of his mosquito curtain, which has not only kept at bay the virulent little insects, but has acted as a purifier of the atmosphere he breathed, the outside being covered with the miasma-impregnated moisture that had arisen during the night.

It is very curious how the sicknesses of these eastern countries come about, but they may often be traced to the exhalations consequent upon animal or vegetable decay. For instance, in a coral island, the side whereon the wind blows may be perfectly healthy until the change of the monsoon, when an epidemic may ensue; and this be entirely due to the fact that where the coral is laid bare by the receding tide, and exposed to the sun, it decays and produces noxious exhalations. So long as the wind sweeps from the native village towards the exposed reef all are healthy;

2 E

but on the change taking place, the vapour is wafted
to the dwellings of the people, and sickness results;
which, however, may be avoided by changing the
sites of the huts.   This is well known to the people,
who are able to escape by exercising care.

Most people who go to the Straits are affected
directly after their arrival by an unpleasant cutaneous
disease.   The treatment of it is, however, very simple,
and it is not an ailment that need be looked upon
with dread, a tolerably copious application of borax
in solution being found to be a specific for its cure.
Moderation and temperance are the two best aids
to health in the peninsula; and these can be easily
supplemented by such little matters as taking care
not to get chilled after the toil of walking through
a hot and moisture-charged atmosphere, that is often
like a vapour-bath; sleeping always with a broad
woollen bandage round the waist, as a protection to
the more vital parts of the organism—such a precaution being invaluable for warding off all attacks of a
choleraic tendency.   Again, it is wise when up the
country to take a little quinine daily as bitters, so
as to keep off fever, for a system so prepared will
often escape when a stronger constitution falls.

To settlers, travellers, or sportsmen, it should be
said: Bear in mind that the simpler your supplies
are the better.   The best kit consists of a waterproof
sheet, a thin cork mattress, and a mosquito curtain.
These are ingeniously fitted in quite a small box by the

Chinese, the box afterwards forming a pillow. For supplies in the way of medicine, which no one should be without, take a sufficiency of quinine, Lamplough's pyretic saline—which is invaluable—and the genuine chlorodyne. These three form a medical armoury that will keep most diseases at bay ; while, by way of fortification, a supply of brandy for medicinal use or burning should form a portion of the medical stores therein : in cases where brandy is wanting, and a good stomachic is needed, a tea made by the infusion of green ginger answers admirably. Lastly, a bottle of Lea and Perrin's Worcester sauce, which is not only a relish, but acts when taken alone by a traveller wanting appetite, as a splendid stomachic, and an excellent " pick-me-up."

For additional provisions, the modern tinned meats and soups are invaluable, affording as they do variety; while their condensed form and convenient shape for packing, afford a wonderful contrast to the old-fashioned casks of salt beef and pickled pork. The convenience of these tinned meats to a person in the jungle can hardly be realised, unless the reader were put to the test. Weary, hot, and hungry, a halt is made, and the preparation of food is a task that is trying; but a tin of sausages is opened, a little brandy or spirit poured into a saucer, ignited, the sausage held in the flame for a few minutes, and there is a hot dish that for piquancy of flavour is indescribable, and outrivals the efforts of the most

2 E 2

famous Pall Mall *chef.* The air and appetite may
have something to do with the enjoyment, but the
simplicity of the cooking is worthy of note.

The sportsman or resident who can handle a gun
can of course make ample additions to his larder
from the surrounding jungle, or the swamps and
lagoons, where teal and wild-duck in many varieties
abound. Snipe absolutely swarm in Province Wellesley, and wherever there is a suitable habitat. In
the above shooting-grounds H.R.H. the Duke of
Edinburgh shot more couples in the course of a few
hours than have fallen to any man since. Deer are
to be found, and wild-boar ham is considered by
some a dainty. There are some, too, who have tried
curried monkey, and declare it to be delicious; and
for those who like to make this addition to their
bill of daily fare there is abundance of supply.
There seems to be something repulsive in the idea
of eating the little semi-human creature; but one
thing in its favour is that the monkey is a fruit-eater,
and in several parts of the world it is a regular
object of diet.

Some rather humorous adventures were met with
during the journey through the state of Perak with
Sir William Jervois, and also during the time of the
little war. When near the river good draughts of
fish were sometimes obtained; but upon one occasion
a halt was made at night, the present supplies were
exhausted, all others were at a distance—there was

nothing to catch, nothing to shoot, and the Governor
had declared that he was starving. The late Mr.
Birch, who was wonderfully fertile in expedient, was
at his wits' end, for there was the fire and no food
to cook. Just when every one was in despair, and
about to accept his fate of waiting for the arrival
of supplies, there was suddenly heard a loud "baa!"

Poor goat! it was speaking its own sentence of
death; for in a twinkling it was seized, slain, the kid-
neys whipped out, roasted on a bamboo, Malay fashion,
and served up to the Governor with sauce and mango
pickle, to his great satisfaction, and the relief of all
concerned.

Better fare was welcomed by a party during the
little war, when the writer was postmaster at Qualla
Kungsa—of which station the engraving gives a very
excellent representation. The reader is looking across
the Kungsa river, which is flowing on to its confluence
with the Perak—the further and larger of the two
rivers represented. The bamboo bridge and landing-
place were all arranged for the coming of the Governor.
About this time, or near to it, the post-runners had to
risk being shot down or speared by the inimical
Malays, who were always on the watch; but upon
the occasion in question the regular communication
remained perfect. The Postmaster - General at
St. Martin's-le-Grand gives accounts from time to
time of the remarkable things that pass through the
post—live, dead, and miscellaneous; but few things

that he annually reports exceed in grotesqueness the contents of the official letter-shaped packet that arrived at Qualla Kungsa, sent by a lady in the Settlements to an officer upon the station. The packet was square and thick and soft, and, on being opened, proved to be a plum-pudding. It need hardly be added that the season was Christmas, though summer-like in temperature, and that the gift was eaten with delight by those who mingled with their thanks to the donor many a thought of the home beyond the seas, and the pleasant meetings and festivities in progress far away.

White clothes are *de rigueur* here, and, with pith helmets, are universally adopted by the Europeans ; but the visitor to Perak, with its hot moist climate, must not forget the value of flannel, which is one of the greatest preservatives of European health. The pith helmets are admirably adapted for repelling heat, and their arrangements for obtaining ventilation are excellent in cooling the head ; but for a European there is no better protection against the sun than a piece of plantain-leaf, big enough to go inside the hat, where its powers are almost beyond belief in keeping down the temperature of the head. So cooling are its properties that it is regularly used for outward applications in the hospitals of the Settlements, while the traders adopt it for wrapping up butter, and preventing it from assuming the quality of oil.

The fowling-pieces and rifles to be taken out by

those who visit Perak and the peninsula, either as
travellers or to stay, must be regulated by individual
taste; but it may be borne in mind that in the Moar
district, north of Johore—regarding which place, since
the death of Sultan Allie, some question as to the
succession has arisen—there is excellent ground for
elephant-shooting, and a tiger may be occasionally
bagged. They may also regulate the calibre of their
pieces, and choose between the "Express" and other
modern rifles in regard to the huge alligators of the
rivers, many of which are of monstrous size, and
almost impenetrable hide.

In the way of settlement, steps are gradually being
taken; for the land, as has been said, offers facilities for
the production of tea, spices, sugar, tobacco, indigo,
and gambier, while on the other hand the mining
presents abundant work for capital. The labour is
the difficulty; but this is to some extent met by the
Chinese, who really are born artisans, and from their
patient industry, aptness in learning, and readiness to
work for moderate pay, promise to become the skilled
labourers of the future.

The maps given in this work contain the mountains, rivers, and villages of the state, as far as it has
been surveyed. It will be useful, though, to give a
few further particulars of the country, which are
founded on good native information, and will be
valuable to anyone making a trip inland; and though
the rivers and places are not named in the maps,

the writer is fully of opinion that future surveys
will confirm this description of the Ulu—interior,
or up-stream, as opposed to the Ilir, or down-
stream.

Soonghy Tekan is a little river that rises near
Kinta and runs into the Soonghy or River Raya,
which is a tributary of the Kinta. When leaving
this part, and flying into the Ulu after the retreat
from Kinta, leaves and roots of trees were all that
Ismail and his fugitive subjects could get by way of
supplies. Their course was from Kinta by Campong
Kapayang, Qualla Tekan, the mouth of the river just
named, Kantan and Kerbu at the sources of the
Plus river, Kerbu, Kernei, and Balla. From Balla,
Baling is easily reached, and then there is a pathway
to a tributary of the Muda river in the Quedah
territory.

Balla and the country beyond it are, strictly
speaking, in the Perak state; but the Patani people
have encroached a good deal beyond their own borders;
and by moving from Kerbu to Balla, it was evident
that Ismail's object was to reach the Quedah state.
Patani proper is arrived at by journeying between the
two ranges Gounong Titiwangsa and Gounong Panjang, where the Perak and Muda rivers rise. Boats
cannot go up the river much beyond Balla; for above
the rapids called Jeram Panjang, previously mentioned, the river Perak becomes a mere torrent.
There is, however, a pathway along its bank which

leads to Patani ; and the natives declare that it can be
reached in seven or eight stages, namely :

1. Ulu Jeram Panjang to Jeram Jambu.
2. Jeram Jambu to Kenering.
3. Kenering to Pelang Gali (inhabited by Patani people).
4. Pelang Gali to Berkuming.
5. Berkuming to Ehril.
6. Ehril to Belong.
7. Belong to Jerum, the boundary between Perak and Patani.
8. Jerum to Jerum Belakap.

Beyond Jerum Belakap are villages named Paropoh,
Tul (which is inhabited by thirty or forty Siamese
families), Nerwat, Hijau, Goar Kapur, and Koon
Panang, which latter is on the Buka river.

CHAPTER XXXVI.

BEFORE closing this work it may not be uninteresting, as so much prominence has been given to the question of Mount Ophir in Malacca being in all probability the Ophir of Solomon, to give a short account of an ascent of the mountain made by the writer some years since, in company with Captain Prothero, then *aide-de-camp* to the Governor, General Cavenagh, and now superintendent of the Andaman Islands. General Cavenagh was the last Governor of the Straits Settlements under the Indian Government, and was a member of the Commission appointed by Her Majesty to inquire into the revenue and expenditure of the Settlements prior to their transfer to the Crown.

The trip was proposed by way of variation to the monotony of a residence in Malacca. Besides which, a natural desire must be felt by every European to inspect a mountain whose name has so many historical associations connected with it, especially when so many facts suggest themselves to the student in proof of its being the genuine Ophir of Scripture; while to the traveller, the knowledge of the common term formerly applied to gold workings in these parts, namely "Ophirs," and the abundance of these ancient mines about the mountain conveys no slight corroborative evidence of the truth of the question.

Mount Ophir is situated in the territory of Moar, in the middle of the peninsula, about fifty miles east of Malacca; and at the time of the excursion to be described had not for many years been visited by Europeans. The time at the command of the little party would not allow of any lengthy preparation being made for the ascent; but considerable facilities were afforded by the resident Councillor of Malacca, who kindly arranged that a small body of about twenty Malays, under the Punghulu, or head-man, of the village of Chabow, should meet the expeditionists at the above place on the day appointed for the start, to act as guides and porters, and to clear the way; the Punghulu, who was an intelligent Malay named Lawih, proving an excellent guide, and of great service during the trip.

The first part of the journey was performed by carriage, and the route was through a place called by the Malays Ayer Panas, or Hot Water, on account of the hot springs. These springs, with some others, are the only traces of volcanic action in the peninsula, and are of the ordinary sulphur-impregnated character.

Bubbles of gas rise from time to time from the bottom
of the springs, which have the character of wells,
being about three feet in diameter, and twice that
number of feet in depth. There are three of these
wells, of which the water in one is much hotter than
in the others, being of so high a temperature as to be
nearly unbearable, while on a level with the surface a
curious deposit of a greenish hue is formed.

The view across the country was very beautiful,
the eye roving over the billowy green expanse of
jungle rising by slow degrees across hill after hill,
till bounded by the triple-crowned heads of Mount
Ophir, rising in softened outline far above the wooded
heights. The first part of the journey had been
through Chinese and Malay villages, but the country
soon grew wilder and more difficult, though very en-
joyable; and pushing on, we reached Jassing soon
after midday, having progressed a little over twenty
miles from Malacca in our morning's run.

Beyond this, as the road lay through padi fields
and water-courses, we could make no further progress,
either by carriage or on ponies; so from here our
journey began in earnest upon foot; and starting
about one, we followed the track through the village
of Rehim, about a mile farther east. After this we
found the land begin to rise till we reached much
higher ground, and plunged at once into the dense
jungle. Here all the beauty of the eastern forest was
on either side of the sun-shaded track, with the

wonderfully-rich foliage flourishing in the hot steaming atmosphere. There were, however, the accompanying discomforts of forest travel, leeches abounding in the moist places, and the track not being altogether free from mud. This dense jungle, which completely robs the traveller of views of the surrounding country, continued till we were about two miles from Chabow, where we were to meet our contingent of Malays and the guide.

On emerging from the forest, the track entered upon an extensive open plain, which had evidently been cleared of jungle in times long gone by ; and now full in our view lay the whole range of the mountains of Ophir piled high in our front, but, on the whole, somewhat disappointing as regarded their height.

It was four o'clock before Chabow was reached, the distance being about eleven miles from Jassing, progress during the latter part of the journey being naturally far more slow—mainly, though, in consequence of one of the heavy downpours of rain which are so common in this part of the world, and which seemed to come rolling down in rain-clouds from the mountain-sides with an impetuosity that it was hard work to withstand. On our approach, though, to Chabow, we were gladdened by the sight of the guide Punghulu Lawih, who, true to the orders he had received, came to the entrance of his campong to give us welcome, and led the way to his house, where the whole of the front portion of his bamboo mansion was placed at the travellers' disposal, and everything possible done to render the sojourn agreeable.

The evening was spent in resting, and making every possible arrangement for the start on the morrow. Packages were disposed for carriage during the ascent, dinner was discussed, and at last, wearied out, the simple couches were sought, with the soft highly-pitched hum of mosquitos making itself heard as these insect pests prepared themselves for their nocturnal banquet upon the tired travellers—intentions, however, carefully frustrated, by turning each couch into a fortress with covered ways formed of mosquito curtains. These effectually kept off the enemy, whose frantic dashes were all repelled, the curtains offering no means of ingress to the insects; but they were powerless to ward off the insidious onslaught of a peculiarly objectionable odour, which not only pervaded the room but soon filled the space within the curtains. This peculiarly strong and singular odour proceeded from the durian fruit in the Punghulu's house, and proved quite sufficient to banish sleep for some considerable time; but at last weariness prevailed, and sinking into a profound slumber we managed to obtain a very fair night's rest before the call came to rise at daybreak, so as to be ready for setting off on the more arduous march at six o'clock.

Before starting came the customary squabble and

fight amongst the bearers for who should get the lightest and most convenient packages to carry; but these minor matters were soon put right by the Punghulu, and at about half-past seven the expedition was under march from the campong, swelling by degrees as it progressed—for such an event was an uncommon one here—and volunteers and friends of the Malays soon increased the party from twenty to forty in number, the greater portion taking as much interest in the novel trip as so many children.

The route lay through Soonghy Dua, and the deserted village of Assahan, a ruined place, which told plainly of its ancient date in the ample testimony afforded by the extensive growth of aged fruit-trees, which abounded in every direction, the clearings between indicating where had stood the houses of the bygone inhabitants of the place. Here we were refreshed by partaking of the finest and largest mangosteen that we had ever seen, growing wild as it were in this desert place, lying about six miles from the campong where we had passed the night.

Passing through Assahan, the direction of our route for the mountains lay fifteen degrees west of north, but about ten o'clock we had to change our way to due east, so as to make for the northern slope of the mountain, by which our ascent was to be made. Soon after this we crossed the Soonghy Chobong, a stream which divides the Malay and

British territory, and at this point we changed again
to a north-easterly direction.

Our intention was to reach the foot of the mountain before nightfall, where we proposed to stay at a
place called Gummi, and therefore pushed on so as to
be there in sufficient time to prepare our hut for the
night, and arrange for the morrow's ascent. Our next
place of call was to be Soonghy Ayer Bangkong, which
we hoped to reach by vigorous walking a little after
noon; but a good track assisted us no longer, for the
latter part of our journey had been through high
lallang grass, so that the miles became wearisome and
slow, as may be surmised, from the want of progress
made upon this second day. Hitherto the track had
been fairly visible, and offered but few obstacles to
ordinary walking; but after threading our way
through the coarse stiff lallang, there was no further
vestige of a pathway, the route before us now consisting of the sturdy brushwood of the secondary
jungle—the undergrowth that springs up after the
primeval forest has been cleared away.

From this point the genuine hard work began; for
the Malays had to come to the front with their sword-
like parangs, and hew and hack a path for us through
the brush. For a good hour this work continued, the
progress being diversified by a fall into a swamp now
and then, when we got through the piece of wilderness and came upon the old track once more. The
Malays then suggested that we should follow in

the steps of former travellers to the mountain, and
encamp for the night at Ayer Bangkong, and on the
left bank of the river ; but we made up our minds to
push forward to the very foot of the mountain, so
that an entire day could be devoted to its ascent.
Ayer Bangkong was reached about the time we
anticipated ; and here the advance party came
suddenly upon a number of the Sakais, or Jacoons,
who proved their wild nature on the instant by
dashing off at full speed into the jungle, as if in
terror at the sight of white men and their enemies
the more civilised Malays.

Mooning was the next place reached, and here our
course had veered to the south-east ; and pushing on,
Gummi was reached by three o'clock, and preparations
immediately made for making ready the little camp.
And now their ability of adapting themselves to
circumstances was strongly shown by the Malays,
who in a very short time had set to work and built
up a rough stage, about two feet from the ground.
Upon the cross-sticks of this they laid strips of the
bark of the Maranti tree, till the structure assumed
the proportions of a capital sleeping-floor, over
which a slight roof of sticks was tied, and again
over this a couple of kadjangs, or palm-leaf mats,
were thrown ; extemporising for us a capital hut
or shed, sufficient to afford a good screen from the
weather.

While the evening meal was being prepared over

2 F

the fire that had been lighted—a meal that was to
consist of a tin of soup and a "sudden death," otherwise a spatchcock—a look round was taken, and a
waterfall was found only a short distance away ; while
upon reaching its foot, where the glistening foam ·
sparkled and played in rainbow tints in the afternoon
light, the geological formation of the rocks over which
the water sprang was examined. These proved to be
of granite, with patches here and there of quartz and
clay-slate. The granite largely predominated, as it
did, in fact, as far down the bed of the stream as could
be explored. Amongst the granite boulders were here
and there deep pools, upon which the Malays made an
onslaught, and soon succeeded in drawing therefrom a
good supply of fish. Their next visit was to the wild
durian trees, from whose fruit they concocted a curry,
and thus from the nature-spread bounty their wants
were very easily supplied.

In spite of the rocky nature of the ground, the
jungle around us was very dense, forming a good
harbour for any of the wild beasts of the peninsula,
if any were near at hand ; but no visit was anticipated, for during the day's journey nothing had
crossed the path larger than squirrels or monkeys,
though every now and then we came across the tracks
of elephants, rhinoceros, bears, deer, and wild-pig.
These, however, were old, and the creatures that had
imprinted them were most probably far away. The

monkeys were plentiful, and were for the most part of the black kind, with a white fringe of hair around the face. Lest, however, we should be troubled by nocturnal visits in a land where the tiger is not unknown, the Malays prepared camp-fires all around us; and choosing one of the most brisk in the centre, piled up the dead wood they had gathered together, and then seated themselves in a knot, with the warm glow reddening the bronze of their faces, and forming a wonderfully picturesque group, as seen against the black background of that forest land.

For hours and hours these people kept up quite a little social entertainment by improvising amusing stories, which they set to their own native music, and sang aloud, after the manner of their *sun-nun-dongs*, to harmonious airs, the whole joining in a chorus of "Aha!" after every line. One of the party then toning down the refrain to a lower key, went on to sing a lament that a high official had lost his leg in the wars, and could not therefore indulge in such an expedition, so as to enjoy the pleasure of a mountain climb. Then another took up the refrain in a higher key, keeping up the idea, and described how that, as this high official could not climb Mount Ophir himself, he had done the next best thing to it—he had sent his Muntri, or secretary, who would no doubt some day be a great man too.

The Malay of this improvised song may not be

2 F 2

without its interest to some readers, and this is the excuse for its insertion here :

Tuan Governor, dia adah satu kaki, sahja.
(*Chorus.*) Aha ! aha !
Dia ta boleh naik Bukit sahja.
Aha ! aha !
Pandi kereem, dia Muntri sahja.
Aha ! aha !
Eang jadi Governor, sundiri sahja.
Aha ! aha !

Improvising songs could not be kept up all night, and by degrees the party dropped off to sleep, till all was silent—a silence only broken now and then by the loud breathing of some sleeper, or the soft whispering of the wind amongst the tree-tops in the jungle. The novelty of the position, however, banished sleep from the European eyes for some time, and we lay listening till the silence was suddenly broken by the shrill note of the *coo-ow*, as the natives call the argus-pheasant, whose cry seemed to rise from the jungle, and was then echoed from the surrounding hills in every direction. The cry of this bird is wonderfully sharp and clear, and, as has been said, it bears a singular resemblance to the savage "coo-ey," its piercing nature being so peculiar that it can be heard at a very great distance.

Sleep overtook the whole party at last, and, forgetful of the dangers to be apprehended from wild beasts, a calm slumber was enjoyed, from which we

woke very early, quite refreshed; and, rising, at once
proceeded to reduce our luggage as much as possible,
so as to get what was absolutely necessary for the
rest of the journey into as small a compass as we could,
it having been decided to leave the remainder here,
in charge of two or three of the older members of
the party. Breakfast was then partaken of, and we
made our start for the real ascent at about eight
o'clock.

Just before setting off, that is to say about a quarter
past seven, the thermometer was examined, when the
mercury stood at eighty-one degrees, a great height considering that the air seemed to be perceptibly colder.

The first part of the ascent lay along the left bank
of the Gummi river, and proved to be toilsome and
precipitous, but it was relieved every here and there
by bits of level ground. Every few yards gained,
though, began to show that much harder work was
in store, and before long the ascent became so arduous
that we could get no foothold in our boots, and these
had to be discarded, the whole remaining part of the
journey, ascent and descent, having to be performed
with no stronger covering for the feet than woollen
socks. Persevering, though, we brought our hands
to the help of our feet, and making use of the various
creepers, gradually dragged ourselves up higher and
higher, till we had topped the first of the hills which
form the Ophir range, descending afterwards into
the valley on the other side, which we reached about

eleven o'clock, after finding the slope on this side
shelving more than on the one by which we had
ascended.

From this valley, the next hill to climb was.
Gounong Padang Batoo, an enormous mass of granite,
offering to us almost perpendicular sides, which were
in places entirely denuded of soil and vegetation. In
other parts, though, the fissures were rich in an abundance of mosses, lichens, and ferns, with a shrubby
plant not unlike the rhododendron in its growth. At
this point the climb became so arduous that one of
the party gave up, and had to relinquish the ascent,
which was made the more difficult by the loads that
it was necessary to bear. Leaving him there, we
pushed on, and finally at one o'clock this granite
mass was climbed.

Water was the first thing thought of, and on
looking about we found to our left the bed of a
mountain torrent; but at this time of the year
it contained very little water, though the well-worn
stones plainly showed that in the rainy season a
heavy torrent must flow through it from higher up
the mountain. The moisture here, though, had its
effect, for the rugged banks were fringed with stunted
vegetation, but it presented a strong contrast to the
lush growths of the steaming jungle.

But very little time was spent here, however, for
there was plenty of arduous work before us, and
tramping on we reached Gounong Tondoh about half-

past two, with the European part of our little expedition very much exhausted; for the mountain here was very precipitous, and step after step could only be won by grasping the trees, shrubs, and climbers, which very fortunately lay ready to hand. At the summit of this mountain is a small plateau some thirty square yards in area, and covered with dense scrub, a few fir trees, and the vegetation peculiar to such altitudes. From here there was a good view of the work yet to be done, the triple peaks of the mountain being visible—Gounong Ledang, the highest, rising very abruptly between the other two.

A rest was however necessary before attempting further progress, and this having been taken, a fresh start was made, with a short descent; and then began a sheer scramble and climb up the face of Gounong Ledang, holding on by points, roots, moss, anything that offered itself to the grasp, till at last, just at four o'clock, we reached the summit of the Ophir range, completely fagged; for the thermometer, when exposed, even at this altitude, registered ninety-six degrees. The crest of the mountain is formed of one large overhanging block of granite, called by the natives Batoo Sardung. The mass is about twenty-five feet high, and its overhanging side offered a fair amount of shelter to our party, for we had determined upon spending the night upon the summit.

The view from this point is grand and extensive, but is on the whole monotonous, on account of the

extent of jungle upon which the eye rests, the billowy
waves rolling off mile after mile in every direction.
Here and there, however, the landscape was relieved
by the vivid green of the clearings, where the rice
grew in its delicate luxuriance.   Moar, Rumbowe,
Jompole, Pahang, all lay in the distance as we
turned from side to side; while far away to the west
was Malacca, with the sea-coast, the Water islands,
and Salangore.

At length, having satiated ourselves with the view
of mountain, jungle, plain, and winding river, our
attention was directed to the little plateau upon which
we stood, and the great block of granite, upon which
former travellers had carved the initials: " W. F.,"
" W. T. L.," and " T. B."   Then came the preparations for encamping for the night.   This proved by
comparison rather cold; for the thermometer fell
rapidly, and at sunrise it only marked sixty-two
degrees, having probably been some degrees lower
during the night.   On rising, the fact was announced
that scarcely any water was to be obtained on the
summit; so, welcome as it would have been, the
Malays had to postpone the preparation of breakfast
until a descent had been made as far as Gounong
Padang Batoo, the great granite mass we passed over
on our way up.   This want quickened the return,
for, arduous as had been the climb up, the descent
was comparatively easy, and we made such progress
that Padang Batoo was reached by half-past seven;

and the meal having been prepared, and a short halt made, we continued our progress down the mountain, and gained our first camping-ground at Gummi by half-past twelve.

At this point we rejoined the portion of the party who had found the ascent too arduous, with the little camp looking very welcome after the toil of the last twenty-four hours. It was determined to proceed no farther that day, and we remained here for the night, so as to be fresh for the long march on the morrow; when, starting early, we made a double journey to Ayer Panas, through Chabow and Jassing, parting from our Malay companions at their campong, where they had met us on our way. They had proved very friendly and helpful, and parted from us with plenty of good wishes expressed on either side.

Ayer Panas was reached at seven in the evening, and we proceeded to the Government bungaloh there, where we put up, and restored ourselves wonderfully after the long day's march by indulging in a bath in the hot springs of the village, the effect of which upon our aching limbs was almost wonderful. The following morning saw us back in Malacca.

By a careful comparison of two aneroid barometers on the summit of Mount Ophir, we made the height above the sea-level to be 4000 feet — a height which does not correspond with that given by Newbold, who places it at 5693 feet, while Crawfurd

gives it as 4300.   Mr. Wallace, however, who
ascended the mountain some years previous to our
own expedition, gives precisely the same result as
ourselves.

Future travellers who may wish to climb Mount
Ophir are recommended to make the attempt on the
north side ; to post ponies to Jassing from Malacca ;
sleep the first night at Chabow, and procure the aid of
the Punghulu of that place, who will provide a good
guide and coolies, at the rate of twenty-five cents a
day.   The second night should be passed at Gumini,
and the third at Gounong Padang Batoo, where there
is a sufficiency of water ; while Gounong Ledang, the
highest peak of Ophir, could be leisurely visited the
next day.

This short account of a hasty trip was written
merely with the view of affording information to those
who might wish to spend ten days pleasantly at
Malacca.   Our visit was much too hurried to admit of
more than a mere cursory inspection of the country,
but it was sufficient to give evidence that a more
leisurely examination of the many points of interest
which present themselves would fully repay those who
commanded plenty of time to attempt the ascent.
The interest that is sure to be taken in the endless
traces, round the foot, of gold workings—some of
which are modern, but many exhibiting traces of the
greatest antiquity—affords plenty of food for considera-

tion as to when the search for the precious metal was first commenced.   To the naturalist generally, whatever may be his particular study—botany, geology, or zoology—there would appear to be a very wide field for research.

CHAPTER XXXVII.

IN treating of the future of Perak many questions of
policy arise, and after all, no single one is equal to
that of precedent; for in the past we have mapped
out for our guidance the smooth waters and the
stormy seas, with the various rocks that have been
the cause of many a wreck. It must not be supposed,
though, that it is intended here to inculcate solely the
oldest and most anti-progressive policy ; for in manag-
ing fresh people, fresh plans must be grafted upon
the old, so as to suit the circumstances of the case.
There is a great deal then to do for Perak : and first
and foremost must be the insuring to the country of
a good government, giving safety to the humblest
coolie therein, as well as protection to those who bring
in their property.   By this means European capital
and Chinese labour will open out the whole peninsula ;
a country which, square mile for square mile, is one of

THE PRESENT RULER OF PERAK—RAJAH YUSUF—AND HIS TWO SONS.

the richest in mineral produce in the whole world. It is only in the course of time that its vast undeveloped resources can be worked; but with this gradually increasing prosperity in the one state, a steady improvement in the systems of the others must follow, so that in time the peninsula may become one vast field of British commerce. It is even possible, and would probably tend greatly to the development of trade, if in the future efforts were made to try and open up a route to China through Siam, lying, as it does, between the peninsula and that vast empire; while already it has been proposed to cut through the Isthmus of Kra, which forms the neck, and so to secure water communication between the Bay of Bengal and the Gulf of Siam.

At the present time the cupidity of their chiefs, and the fear of exciting their jealousy, prevent the Malays from attempting to improve their condition, or raising any structure better than the ordinary hut. They grow just sufficient for their wants, acquire one or two buffaloes; and it is only when they get near the towns, and under the salutary British rule, that they attain to a position in any way resembling comfort; and doubtless this oppression has much to do with the careless indolent habits of too many of the people. That they approve of the protection and example of British rule is constantly being shown. Already in Laroot cases are tried magisterially, and there is a well-built prison to confine offenders; while the people

gladly seek the court, because they feel sure of justice
—a something that they find as novel as it is beneficial
to them all. Again, they must see for themselves
that they, the Malays of Perak, suffer by comparison
with their neighbours of Province Wellesley, who, existing under British rule, are better fed, and live in
peace and content. A great deal may be done by
encouraging them to contribute to the resources of
their own country by various agricultural pursuits,
and by securing to them more freedom under their
chiefs.   By this means a sure, even though slow,
advance may be made ; and one certainly more advantageous to the country than a wholesale annexa-
tion, and bringing the territory under British rule.

But much has yet to be done by the Government,
who will have to give attention to the food-supply of
the country before very long.   Then the works
connected with irrigation and water-supply for other
purposes will have to be taken in hand.   Water would
bring many parts of Malacca into value, by rendering
the barren fertile ; and though some attention has been
given to the economical use of water in the mines of
Perak, it will have to be further considered when the
mines come to be extended.   Fortunately however the
water is there ; it is only the question of storing and
directing that has to be dealt with.

A great step in the direction of settling Perak
might have been taken most advantageously by the
Government in encouraging the Indian convicts, now

on ticket-of-leave at Singapore, to go up the country, furnishing them with money for the purpose, and giving them tracts of land to cultivate. For the most part these men are agriculturists or herdsmen ; and by giving these settlers a start a great deal would have been done to render them useful to the state, and give additional security to life ; while in making the place better, they would have been forming a nucleus to which there would have been some encouragement for other people to flock. As it is, there is a natural reluctance amongst those who have all the desire to settle to go and make themselves the pioneers of the new civilisation. These convicts, by the way, are the remainder left after the cessation of the receipt of prisoners at Singapore ten years ago. Many of them are Madrassees or Klings, and are now, for the most part, decent people, to whom the character of criminal attaches merely as connected with old offences, expiated, and to a great extent condoned.

As it has taken time for the Malays who live under our government in the Settlements to become acquainted with the justice of our laws, and the firm and equitable collection of the revenue, with protection to life and property religiously insured on all hands, so must we expect that in Perak, and such other native states as we may take under our protection, there must be a great deal of tedious delay before we shall find the mass of the chiefs and people yielding due respect to the laws and institutions which are

so adverse to their own, and which strike at the root
of the profit and advantage which accrue to them as
gained by fraud and oppression. It requires a display
of great judgment, with a large amount of temper and
patience, on the part of those who are deputed to the
carrying out of these important duties; so that more
by example and suasion, than by the exercise of coercion, they should carry on their intercourse with the
Malays.

According to the Malay saying—*nanti-palla-han*
—the lizard gives the fly time to say its prayers
before he makes his final spring to devour his prey;
and setting aside the seizure of the prey, this must be
our policy with the Malays; we must give them
time—deal with them firmly but gently, and all
will be well. It may be argued that we gave the
Turks time, and what has been the result? If we had
kept them to their Constitution—which, it is true, was
given under pressure—it is possible that there would
not have been this bloodshed. The Malays have been
punished for their gross outrage; and this being at an
end, now what is necessary is to insure them good
government, and then—give them time, when there
is no fear but that in Perak and other states we may
have as loyal and trustworthy a set of people as now
exist in Province Wellesley and Malacca, and in the
towns of Singapore and Penang.

By encouragement and teaching, the Malays are

not incapable of being led on to industrious pursuits ; but even in this the giving-time policy should be adopted, and they should at first be allowed to derive profit from their produce in the way that comes most natural to them, and in accordance with their customs for generations past. There exists no reason why the Malay should not become in all points a good citizen ; and though he may not possess the native intelligence of the Chinese as a trader and artisan, nor the shrewd cleverness of the Kling in his business and monetary transactions, he will be found no whit behind them in agricultural pursuits ; and both in Perak and elsewhere, as he gradually learns the value of our institutions, he will follow in the footsteps of those of his countrymen who are now our fellow-subjects, and than whom none could be more loyal and devoted to the British Crown.

It is questionable whether great blame does not attach to us as a nation for the little we have done during our long occupation of the settlements of Penang, Malacca, and Singapore, towards the pacification and improvement of the states on the peninsula. We have been too often content to merely draw from them the products that suit us in trade, while so long as the commerce was in a flourishing condition, the improvement of the people and the introduction of the arts of civilisation were neglected. We have perhaps held back on political grounds, and from

2 g

the fear that if we became entangled in the "native question," we should either have to retreat with loss of prestige, or have to carry out a policy which would drive out the native chiefs and government, but would necessarily only be effected by resort to arms, or at least by a display of force which would either cast a burden upon the Settlements which they could ill afford, or fall upon the imperial revenues—a state of affairs to which the British taxpayer would readily object.   The medium policy of placing an English Resident at the native courts, so common on the continent of India, was never undertaken, singularly enough, when the Settlements were under Indian rule ; and when attempted but two years ago in Perak led to disastrous consequences for the time, the outcome of causes which were, however, preventible.   In Salangore, on the contrary, as in other states, it has hitherto been continued with marked success ; and if in the future we are judicious, and avoid taking steps which might lead the people to believe that we intended to meddle with their established customs—points upon which they are extremely jealous of interference—the resident system will doubtless be carried on in Perak with equally good results.

The effect of such a mild form of policy will not only be vastly advantageous to ourselves, in bringing a large mass of people into a more civilised state, and opening up to our commerce the mineral and other

wealth of this country; but we shall be able to take
to ourselves the satisfaction of having at least done
our duty in bringing no inconsiderable portion of the
earth's surface under the benign influence of British
rule, and within the reach of that Christian truth
without which no people can be fully civilised, and
the spread of whose knowledge it is Britain's privilege
and glory to foster and encourage.

In the earlier chapters of this work allusion was
made to the failure of Mr. Muntinghe's commission at
Palembang, which was due to his want of knowledge of
the Malay character, and too great eagerness to en-
force a novel system that, though perhaps admirable
in Java, was utterly unsuited to the people amongst
whom he wished it to take root.   Contrast with this
the excellent management, in his successful dealing
with the people, of one whom the writer is proud of
being able to say he could call a friend—the late Sir
James Brooke, of Sarawak.   Singly and unaided did
this English gentleman, animated from first to last by
the highest motives, gain the respect and affection of
every Malay with whom he was brought in contact,
both among the chiefs and the people.   Fear of
him existed only in the hearts of those who, in
direct opposition to his mild counsel and sugges-
tions, persistently endeavoured to maintain a system
of cruel piracy and oppression.   Even, however, in
dealing with these last he tempered his justice with

mercy, knowing full well that time is necessary for
the eradication of a national vice; and that it would
be simple madness to attempt to change, as by the
touch of a wizard's wand, that which had been the
growth of centuries — in other words, the whole
character of a nation.

Sir Andrew Clarke, when Governor of the Straits
Settlements, was animated by a similar spirit, and, by
his wise policy, paved the way for peace and good
government in Perak; and had he not been summoned away to a higher appointment, it is probable
that many of the troubles in Perak would not have
had place. He was possessed of a wonderful faculty
of dealing with the natives, whom he won to his side
by his frankness and openness of manner, through
which, though, always shone firmness of character,
mingled with a high sense of justice, and that which is
due from man to man. He was in favour of the Resident principle—the presence with a native ruler of
one who would advise and lead towards right, without
seeming to control, and always exerting his influence
for good with both chiefs and people.

This is undoubtedly the course that should be
followed out, and the various chiefs taught how to
increase the value of their country by good government and improvement, as they invited co-operation
by making life and property safe. For, given such a
country and such a people, by good advice, an ad-

ministration may be brought about similar to those of Johore and Quedah, where, from their contiguity to our civilisation, this has permeated their own; and in consequence we have native princes ruling by our laws, and keeping down the evil principles of their states, with magistrates, stations, regular trials, and convict gaols, while on the other hand peace and prosperity have a permanent reign. This has been the result of time, and of letting the people see and learn the value of our institutions, the chiefs' power increasing with the progress of their land.

In conclusion, it must never be forgotten that whatever may be the future of Perak, and however great a position it may reach in the scale of civilised countries, it was the death of one man that first drew the attention of our home Government fully to the state for its development and ultimate prosperity. For these, he who literally acted as the pioneer of its civilisation unceasingly toiled; falling, though, in the dawning of that day of progress for which he had so earnestly laboured, when the bright sun of western light was beginning to brighten the waving palms of this far distant forest land. Though his family will never cease to bewail his loss, there is a mournful satisfaction in knowing that he laid the foundation of a better government in Perak; and that as our influence over the peninsula still further extends, his memory will ever be associated with the advance and civilisation of this portion of Her Majesty's domains; while those who loved him can always say—He had the progress of Perak thoroughly at heart, and its prosperity was the work of

J. WHEELER WOODFORD BIRCH.

FINIS.

www.ingramcontent.com/pod-product-compliance
Lightning Source LLC
Chambersburg PA
CBHW031811270326
41932CB00008B/386